AF522608

JASSIDS
AND
THEIR CONTROL

By

Dr. T.V. Sathe
Department of Zoology
Shivaji University
Kolhapur - 416 004
(Maharashtra)
(INDIA)

&

Dr. Chandani Subhash Kamble
Department of Zoology
Shivaji University
Kolhapur - 416 004
(Maharashtra)
(INDIA)

DISCOVERY PUBLISHING HOUSE PVT. LTD.
INDIA

Published by:

Namit Wasan

DISCOVERY PUBLISHING HOUSE PVT. LTD.

4383/4B, Ansari Road, Darya Ganj
New Delhi-110 002 (India)
Phone : +91-11-23279245, 43596064-65
Fax : +91-11-23253475
E-mail : discoverypublishinghouse@gmail.com
namitwasan9@gmail.com
sales@discoverypublishinggroup.com

website: www.discoverypublishinggroup.com

***First Edition:* 2017**

ISBN: 978-93-5056-846-0

Jassids and their Control

Printed at:
Infinity Imaging Systems
Delhi

Preface

Biodiversity plays an important role for sustainable development of a region or a country. Jassids are highly destructive to economically important crops including: agriculture, horticulture and forest.

Jassids are herbivorous insects, they cause serious damage either directly by sucking the cell sap or indirectly by transmitting plant pathogens including viruses and phytoplasmase. They secret honeydew likes: sticky substance over the plant body and cause sooty moulds. The sooty mould on the leaf affects photosynthesis and further growth and yield of the crop. Therefore, any advanced knowledge on the biodiversity will add great relevance in jassid management and protecting various crops of the region from jassids. However, very little attention is paid on their diversity from western Maharashtra. Hence, in the present work, description of jassids, their abundance, host plants and distribution from Western Maharashtra specially, Kolhapur, Sangli and Satara have been given. I feel that the work will be helpful to students, teachers and scientists in the field of insect pest management and environmental sciences.

Dr. T.V. Sathe

Dr. Chandani S. Kamble

Contents

1 Introduction

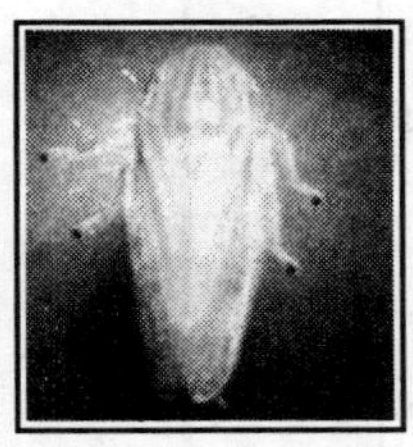

India made significant development towards economic growth, modernization and self-reliance in various areas. Since last fifty years including most indicators of human development (Dreeze and Sen, 1995). The average expectancy of life has gone up from an estimated 30 to over 60 years. The death rate declined as 27.4 per thousand and as per population census of India 2011. The literacy rate of India has shown improvement 9 per cent. Literacy of India was 74.04 per cent in 2011 and 65.38 per cent in 2001. However, India made worst progress in elementary education than even the average of poorest countries in the world. In India 82.14 per cent adult literacy was noted in 2001 (http://www.indiaonlinepages.com/population/literacy) the level is well below the world average literacy rate of 84 per cent (Crossette and Barbana (1998).

Indian population is critical issue for its stabilization which affects the economic growth and benefits of common man. The current population of India in 2015 is 1.28 billion (www.indiaonlinepages.com). Requirement of land to a common man is decreased considerably due to increased population. India supports about 15 per cent of the world's human and animal population holding only 2.4 per cent of land area.

The compound growth rate of India's population is 1.25 per cent (www.indexmundi.com). The environment quality and life style of the animals have direct relation with the sources like: water, soil, forestry etc. Due to the increasing availability of health services, food sheltering and quality of water supply, life expectancy of birth has considerably increased in India (Fig. 1.1).

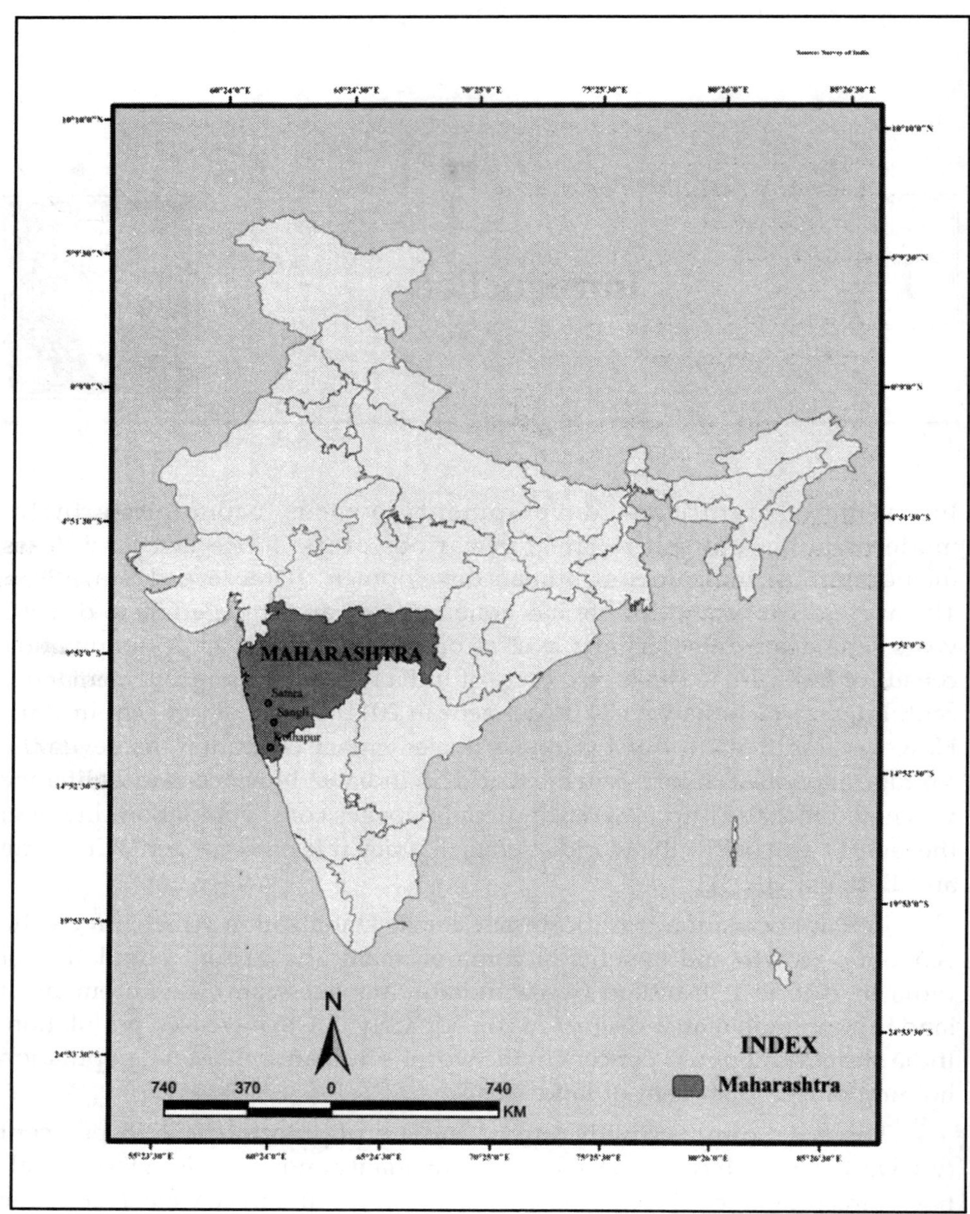

Fig. 1.1: **Map of India Showing Maharashtra**

Socio-economic development of any nation is largely dependent on agriculture, forestry and industry. Forestry is important component of an environment which has direct or indirect relationship with the humans as a versatile assemblage of biodiversity. Forestry maintains the ecological balance and life support system essential for food production, health and human development since it provides timber, wood, fuel, fiber, grasses and non wood forest products which also supports industrial and commercial activities. Out of 329 million hectares of geographical area of India, actual forest cover exist only 76.52 million hectares.

Forestry is admixture of plants and animals and acts as harbor for diversity. However, due to deforestation it is in serious danger. The major cause of biodiversity and species extinction is deforestation. According to Radhakrishnan (2003) some of the life forms have totally vanished while, some others are categorised as endangered. About 3120 species of plants and 172 categories of animals of our country are listed in the IUCN's Red list threatened category (Radhakrishnan, 2003).

The Western Ghats (Fig. 1.2) is biodiversity rich area of Maharashtra which is extended from the southern tip of the Peninsula (8° N) Northern about 1600 km., to the mouth of river Taphi (218° N) with 1600 km., area and with prominent range of mountains located as altitudes between 900 and 1500m above the sea level except the 'Phalghat gap' which is almost the central part of Western Ghats found in Kerala State, having very low altitude, usually less than 144m above the sea level.

The Western Ghats has occupied 159000 sq. km., area of five states (Fig. 1.2), including: Maharashtra, Goa, Karnataka, Kerala and Tamil Nadu. Due to conducive environment, the Western Ghats is one of the biodiversity rich area of India. The Western Ghats in Maharashtra is scattered in nine districts namely: Dhule, Pune, Satara, Sangli, Kolhapur, Sindhudurg, Ratnagiri, Raigad and Thane but, the present work was restricted to Kolhapur, Sangli and Satara districts only.

Kolhapur district of Maharashtra covers an area of 7585 sq. km., with total forest coverage of about 1672 sq. km., and 563 sq. km., as reserved forest and 417 km., as a protected forest. The forest area is about 22 per cent of total geographical area of the district. Subtropical evergreen, the moist deciduous and semi-evergreen and the dry deciduous forests are the main types of forests in Kolhapur districts.

Kolhapur district shows three distinct parts *viz;* Eastern ranges, Central ranges and Southern ranges. Eastern and Southern ranges have black soil while, Western ranges are mostly hilly and have red soil and mostly with thick forest coverage. The district receives the rainfall from 700-6000mm. From Western Ghats, east wardly Hiranyankeshi and Ghataprabha. Kolhapur districts is having 12 Tahsils out of which Karvir, Panhala, Hatkanangale, Shirol, Shahuwadi, Gaganbavda, Radhanagari, Kagal, Ajara, Gadhinglaj and Chandgad have been selected for diversity, abundance and distributional studies.

Satara district of Maharashtra (Fig. 1.3) has an area of 10,492 sq. km., which form a part of Deccan plateau between latitude 17°5′ and 1801′N and longitude 73°33′ and 74°74 E. It is bounded by Sangli from southern region and Pune from northern region. Satara district shows 11 Tahsils namely: Patan, Satara, Medha, Wai and Mahabaleshwar which comes under hilly region. Satara district is located at altitude of 900 to 2150m from sea level. The famous Koyana dam and Koyana wild life sanctuary are part of Satara district. In present study Karad, Patan, Satara, Khandala, Wai, Dahiwadi and Mahabaleshwar have been selected for jassid diversity studies since, they have important in the view point of geography and topography.

Mahabaleshwar tahsil lies between 73°37′ and 74°47′ E longitude and 17°52 and 17°59 N latitude at the height of 4719m located in basaltic province of Deccan and clothed with mantle of evergreen forests and it is visualized as picnic spot.

Sangli district is (Fig. 1.3) lies between 16°45′ and 17°38′ N latitude and 73°42′ and 75°4°′ E longitude. This district is bounded by Bijapur district of Karnataka State from East side and by Ratnagiri, from west and from north Satara. While, Kolhapur (MS) and Belgaum district of Karnataka State and Solapur district are in association from the southern boundaries. Krishna basin and Bhima basin are important parts of this district. Topography, climate and rainfall divides the district as follows:

1. Western hilly area of Shirala tahsil of heavy rainfall.
2. The basin area of Krishna, Warna and Yerala.
3. An eastern drought prone area which comprises eastern part of Miraj and Tasgaon tahsil, North Eastern part of Khanapur and whole of Atpadi, Kavathe Mahankal and Jath tahsils.

The maximum temperature of the district ranges between 31.1°C in July to 41.5°C in April. Similarly, the minimum temperature ranges from 10.3°C in December to 21.5°C from April to June. The district Sangli have 76 major and minor irrigation projects and is admixture of low and heavy rain fall and hence the biodiversity. For the present study Shirala, Palus, Kadegaon, Vita, Sangli, Miraj, Kavathe-Mahankal and Jat have been selected.

According to, UNEP (1995) biodiversity is the variety and variability among living organisms residing in terrestrial, marine and other aquatic ecosystems. The broad specialised branches of biodiversity refer to species diversity, ecological diversity and genetic diversity. Species diversity is the

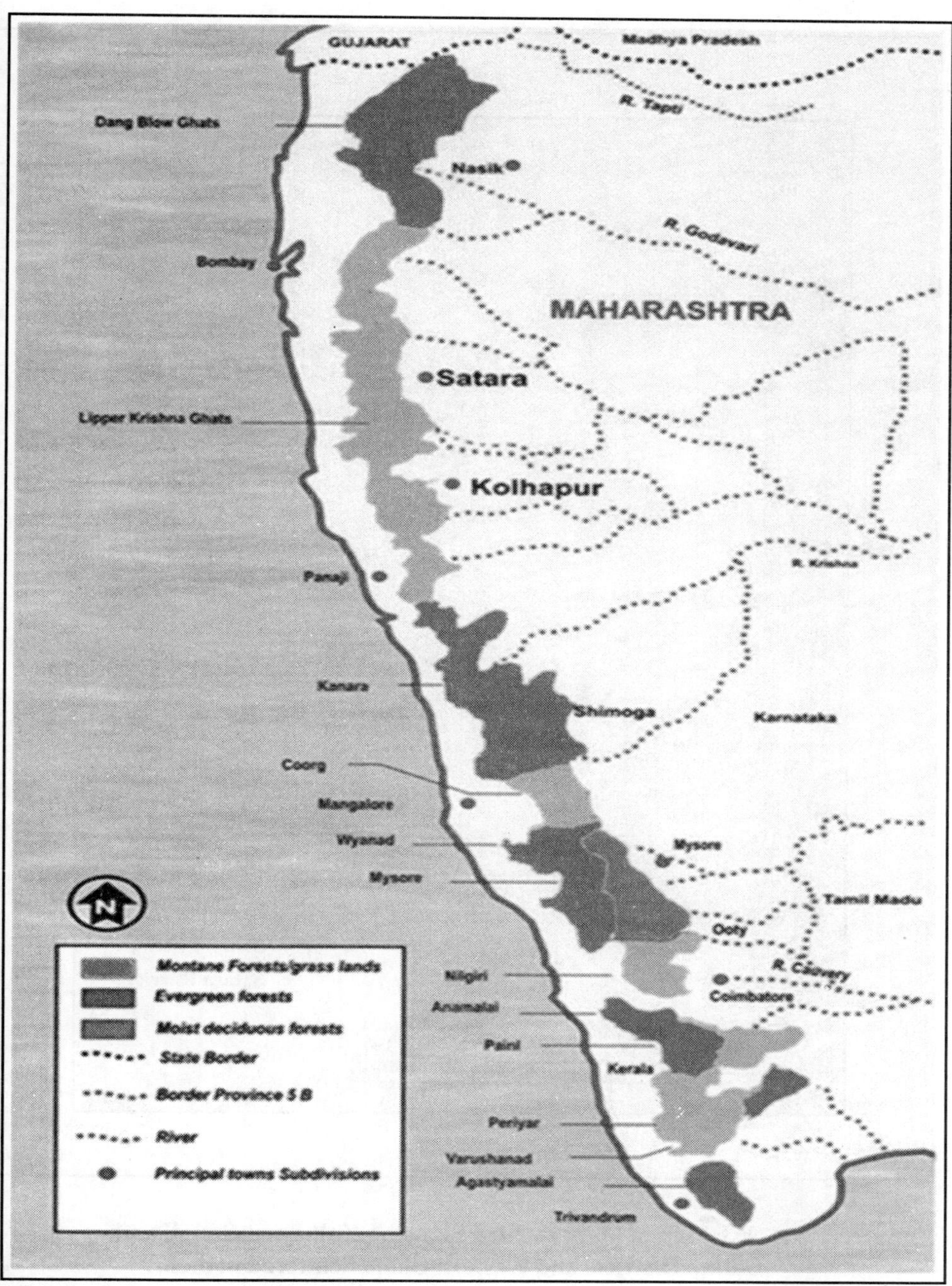

Fig. 1.2: **Map of Western Ghats**

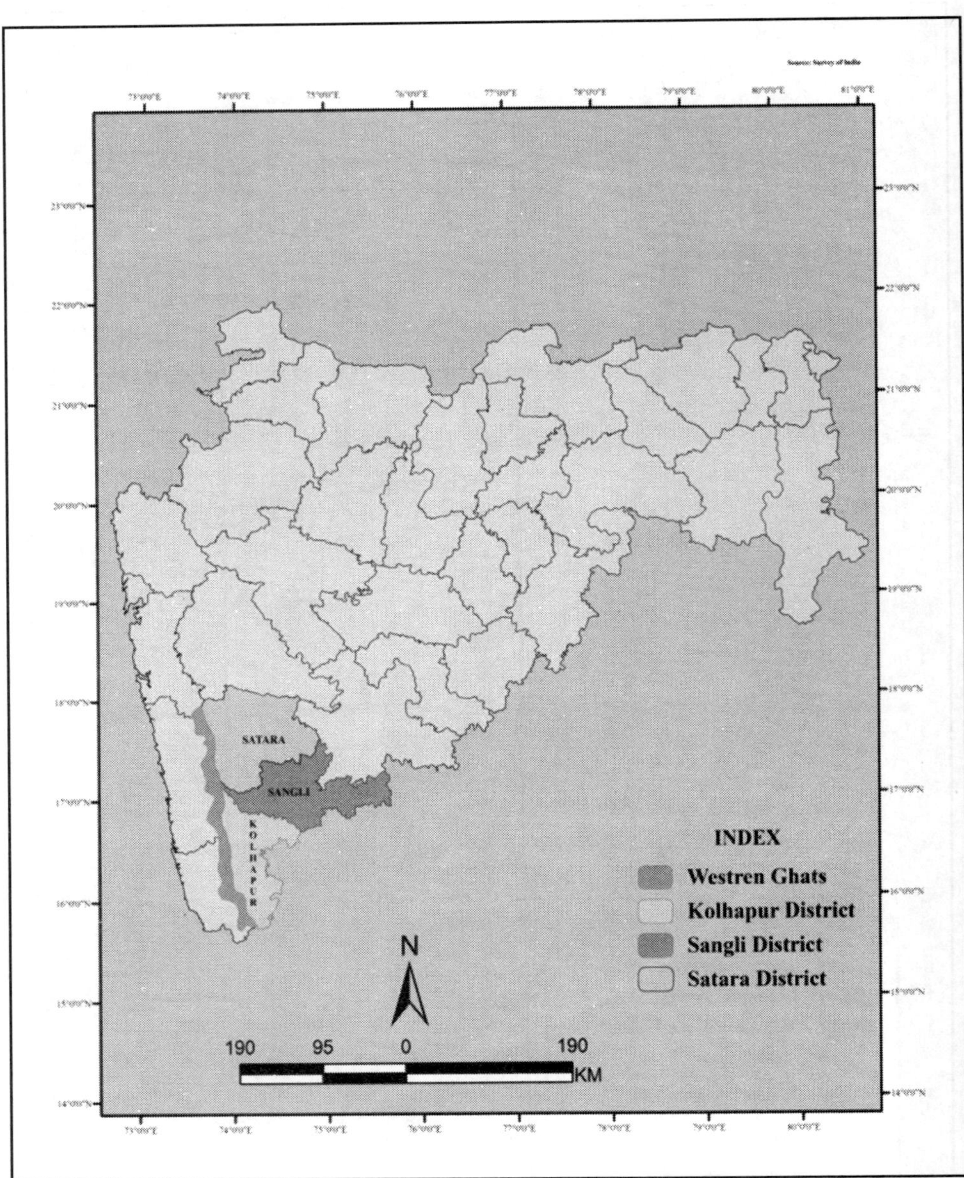

Fig. 1.3: **Map of Maharashtra Showing Kolhapur, Sangli and Satara Districts and Western Ghats Scattered in them**

basic and simplest level of biodiversity. Ecological diversity is the diversity of ecosystem/habitats/biomes/bioregions/landscapes/communities that don't really exist as discrete unit but are part of much wider system (Krebs, 1989). Genetic diversity is the total number of genetic characteristics in the genetic makeup of a species. It is distinguished from genetic variability, which describes the tendency of genetic characteristics to vary. (https://en.wikipedia.org/wiki/Genetic_diversity).

The existing biodiversity is a product of over 3.5 billion years of elevation, involving speciation, migration, extinction and human influence. Humans are responsible for the loss of biodiversity much faster than the natural rates of extinction. Many species are on the verge of extinction with higher risk in India because of a high degree of endemism. Hence, biodiversity conservation and protection is not only a national but also a global issue. Myers (1988) identified ten regions of hot spots that are characterised by high concentration of endemic species and are experiencing usually rapid rate of extinction or loss. Further, Myers (1990) added eight hot spots, four in tropical rain forest and four in Mediterranean region, making a total 18 hotspots globally. Currently the world contains 35 hot spots of biodiversity of which the Western Ghats is very prominent.

From the world, more than 17,00,000 species of microorganisms, plants and animals have been identified and described (Chapman, 2009). During the last 25 years 20,000 species have been identified and named per year. It is estimated that these can be between 10,000,000 and 13,000,000 species on earth, of which insects alone accounts to 8,000,000 species (Nieuwenhuys, 2008). Insects play a very crucial role in agriculture economy by affecting agricultural productivity.

According to Rodger and Panwar (1988) the floral wealth of Western Ghats is very rich and likely the fauna of reptiles, amphibians, mammals and insects too. In Western Ghats more than 4,500 species of flowing plants are occurred. The diversity of flowering plants in Western Ghats is equally rich. From Peninsular India, Rodger and Panwar, (1988) reported 518 rare or endangered species of animals. They also reported richness of the biodiversity with more than fifteen plant species.

The Western Ghats is characterised by a very rich faunal diversity. Many of them are highly endemic. Several reptiles and birds species are confined to only Western Ghats. Rodgers and Panwar (1988) listed many important species and groups of animal species found in Ghats while, Balakrishnan and Alexander (1984) studied wild mammals from Kerala, Western Ghats.

From Western Ghats several workers studied the insect fauna. Laresn (1987) reported 299 butterflies from the Nilgiri mountain of Western Ghats. According to Nair *et al.* (1973) a total of 314 species of butterflies have been recorded earlier from the Western Ghats region. Joseph (1984) studied the life cycles and eco-developments of insets of Western Ghats. The Western Ghats are focal points of endemic biodiversity of certain butterfly species. Wyner Blyth, (1957) listed *Colis hyale* as an endemic species. Butterflies in the Western Ghats belong to five families, 116 genara and 330 species. Of these, 37 species are endemic. These 330 species of butterflies depend on over 1000 species of plants for feeding and breeding. Diversity of butterflies in the Western Ghats are thus related to not only adult feeding habitats, but also larval food plants.

Sathe *et al.* (1986, 1987) reported 33 species of butterflies from Western Ghats of Maharashtra out of which 8 species were rare. Shivramkrishnan *et al.* (1990) observed many hill streams of Western Ghats for recording may flies. 17 insect pests feeding on mulberry plants in Amboli (Western Ghats) have been reported by Sathe and Mulla, (1995). Gaonkar (1996) reported 330 species of butterflies from the Western Ghats while, Satish (1996) recorded 13 species of moths and 16 species of butterflies from Shimoga. 13 species of Sphingid moths belonging to six genera *viz; Acherontia, Herse, Theretra, Macroglossum, Hippotion* and *Campsogene* from Western Ghats of Maharashtra have been described by Sathe and Pandharbale, (1999). Pandharbale and Sathe (2001) also described a new species of Syntomid moth, *Syntomis vitex* from the environment of Western Ghats of Satara districts.

From Radhanagari Wilds Life Sanctuary Bhoje and Sathe (2003) reported 80 species of butterflies. The diversity of higher taxa of aquatic insects in three hill streams of Western Ghats of Southern parts have been studied by Nagendran and Smija, (2004). According to them the order Ephimerida was dominated in above mentioned area. Recently, Sathe (2004) noted that lady bird beetles like: *Menochilus sexmaculatus* (Feb.), *Coccinella yamini* S.&B. found migrating to hilly regions of Western Ghats of Maharashtra along with aphids. Pandharbale (2004) described 31 species of moths from Western Ghats of Satara, out of which 16 species have been newly described. Sathe and Pandharbale (2005) recorded 130 species of moths from the Western Ghats of Satara district. 151 species of dragonflies and damsel flies have been reported from Koyana dam and around area by Shinde (2006; Sathe 2010). Out of which 17 species of dragonflies have been newly described. Sathe and Shinde (2006) studied diversity of 80 butterflies from Western Ghats of Kolhapur district. Recently, Sathe (2010) reported 40 damselflies predating on as various small insects from Koyana dam and around area.

Sathe (1992) reported 28 species of aphids on economic plants from Western Ghats. Similarly, Jadhav and Sathe (2006a, b) recorded 21 species of aphids from Western Ghats of Satara districts and 19 species Poona district.

Although, several types of insects reported from Western Ghats, very little is known on the jassids of Western Ghats except the work of Sathe *et al.* (2014). Jassids have also been reported from agro-ecosystems from plain region of Maharashtra. (Sathe *et al.* 2014).

Indian agriculture plays a very crucial role in fulfillment of nutritional requirement for increasing population and nation's economy. According to Singh and Sadhu (1986) India cultivates a wide variety of food crops including: cereals, pulses, oil seeds, vegetables, fruits, fiber and other crops. In last fifty years, cropping intensity increased from 1.11 to 1.36 (Paroda, 1993). India made significant progress in different crops by releasing first hybrids in the world producing higher productivity and possessing resistance to various biotic and abiotic traces. H-4 was the first such intraspecific cotton hybrid which was released by India very first in the world for commercial use. India also released commercial hybrids in castor and jowar. Although, several hybrids are released by India in various crops, the expected yield of the crops is not achieved so far because of the destruction to the crops by insect pests. New hybrid varieties in several agricultural, horticultural and floricultural crops are also responsible for increasing the pest complex in various ecosystems. A very large number of insects cause damage of the various parts of crop plants including: stems, leaves, flowers, seeds and roots. Many soil inhibiting insects damage roots and kill the plants causing serious losses in the crops, many more cause damage to crops by boring the roots or stems or fruits and several acts as defoliators (which feed upon the leaves). Leaf mining and formation of galls by insects are common phenomenon in agro and forest ecosystems. However, cell sap sucking insects like: aphids, jassids, delphacids, psyllids, membracids although they are small sized cause enormous damage to agriculture and forest crops resulting in 100 per cent destruction to the yield of crops (Sathe, 2012).

Jassids belongs to family Cicadellidae of sub-order Homoptera of order Hemiptera and found affecting different crops like: cotton, sunflower, soybean, sugarcane, vegetables, groundnut, mango, etc. 22,000 species of jassids have been described from the world. From India 5216 species have been reported (Ishihara, 1969).

Jassids have a rich morphological diversity. They vary in size from 2mm to 30mm. Jassids are small, wedge shaped insects of various forms, colour and sizes (Chowdhury *et al.* 2011). All jassids exhibit sexual reproduction except *Agallia quadripunctata* (Prov.) which shows parthenogenetic reproduction (Rao, 2001). Dispersal of jassid is usually by directional flights, they over winter either as eggs or adults (Rao, 2001). Jassids also exhibit a wide range of variation with regards to acoustic signals, nutritional behaviour, season and genetics and host plants. Their variation is also due to photoperiodicity and geographical position of the concerned groups (Rao, 2001).

Jassids (Hemiptera: Cicadellidae) walk diagonally and suck the cell sap with the help of piercing and sucking type of mouth parts. While sucking the cell sap, they inject toxins into the plant body which results yellowing and curling of leaves and dropping down of flowering and fruiting bodies. They secrete honey due like sticky substance which create sooty mould on leaves and affect photosynthesis, growth and finally the yield of the crop (Sathe *et al.* 2014). Jassids essentially feed on leaf tissues and fluids. Uncontrolled jassid populations can seriously damage leaves, resulting in loss of chlorophyll and premature leaf abscission. If left unchecked, severe yield losses due to shriveling of fruit may occur (Martinson *et al.* 1997). They also cause the damage to crop plants by transmitting virus diseases besides reducing the vitality, vigour and fruit-bearing capacity and also forming malformations. 115 species of Cicadellids have been reported to transmit 86 plant pathogens (Ishihara, 1969).

Jassids have 3 distinct stages of life cycle *viz;* egg, nymph and adult. Jassids are also known to produce sound for intraspecific communication (Ossiannilsson, 1949), although most sounds are quite weak and usually have to be amplified to be heard. These sounds probably are for species recognition and sexual selection. Some species have a broad range of food plants while others may be quite host specific. In temperate high latitudes they usually have a single generation per year, but in warmer climate species generally, have multiple generations per year. Most species are sexual, but a few, typically from high elevations or high latitudes, appear to be parthenogenetic (Oman 1949). Climatic factors adversely affect the insect development, life cycle, propagation and outbreaks (Prasad and Logiswan, 1997, Pedigo, 2004).

Hosts of Jassids

Although jassids are small sized, they affect a very large number of host plants.

Major hosts include: cotton (genus *Gossypium*), paddy (*Oryza sativa*), okra (*Abelmoschus esculentus* (L.), groundnut (*Aracis hypogea*), soybean (*Glycine max* (L.) Merr.), sunflower (*Helianthus annus* (L.), Brinjal (*Solanum melongena*), potato (*Solanum tuberosum*), green bean (*Phaseolus vulgaris*), cluster bean (*Cyamopsis tetragonoloba*), pea (*Pisum sativum* L.), mungbean and Pigeonpea (*Cajanus cajan* (L.) Millspaugh), cow pea (*Vigna sinensis*), chickpea (*Cicer arietinum* L.) Almost all Vegetables like: Cabbage and Cauliflower (*Brassica oleracea*), tomato (*Solanum lycopersicum*), cucumber (*Cucumis sativus*), chilly (*Capsicum annum*), onion (*Allium cepa*), mustard (*Sinapsis arvensis* L.), Aster, castor (*Ricinus communis*), cereals like wheat (*Triticum, aestivum* L.), maize (*Zea maize*), sorghum (*Sorghum vulgare*), barley (*Hordeum vulgare* L.), sugarcane (*Saccharum officinarum* L.), common beans (*Phascolus vulgaris* L.), sugar beet (*Beta vulgaris*), Gram (*Cicer arientinum*, L.), fruits like: mango (*Mangifera indica* L.), apple (*Malus malus*), carrot (*Daucus carota*), peach (*Prunus persica*), oats (*Avena sativa*), finger millet (*Eleusina coracana* Gaerth), Isabgul (*Plantaego ovata*), Cumin, (*Cummin cyminum*), bottle gourd (*Legenaria siceraria*), red carrot (*Dacucus carota*), China Rose (*Hibiscus rosasinensis* L.), several grasses including durva lawns (*Gynodon dactylon* L.), garden plants, plantations crops etc.

Natural Enemies of Jassids

The jassids have several natural enemies in the form of parasitoids and predators. *Cheilomenes sexmaculatus* (Fabricius), *Chrysoperla carnea* (Stephens), *Arescon enocki*, *Anagrus* sp. coccinellids, spider mite *T. cinnabarinus,* lady bird beetle, Lizards, spiders and several other insects predators on jassids and suppress the population of jassids in various ecosystems.

As Western Maharashtra specially, Kolhapur, Sangli and Satara districts is agricultural source and the Western Ghats is one of the 35 hot spots of the world in biodiversity. Therefore, diversity, abundance and distributional studies of jassids will add great relevance in conservation and protection of economic crop plants and general plant diversity of Western Ghats. Keeping in view all above facts, the present topic is selected.

2 Review of Literature

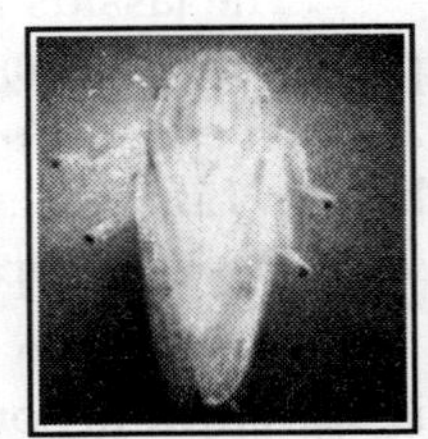

Most of the work published by scientists on the classification and diversity of the Cicadellidae has appeared in a large series of short publications, monographs and books. Review on morphological and taxonomical diversity and abundance of jassids is given below.

Cicadellidae in the World

Review of the literature indicates that, Latreille (1802) and Fieber (1806, 1852-85), made significant contribution on the family Cicadellidae. Walker (1851, 1857, 1862) listed very large number of species. He studied several species of jassids of homoptera from the collection of the British Museum. The first effort towards a synthesis of the Cicadellinae species was that of Signoret (1853a-c, 1854a-d and 1855a-d) who published redescriptions of a number of species and descriptions of a large number of new species. Stal (1869) published work dealing to genera of the subfamily Cicadellinae. Edwards (1877-1928), Van Duzee (1889-1938), Ball (1901) contributed on the North American species of jassids. Buckton (1903) worked on Membracidae and published a monograph related to jassids. Kirkaldy (1906) studied jassids and their natural enemies. Distant (1908, 1918) taxonomically treated a large number of species from oriental region. Runner and Bhiss (1923) worked on the three banded leafhoppers and other leafhoppers injuring grapes. China (1938) selected type species for the genera of Cicadellaria which has been characterised only in Melichar's key, except in those cases where the type-species were undescribed.

Melichar (1924, 1925, 1926, 1932, 1951) has made a comprehensive classification of the subfamily Cicadellinae. He divided the subfamily into two sections, Proconiaria and Cicadellaria and placed 54 genera in the

Proconiaria and included 101 genera to the Cicadellaria. He also provided keys to the subfamilies and genera. Zachvatkin (1924-48), China (1927) and Oman (1930-71) studied several genera and species of jassids. Bohart and Mitchell (1943) studied one new species of the genus *Halictophagus* with a key to general species in North America. Poos and Wheeler (1943) worked on the host plants of leafhoppers of the genus *Empoasca*. China and Fennah (1945) studied the genera *Tettigonia* Geoff, *Tittigonia* F., *Tettigoniella* Jac. and *Iassus* Fab. while, Hepner (1946, 1947) studied a new subgenus and several new species of *Scaphytopius*. Evans (1947, 1948) published a list of Cicadellids. Oman (1949) placed the Nearctic species of Ciccadellidae into various genera, partly on the male genitalia structure.

Ossiannilsson (1949) worked on jassids produced sound for the intraspecific communication. Kramer (1950) studied the morphology and phylogeny of Auchenorhynchous Homoptera including jassids. Wagner (1950, 1964) contributed on the genus *Macropsis* with 8 species, he gave illustrations and descriptions. Nielson (1951-68, 1982) revised the subfamily *Coelidiinae.*

Ross (1957, 1968) studied the evolutionary development in the leafhoppers, grouped under family Cicadellidae. Ross (1968) also studied the evolution and dispersal of the grassland jassids of the genus *Exitianus* (Cicadellidae: Homoptera) with keys. Young (1958, 1963, 1964 and 1965) worked on the species of *Homalodisca* in the United state and types of Cicadellidae in the Naturhistoriska Riksmuseet in Stockholm and some Cicadellinae lectotypes of Breddin species. Metcalf (1962-68) gave a general catalogue of Homoptera-Fascicle VI, Cicadelloidea (17 parts) from agricultural research service, North Kerolina. Carpriles (1964) contributed on Idiocerinae jassids II. The Indian and Phillippine species of *Idiocerus* and the genus *Idioscopus* have been attempted by Carpriles (1964). Emeljanov (1964) reported several new genera and species of Cicadellidae from middle Asia. Hennig (1965) studied the phylogenetic systematics of jassids. Metcalf (1965) prepared a general catalogue of Homoptera, Fascicle VI, Cicadelloidea Part I, Tettigellidae.

Pollard and Yonce (1965) studied the significance of length of tibial spines in some leafhoppers. Kramer (1966) revised the new world's jassids of the subfamily Ledrinae. Vilbaste (1968, 1982) provided the preliminary key for the identification of the nymphs of North European Homoptera, Cicadinea II. Ishihara (1969) reported about 115 species of Cicadellids. He also added on pathological role of them. Knight (1970, 1983 1987) studied the family Cicadellidae and revised the genus *Hishimonus* Ishihara. Chauri (1971) revised the genus *Nephotettix* (Homoptera: Cicadelloidea: Euscelidae). Nast (1972, 1976 and 1985) worked on Palaearctic Auchenorrhyncha (Homoptera). Morrison (1973) worked on the subfamily Hecalinae

(Homoptera: Cicadellidae) from Oriental region. Nei (1973, 1978) analysed the genetic diversity in subdivided populations of jassids. Hamilton (1975, 1984) worked on the genera of jassids.

Logvinenko (1975) studied jassids of Ukraine while, Walter (1975, 1978) and Anufriev (1977) studied the jassids of subfamily Euscelinae. Barnett (1977) revised the Nearctic species of the genus *Scaphoideus* while, Nielson (1977, 1982) revised the subfamily Coelidiinae (Homopera: Cicadellidae) with 11 tribes. Kameswara *et al.* (1978) studied the genus *Moonia* of Cicadellidae. Linnavuori (1978) also studied the family Cicadellidae. Alam and Alam (1979) studied hopperburn by the orange-headed leafhopper in Bangladesh. Young (1979, 1986) worked on the genus *Cofana* (Homoptera: Cicadellidae). Hamilton (1980-82) reported a number of jassids from the Oriental, Palaearctic and Nearctic regions. Sohi (1983) worked on the Oriental Typhlocybinae with special reference to pests of cotton and rice. Wilson (1983) studied the genus *Paramesodes* Ishihara (Homoptera: Archenorrhyncha: Cicadellidae) with description of 8 new species. Stewart (1986) described the nymphs of *Eupteryx* by providing key. Theron (1986) contributed on new genera and species of southern African Coelidiinae with description of new tribe Equeefini. Freytag (1987, 1989) reported 2 new genera, *Brevicisana* and *Minimana* and 4 new species of Gypoininae (Homoptera: Cicadellidae). He also added 3 new genera and 6 new species from South American Gyponine. (Homoptera: Cicadellidae). Thapa (1989) worked on some higher Himalayan Typhlocybine jassids (Homoptera: Cicadellidae).

Hayashi and Arai (1990) reported 5 new species of the genus *Pagaronia* Ball from Central Honshu. Oman *et al.* (1990) studied the leafhoppers of Cicadellidae and provided bibliography, generic checklist and index of the world. They also proposed a provisional higher classification of jassids recognizing 40 subfamilies and 121 tribes of Cicadellidae. Webb and Heller (1990) studied the genus *Pseupalus* in the world tropics with a checklist of the Afrotropical and Oriental paraliminini (Homoptera: Cicadellidae: Deltocephalinae). Cai (1992, 1993, 1994) described 5 new species of the genus *Tituria*, a new species of the genus *Confucius* and a new genus and 2 new species of Ledrinae. Dietrich (1993, 1994) worked phylogenetic analysis of jassids (Homoptera: Cicadellidae) family-groups. Dietrich and Deitz (1993), Godoy and Webb (1994) worked on subfamilies of Cicadellidae from Coast Rica. Blocker *et al.* (1995) reviewed the Nearctic Deltocephalinae. Dietrich and Vega (1995) worked on systematics of the genus *Draeculacephala* Ball (Homoptera: Cicadellidae). Fang *et al.* (1995) studied the cladistical analysis of Nearctic Deltocephalinae. Skimmer and Camacho (1995) worked on the genetic diversity within a potato leafhopper (Homoptera: Cicadellidae) population infesting alfalfa.

Cai and He (1997) studied the newly recorded genera of jassids from China. Meidalani (1998) studied new species of Neotropical genus *Bythonia*. Rakitov (1998) worked on the differentiation of Cicadellids leg chaetotaxy. Dmitriev (1999, 2001, 2002a, 2002b, 2003, 2004) studied the larvae of European species of *Elymana* DeLong (Homoptera: Cicadellidae) and the larvae of some species of the subfamily Eupelicinae (Homoptera: Cicadellidae) and general morphology of jassid nymphs of the subfamily Deltocephalinae (Hemiptera: Cicadellidae) from European, Russian and adjacent territories. A key to the tribes Drabescini, Scaphytopiini, Hecalini, Limotettigini and Opsiini for larvae of the jassids of subfamily Deltocephalinae (Homoptera: Cicadellidae) has been given from European, Russian and adjacent territories. The tribes Deltocephalini, Stirellini and Paralimnini were also provided. McKamey (2000, 2005) gave checklist of leafhoppers 1758- 1955 (Hemiptera: Cicadellidae) with synonymy and distribution.

Nicholls *et al.* (2000) studied the abundance of jassids from a northern California organic vineyard. Yh *et al.* (2000) worked on freeware for Population Genetic analysis. Khaing *et al.* (2002) studied special distribution pattern of cotton jassids. Tishechkin (2002) reviewed the species of the genus *Macropsis* Lewis. Holzinger *et al.* (2003) worked especially on the Auchenorrhyncha of Central Europe while, Wallace and Deitz (2004) worked on phylogeny and systematics of the subfamily Centrotinae. Wang and Li (2004) studied three new species of the genus *Scaphoideus*. Li and Dai (2004) described 6 new species of *Scaphoidius* from China. Backus *et al.* (2005) have taken an overview of insect taxonomy, behaviour and phylogeny. Zenner *et al.* (2005) gave preliminary key to the nymphs of the families and subfamilies of the German jassid fauna, it covers 4 subfamilies of Cicadellidae and 13 subfamilies.

A taxonomic studies on the leafhopper genus *Scaphoidella* Vilvaste (Homoptera: Cicadellidae: Deltocethalinae) has been made by Zhang and Dai (2006). Knight and Fletcher (2007) studied new deltocephalinae jassids genus *Melanettettix* from Melanesia. Xing *et al.* (2008) studied a new species of the genus *Scaphoidella* from Hainan Province in China. Zahniser and Dietrich (2008, 2010) studied morphology-based phylogeny of the leafhopper of subfamily Deltocephalilae and related groups (Homoptera: Cicadellidae), based on molecular and morphological data with a revised family-group classification. Zahniser (2008) studied systemics of the leafhopper subfamily Deltocephalilae (Homoptera: Cicadellidae) and the tribe Chiasmini. He highlighted the phylogeny, classification and biogeography. Li and Xing (2009) reported a new species of the genus *Scaphoidella* Vilbaste (Hemiptera: Cicadellidae: Euscelinae) from China. Zhang *et al.* (2010) reviewed the genera of *Emposca* and *Dworakowska* with description of some new species from China. Saguez *et al.* (2012) studied diversity and abundance of leafhoppers from Canadian vineyards. Hafizal and Idris (2014) worked on temporal population abundance of leafhoppers (Homoptera: Cicadellidae) and plant hoppers (Homoptera: Delphacidae) as affected by temperature, humidity and rice growth stages. Qin *et al.* (2014) studied the genera of *Emposcini* and provided the key to the species from China. Very recently, Xing and Li (2015) reviewed Chinese species of the leafhoppers of the genus *Scaphoidella*.

Cicadellidae of India

Atkinson (1885) provided notes on Indian Rhynchota No. 3. Distant (1908, 1916 and 1918) made significant contribution on the jassid fauna of British India. Hussain and Pruthi (1923) provided short notes on life history of mango hoppers (*Idiocerous*) in Punjab. Pruthi (1930, 1934, 1936, 1940) has also gave significant contribution on the Indian Jassidae (Homoptera - I, II, III) with description of several species from North India. The contribution of Ghauri (1936, 1963, 1967, 1971, 1975) have also strengthened the literature on jassids. He worked on several subfamilies of the family Cicadellidae from India. Mathur (1953) provided a systematic catalogue of entomological collection of the forest research Institute. Menon and Das (1958) worked on taxonomy of Indian Membracidae including jassids. Rao (1967, 1973, 1981, 1986 and 1990) significantly reported jassids with descriptive notes on Homoptera: Cicadellidae from the Meghalaya. Datta (1969, 1972, 1973 and 1988) studied taxonomy of Indian Cicadellidae (Homoptera - I and II) similarly, Dworakowska (1969ab, 1970, 1976, 1977, 1979-81) also made significant contribution on the jassids of Oriental region with a remark on synonymy. He revised the family Typhlocybinae.

Singh (1969) described 15 new species of jassids (Cicadellidae) from Himachal Pradesh and Chandigarh. Bindra and Singh (1970) worked on biology and bionomis of a jassid *Orosius albicintus* Distant. Ramkrishnana and Menon (1971, 1972) studied Indian Typhlocybinae (Homoptera: Cicadellidae) with 8 new genera and a new record of tribe Dikraneurini. Sohi (1972, 1983-84) classified subfamilies of Cicadellidae and added good number of new species of Typhlocybinae. Datta and Ghosh (1973, 1974) reported three new species of Typhlocybinae (Homoptera: Cicadellidae) from the Himalayan region. Dworakowska and Viraktamath (1975, 1978, and 1979) also studied some Typhlocybinae from India. Viraktamath (1976-90) contributed some new species of the genera *Doratulina* and *Bumizana* (Homoptera: Cicadellidae) from Karnataka. He also added *Jogocerus* gen. nov. and new species of *Idioscopus* from southern India. Anufriev (1977) reported two new species of Auchenorrhynchous from the Temperate Asia. Malhotra and Sharma (1977) provided the key to identification of common jassids (Homoptera: Cicadellidae) of J and K state. Datta *et al.* (1978, 1984) also made significant contribution on Cicadellidae. Gangopadhyay, (1980) studied new species of *Idioscopus* from southern India.

Ghosh *et al.* (1986, 2000) worked on Cicadellidae of India and accounted 41 species belonging to 35 genera and 5 families from Calcutta. Nath *et al.* (1986) provided a key for the identification of jassids, occurring on rice in west Bengal. Ghosh and Ghosh (1994, 1998) studied the fauna of west Bengal, and Meghalaya comprising 38 species belonging to 27 genera distributed over 12 subfamilies, it is based on recent as well as the old collections made by different survey party members of Zoological Survey of India.

Prasad and Logiswan (1997) studied climatic factors affecting the insect development. Biswas and Ghosh (1998) also worked on Indian jassids. They reported first consolidated account of 19 species belonging to 11 genera from Meghalaya. Rao (2001) worked on general observation, economic importance and systematic list of jassids and effect of human activity.

Sathe and Margaj (2001) studied on cotton pests including jassids and biocontrol agents. Ghosh and Ghosh (2004) worked on taxonomy of Cicadellidae (Insecta: Homoptera). Dietrich (2005) provided keys to the subfamilies of Cicadomorpha and to the subfamilies and tribes of Cicadellidae (Hemiptera: Auchenorrhyncha). Ghosh and Bal (2007) also made significant contribution on taxonomy of Cicadelloidea (Insecta: Hemiptera). Their work has included 22 species belonging to 16 genera scattered in 6 families of the superfamily Cicadelloidae, all the species are being recorded for the first time from the state. Dai *et al.* (2009) reviewed the leafhopper genus *Scaphotettix* Matsumura (Hemiptera, Cicadellidae, Deltocephalinae) with description of a new genus. Chandra *et al.* (2012) studied diversity of grassland Auchenorrhyncha (Cicadidae, Cercopidae, Cicadellidae) in Madhya-Pradesh and Chhattisgarh, India. Very recently, Kamble and Sathe (2015b) described a new species of the genus *Scaphoideus* (Hemiptera: Cicadellidae) for the first time on Grapevine from India.

Saha *et al.* (2012) studied seasonal incidence and enzyme-based susceptibility to synthetic insecticides in two sucking insect pests of tea. Shahid *et al.* (2012) worked on seasonal occurrence of sucking insect pests in cotton ecosystem of Punjab. Pachundkar *et al.* (2013) studied an evolution of various synthetic insecticides against sucking insect pests of cluster bean. Chandra (2014) studied the fauna of Achanakmar, Amarkantak Biosphere Reserve, Chhattisgarh and Madhya Pradesh. Praveen *et al.* (2014) prepared new records of jassids from Chhattisgarh. Kamble *et al.* (2014) studied the vertical destructive pattern of *Amrasca biguttula* (Ishida) on sunflower and its control in Kolhapur district of Maharashtra. Sathe *et al.* (2014) worked on biodiversity of jassids from agro-ecosystems of Kolhapur district, India. They reported 22 species of jassids. Kamble and Sathe (2015a) worked on colour preference of sugarcane jassids *Cofana spectra* Distant (Hemiptera: Cicadellidae). Sathe and Kamble (2015) also studied the impact of Environmental factors on population of *Idioscopus clypealis* (Hemipera: Cicadellidae) on mango. Review of literature indicates that very little attention is given on the diversity, occurrence and damage of jassids from Western Maharashtra although this area is very rich in biodiversity.

3 Collection and Preservation Methods of Jassids

Establishing and standardizing methodologies for scientific work is continuous process. Correct methodology always provides good results. Hence, biodiversity of jassids have been studied by adopting following materials and methods.

MATERIALS

1. *Glass Cages* (Fig. 3.1 and 3.2): Jassids have been reared in two types of glass cages of size, 25 × 25 × 30cm. (Fig. 3.1 and 3.2) with quadrangular shape under laboratory conditions (27 ± 1°C, 75 - 80 per cent R.H. 12 hr. photoperiod). Each cage consisted wooden base and glass walls except in one cage (Fig. 3.1) door was designed with muslin cloth as a sleeve for handling the insects and in the second type (Fig. 3.2) the door was of glass. The nymphs and adults of jassids were reared on host plant twigs which were immersed into the water in glass jar and the glass jar was kept in glass cage.
2. *Glass Troughs* (Fig. 3.3A and 3.3B): Two sized, 25 × 10cm (diameter and height) (Fig. 3.3A) and 22 × 9cm (Fig. 3.3B) glass troughs were used for rearing the jassids. For protection and prevention of jassids from escape, glass troughs were covered with muslin cloth.
3. *Plastic Containers* (Fig. 3.4 and 3.5): 18 × 6cm (height and diameter), 13 × 5cm, 6 × 4cm (Fig. 3.4) sized containers were used for rearing the jassids and keeping them live for the purpose of scientific studies. The containers were perforated with small holes for aeration for jassids.

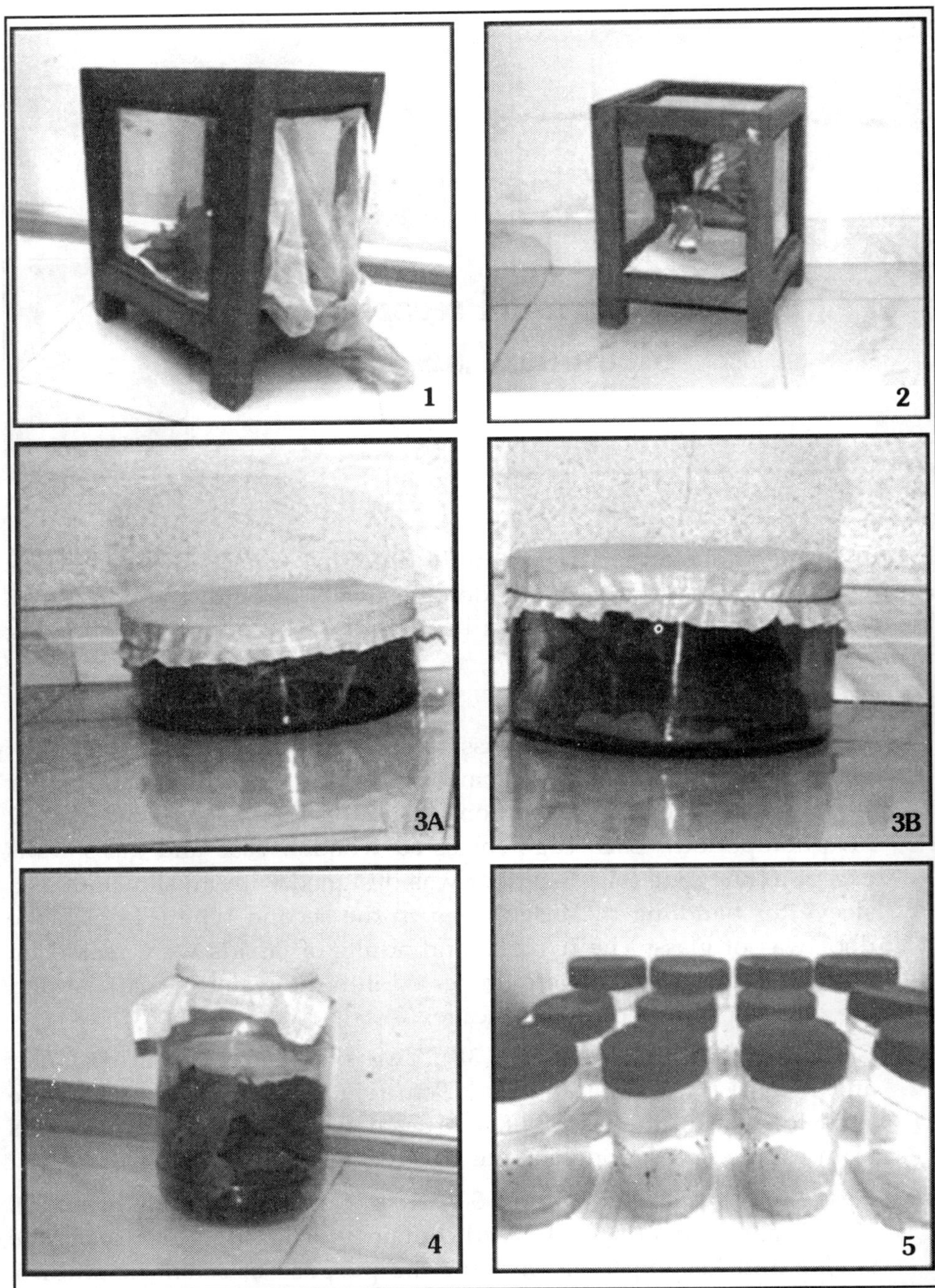

Plage - I: Fig. 3.1: **Glass Cage Type-1,** Fig. 3.2: **Glass Cage Type-2,** Fig. 3.3A & B: **Glass Troughs,** Fig. 3.4 & 3.5: **Plastic Containers**

4. *Petridish* (Fig. 3.6): A petridish (10 × 1.5cm in diameter and height) (Fig. 3.6) was used for rearing and handling the jassids.
5. *Test Tube* (Fig. 3.7): Test tube of size, 15 × 1.8cm (length and diameter) has been used for handling the jassids.
6. Specimen Bottles (Fig. 3.8): For preserving and handling the nymphs and adults of jassids. The mouth of bottles has been closed by rubber cork for keeping specimens air tight and safety. Specimen bottles of size, 6 × 2cm (length and diameter), 5 × 2cm and 4 × 2cm were used.
7. *Forcep* (Fig. 3.9): Forcep has been used for handling the jassids.
8. *Insect Collecting Net* (Fig. 3.10): Jassids have been collected with the help of insect collecting net (Fig. 3.10).
9. Camera Canon SX 600 HS (Fig 3.11): Photographs have been taken with the help of Canon SX 600 HS megapixels. Photographs of jassids on host plants and their habitats have also taken by above Camera.
10. *Lens* (Fig. 3.12): Lens has been used for observation of jassids in field and under laboratory conditions.
11. *Brushes* (Fig. 3.13A, B and C): Camel hair brushes No. 00 (Fig. 3.13A), No. 4 (Fig. 3.13B) and No. 8 (Fig. 3.13C), have been used for preparation of slides and collecting jassids from various host plants.
12. *Lens* (Fig. 3.12): Lens has been used for observation of jassids in field and under laboratory conditions.
13. *Brushes* (Fig. 3.13A, B and C): Camel hair brushes No. 00 (Fig. 3.13A), No. 4 (Fig. 3.13B) and No. 8 (Fig. 3.13C) have been used for preparation of slides and collecting jassids from various host plants.
14. *Polythene Bags* (Fig. 3.14): Jassids were temporarily kept in polythene bags of size 18 × 12cm (length and width) during the field condition and bags were punctured with fine point for aeration to jassids.
15. *Slide Boxes* (Fig. 3.15): 28 × 22 × 3.5cm (length, width and height) sized insect slide boxes were used for keeping the slides of jassids. The slides have been appropriately labeled.
16. *Slide and Cover Slips* (Fig. 3.16): The whole mounts and other body parts like antenna, hind leg, wings and genitalia were taken on slides for which ordinary slides and cover slips were used.
17. Bulb (Fig. 3.17): An anchor cool daylight bulb of 20 W - 3U. 240 V - 50/60 Hz. Lumen 1120 B22-6500K. was used for trapping/attracting jassids.

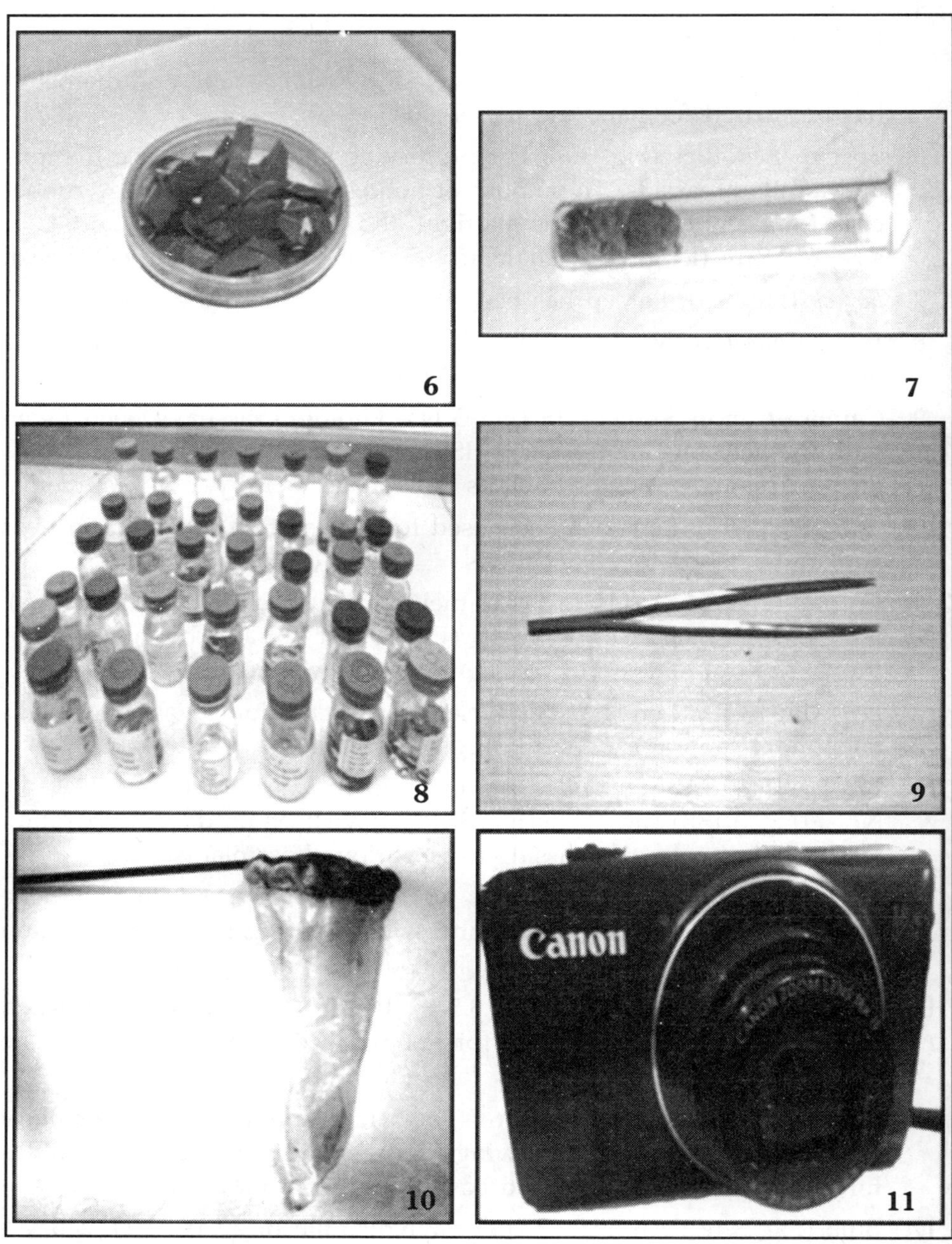

Plage - II: Fig. 3.6: **Petridish,** Fig. 3.7: **Test tubes,** Fig. 3.8: **Specimen Bottles,** Fig. 3.9: **Forcep,** Fig. 3.10: **Insect Collecting Net,** Fig. 3.11: **Camera Canon SX 600HS**

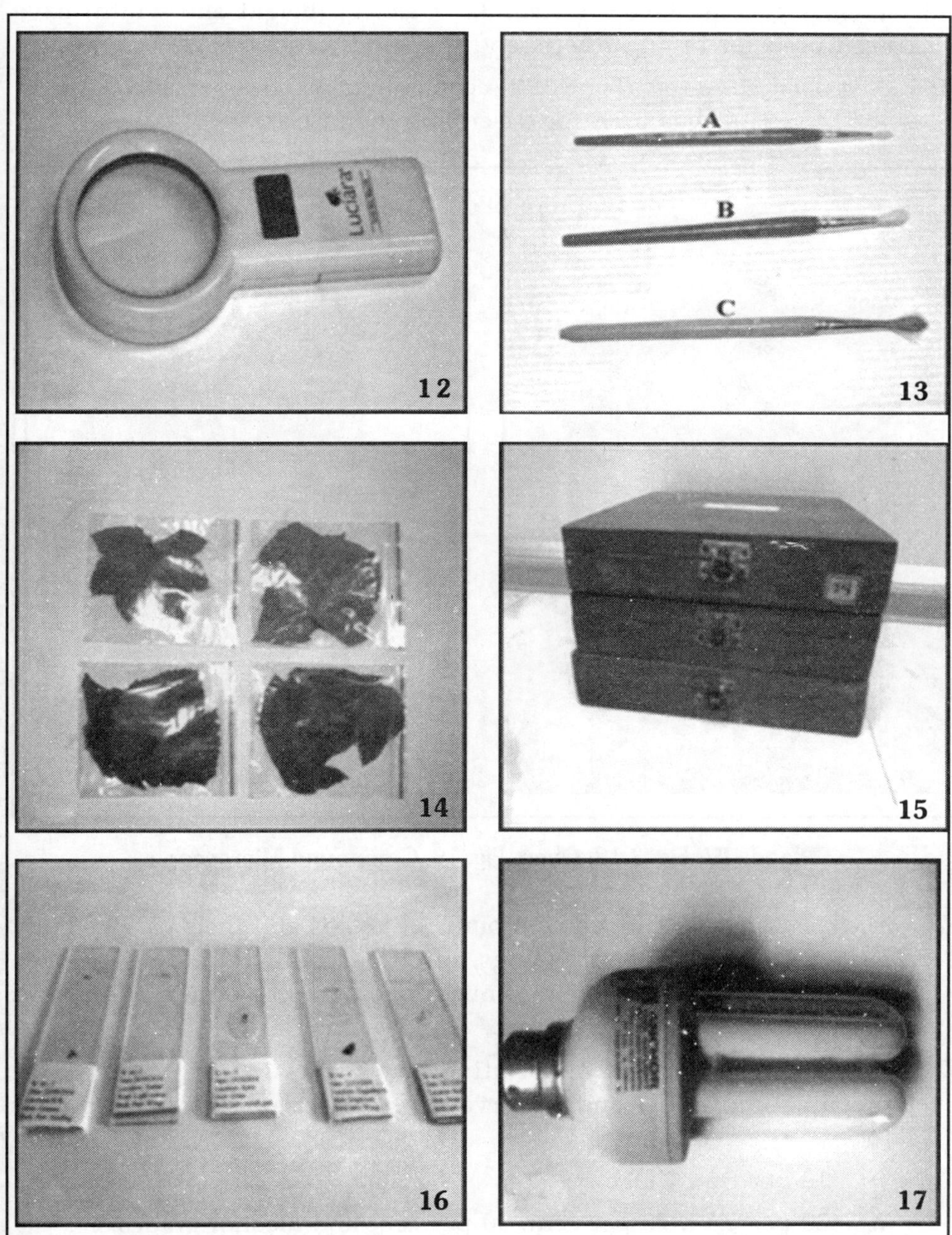

Plage - III: Fig. 3.12: **Len,** Fig. 3.13A, B&C: **Brushes,** Fig. 3.14: **Polythene bags,** Fig. 3.15: **Slide boxes,** Fig. 3.16: **Slides & Coverslipes,** Fig. 3.17: **Bulb**

18. *Oven* (Fig. 3.18): Oven of size, 3.6 × 2.4feet (height and width) have been used for drying insects and the slides of jassids.
19. *Compound Microscope* (Fig. 3.19): A compound microscope with objectives 10 × 45 × 100 was used for describing the insects.

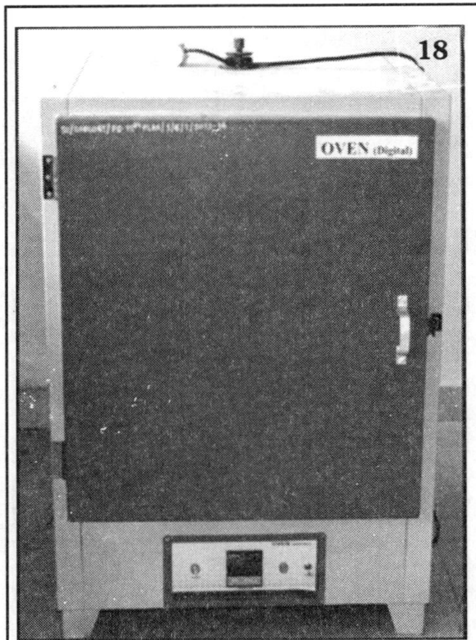

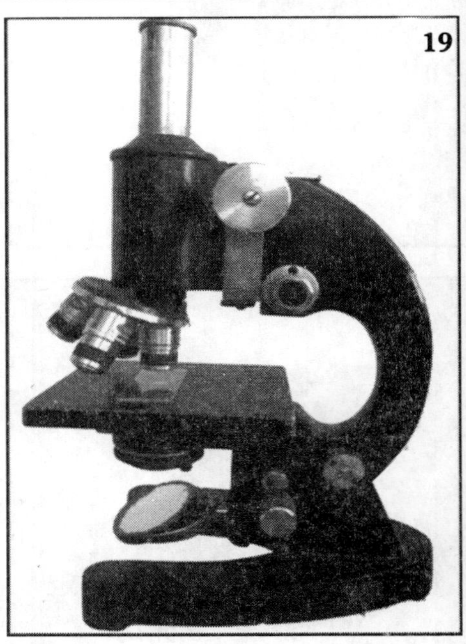

Plage - IV: Fig. 3.18: **Oven,** Fig. 19: **Compound Microscope**

20. *Microphotographs*: The whole mounts of jassids and their various body parts *viz*; head, antenna, wings, hind leg, genitalia etc., have been photographed with the help of micro-photographic camera (Canon SX 600 HS).
21. *Chemicals*: For studding biodiversity of jassids, especially, for preparation of slides and preservation of insects, chemicals used refer to:
    - *(i)* 10 per cent KOH;
    - *(ii)* 30 per cent, 70 per cent, 90 per cent and alcohol grades;
    - *(iii)* Xylene;
    - *(iv)* D.P.X./Canada Balsam.

METHODOLOGY

Preparation of Slides

The slides of Jassids have been prepared as per the following method:

Jassids were collected from the fields on various crop plants with the help of camel hair brush or swift insect net. The infested plant twig along with the insects (nymphs and adults) was collected in polythene bags. The nymphs of the insects thus collected were reared in the laboratory in glass cages (25 × 25 × 25) cm in which twig was immerged into the water in beaker. The nymphs were allowed to develop into adults. Such adults, sometimes have been considered for preparation of slides. The field collected jassids/laboratory jassids have been passed through various grades of alcohol, namely 30 per cent, 50 per cent, 70 per cent, 90 per cent and absolute for dehydration. The dehydrated jassids have been cleaned in xylene and mounted in DPX. The slides have been dried at 60°C for at least one week. Such slides were used for morphological studies of the insects.

From Kolhapur, Sangli and Satara (Western Maharashtra), extensive collection of jassids was made from various study spots including Ghats, during the year 2013-15. A very large number of jassids were collected from Forest ecosystems of above three districts. The collection of jassids was made early in the morning and evening.

Morphological Diversity

The morphological diversity of jassids was studied with the help of Compound microscope. Various body parts such as head, thorax and abdomen and their appendages were taken into account for morphological diversity. Detailed descriptions were made on the species collected from the study area and identified by consulting appropriate literature cited in bibliography.

The measurements were taken by ocular micrometer and expressed in millimeter (mm).

- *Body length*: Body length was considered from the tip of head to the tip of abdomen of jassid.
- *Body width*: Body at maximum width was considered for measurement.
- *Antenna*: Length of antenna of jassid from base of first segment to the tip of flagellum was counted. Similarly, other appendages of the body have also been measured in mm.

The jassids were collected in the early morning and evening from agricultural and forest study areas. The collection of jassids were also made at night by the light source, with sticky card sheets (Kamble and Sathe 2015) and used for diversity studies.

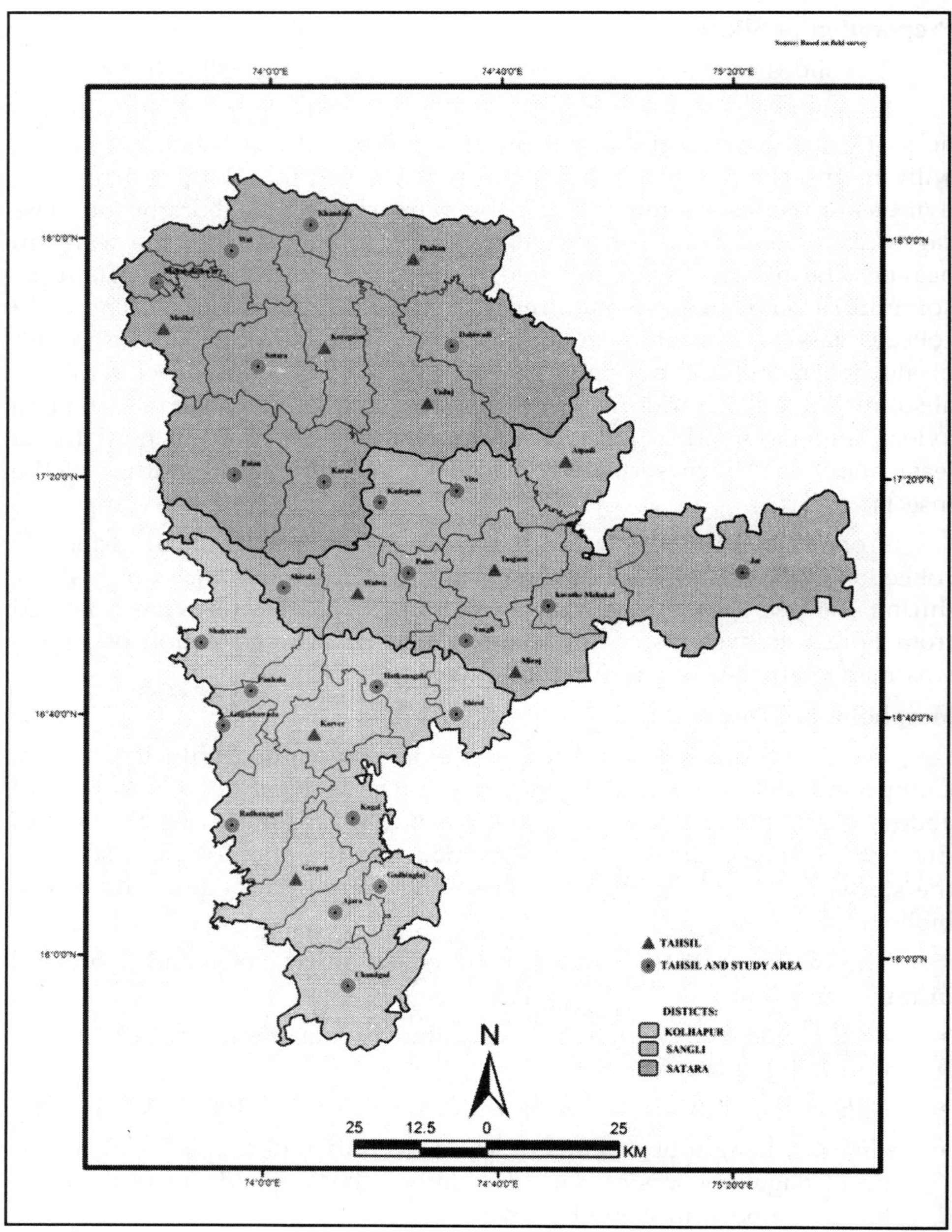

Fig. 3.20: **Map of Districts - Kolhapur, Sangli and Satarna (Study Area)**

Sampling of Jassids

Sampling of jassids were made by 'One man one hour search method' from study area by insect swift net method (Sathe *et al.* 2014) from Western Maharashtra (Districts: Kolhapur, Sangli and Satara only). Distribution and seasonal abundance of jassids have been studied by visiting selected study areas at 15 days interval and by 'One man one hour swift insect net collection method' and keeping the records of their availability in the fields.

Extensive survey of jassids was made during the years 2013-15 from various collection spots of Western Maharashtra (Figs. 3.20-3.32) specially Shahuwadi, Panhala, Gaganbawda, Radhanagari, Hatkanangale, Shirol, Karvir, Kagal, Gadhahinglaj, Ajara, Chandgad of Kolhapur District and from Miraj, Shirala, Palus, Jat, Kavathe Mahankal, Kadegaon of Sangli District while, from Satara district Dahiwadi, Karad, Khandala, Patan, Satara, Mahabaleshwar and Wai were taken into account. Both agro and forest ecosystems were considered for the survey of jassids.

Host Records

For the host plant record, jassids feeding on host plants were noted and collected from the field and later, both plants and insects were identified by consulting appropriate literature cited in under bibliography.

Host Plant Damage

Host plant damage by jassids was studied under field condition by spot observations, the features of leaves, flowers and fruits, sooty moulds if any on plant body and growth of the plants by height and general health were taken into account.

Preparation and Examination of Genitalia

1. The apex of the abdomen/preferably the whole abdomen was carefully removed.
2. Abdomen was heated in 10 per cent KOH for 2 to 3 min.
3. Muscles and soft connective tissues were removed.
4. Abdomen was made sufficiently transparent to see the internal structures.
5. Care was taken for not to heat the genitalia for too long for avoiding excess transparency to genitalia.
6. Once the matter cleared, the genitalia was removed from the KOH and washed thoroughly twice in distilled water to ensure that all trace of the KOH was removed.
7. The genitalia then transferred to 70 per cent ethanol for examination and eventually into a small rubber topped plastic tube of glycerin for storage.

Plate - V: Fig. 3.21: **Study Spot: Gaganbawada,** Fig. 3.22: **Study Spot, Sangli,** Fig. 3.23: **Amba Ghats,** Fig. 3.24: **Amboli Ghats**

Plate - VI: Fig. 3.25: **Author Collecting insect - Gadhinglaj,** Fig. 3.26: **Author at study spot - Gaganbawada,** Fig. 3.27: **Jassids on *Cajanus cajan* (L.,),** Fig. 3.28: **Jassids on *Heltantus amannis* (L.,)**

Plate - VII: Fig. 3.29: **Jassids on *Abelmoschus esculantus* (L.,)**, Fig. 3.30: **Jassids on *Arachius hypogea* (L.,)**, Fig. 3.31: **Jassids on *Gossypium sp.***, Fig. 3.32: **Jassids on *Phaseolus Vulgais* L.**

Distributional Records

On the basis of number of jassid collected and availability of jassids, distributional records were made from various places of Western Maharashtra at 15 days interval. One man one hour search method was adopted for making distributional records.

4 Diversity of Jassids

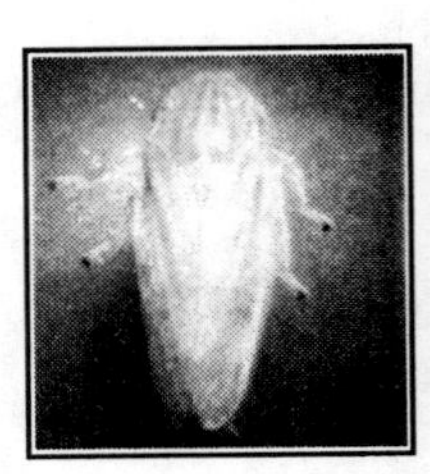

INTRODUCTION

As a part of the largest group of the animal kingdom, insects are divided into 29 orders that are in turn broadly grouped into Apterygota or wingless (ex. Silverfish, springtail, etc.,) and Pterygota or winged (ex. Bugs, butterflies, moths, beetles, flies etc.,) forms. From invertebrate animals, only the insects have the flying capacity. They appeared on the earth around 360 million years ago. Insects are supposed to be the most successful groups of animals, surviving on the earth and are significantly managed by the man for his needs as nutrition, medicine and economical products like: silk, honey, wax, colour, etc. (Atwal, 1976; Sathe, 2005).

About ½ million species have been recorded in the scientific literature and several million insects are awaiting their discoveries mainly in tropics (Chelliah and Ganathilagaraj, 1993). Since India is considered to be one of the richest centers of biodiversity in the world, more than 60,000 species of insects have been described in the country (Ananthakrishnan 1993; Gupta 2004). Biodiversity has never been an attractive profession, but in recent years, it has been attracted the attention of scientists due to its importance in the development of a region or a country. Hence, financial agencies are coming forward for financial assistance to biodiversity studies. Biodiversity experts and taxonomist are presently needed in several institutes such as: Universities, Research Institutes, Museums, Central and State Government agencies, Industries, Zoos etc., for identification and utilization of flora and fauna for the betterment of nature and humans. Therefore, in the present study, morphological and faunastic diversity of jassids has been studied.

Morphological Considerations

The body of jassid is divisible into the head, thorax and abdomen (Fig. 4.1).

- *Head* (Fig. 4.2, 4.3): According to Dietrich, (2005) the term face is used to refer to the anterior part and the term crown refers to the dorsal part, although in different groups these areas are made up of parts of different sclerites. Some authors (Blocker and Triplehorn, 1985) use crown and vertex interchangeably, but the term vertex is correctly applied only to the pair of sclerites posterolaterad of the frontal sutures and bearing the lateral ocelli. The rostrum (or beak), the modified labium, varies in length in different species. The clypeus is almost always divided by the clypeal (or transclypeal) suture into two sclerites, the anteclypeus (clypellus) and post-clypeus, both of which vary in texture and proportions in various forms. The post-clypeus is usually not clearly divided from the frons dorsally, hence, the term frontoclypeus is often used to refer to the combined sclerite, which is usually the largest structure of the head in anterior view. Immediately lateral of the clypeus on the lower part of the face is a pair of mandibular plates called the Lora (singular-lorum), which vary in size, shape and relative position in different species. The lorum is situated on the maxillary plate. In most jassids, the gena and maxillary plate are fused, but in some cases maxillary plate and gena separated by a distinct suture or cleft. The antennae (Fig. 4.4) of jassid consist of two short basal segments and an elongate flagellum, which varies in length and shape and may be sub-segmented. The base of the antenna may be partly covered dorsally by an outgrowth of the vertex called the antennal ledge, which also varies in shape and may extend onto the frontoclypeus. The size and shape of eyes and the ocelli vary in their position may be different in different species. The frontal sutures are reduced or lost in various taxa and their relative shape and position also varies.
- *Thorax* (Fig. 4.5): The pronotum of jassid varies in shape, ornamentation, texture and proportions. The mesonotum and scutellum, divided by the scutellar suture vary in proportions and the degree of concealment to pronotum. Important pleural sclerites include the proepisternum, the mesepisternum and mesepimeron which vary in proportions or structures. The forewing or tegmina (Fig. 4.6) and hind wing (Fig. 4.7) vary in proportions, texture and venation. The branching pattern of veins and the shape and texture of the cells helps in identification. The legs (Fig. 4.8) vary in shape, proportions, spination and chaetotaxy (Rakitov, 1998). According to Rakitov (1998) longitudinal rows of setae are labeled according to their position assuming that the leg is extended perpendicular to the mid-saggital plane of the body; *i.e.*, anterodorsal (AD), posterodorsal (PD), anteroventral (AV) and posteroventral (PV). The front femur of leafhoppers often bears additional anteromedial (AM) and intercalary (IC) setal rows.

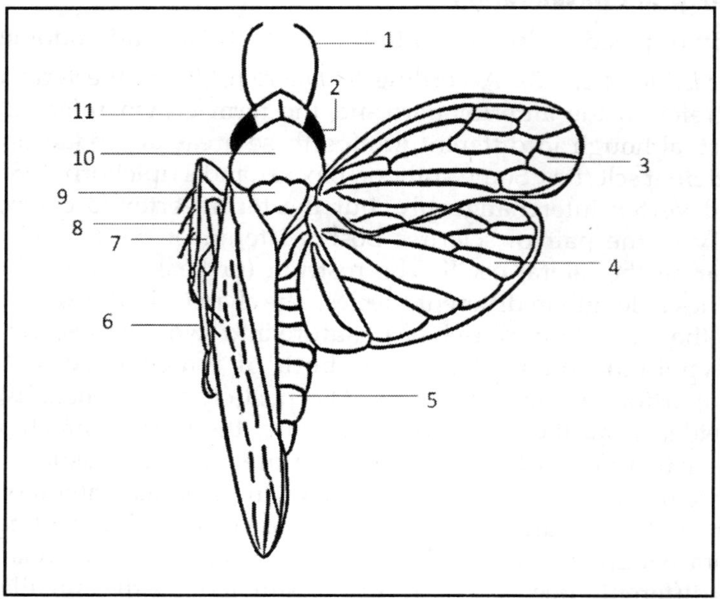

Fig. 4.1: **Body of Jassid: Dorsal view:** 1 - **Antenna,** 2 - **Compound eye,** 3 - **Forewing,** 4 - **Hindwing,** 5 - **Abdomen,** 6 - **Hindleg,** 7 - **Midleg,** 8 - **Foreleg,** 9 - **Scutellum,** 10 - **Pronotum,** 11 - **Crown**

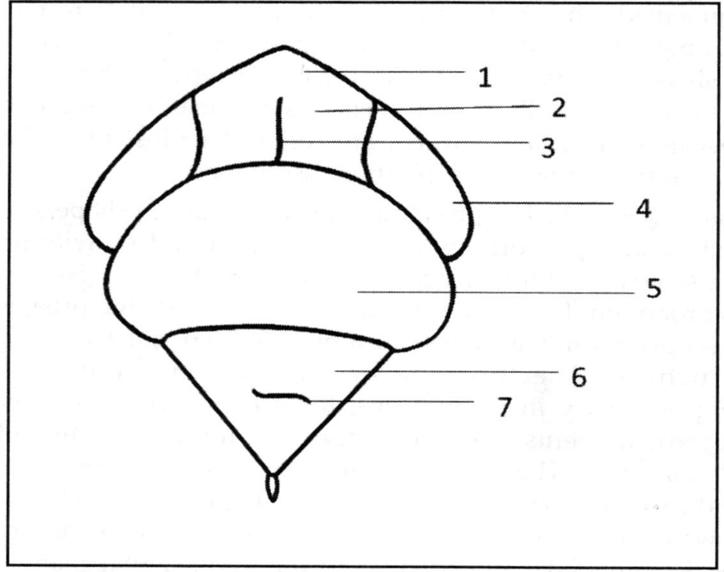

Fig. 4.2: **Dorsal view of head and pronotum of jassid:** 1 - **Vertex,** 2 - **Crown,** 3 - **Coronal suture,** 4 - **Compound eye,** 5 - **Pronotum,** 6 - **Scutellum,** 7 - **Scutal suture**

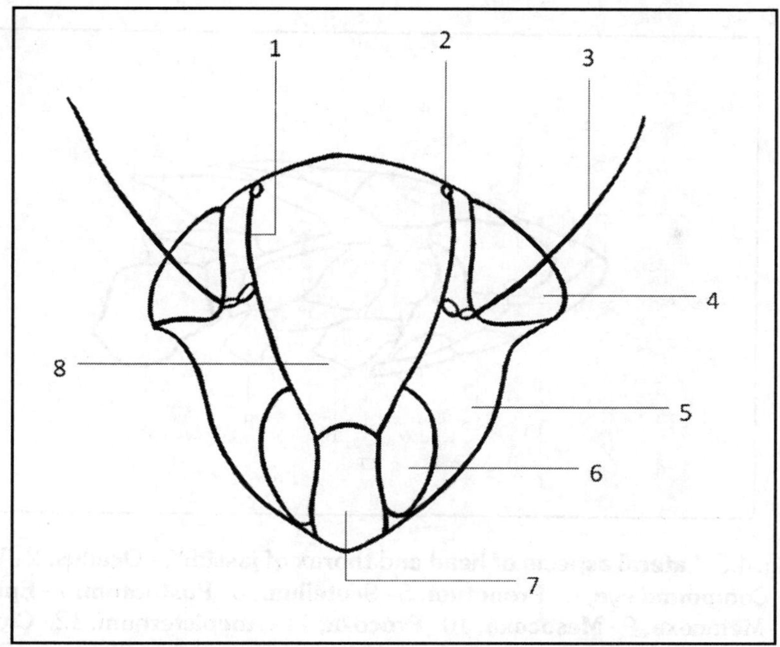

Fig. 4.3: **Head: anterior view (face) of jassid:** 1 - **Lateral frontal suture,** 2 - **Ocellus,** 3 - **Antenna,** 4 - **Compound eye,** 5 - **Gena,** 6 - **Lorum,** 7 - **Anteclypeus,** 8 - **Frontoclypeus**

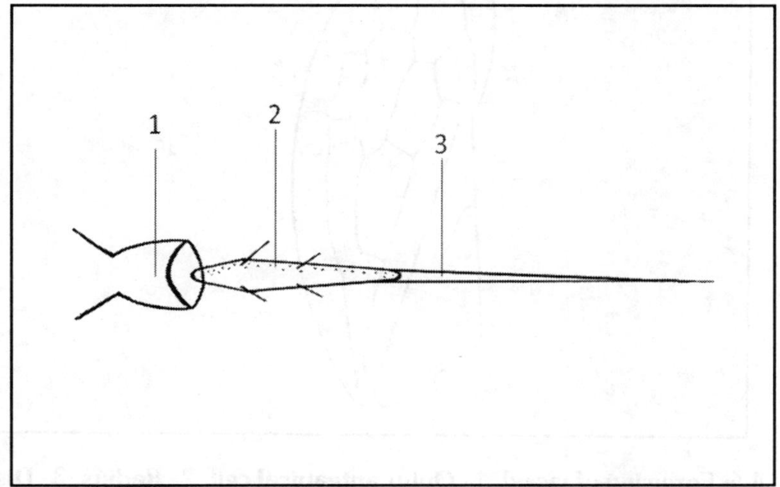

Fig. 4.4: **Antenna of jassid:** 1 - **Scape,** 2 - **Pedical,** 3 - **Flagellum**

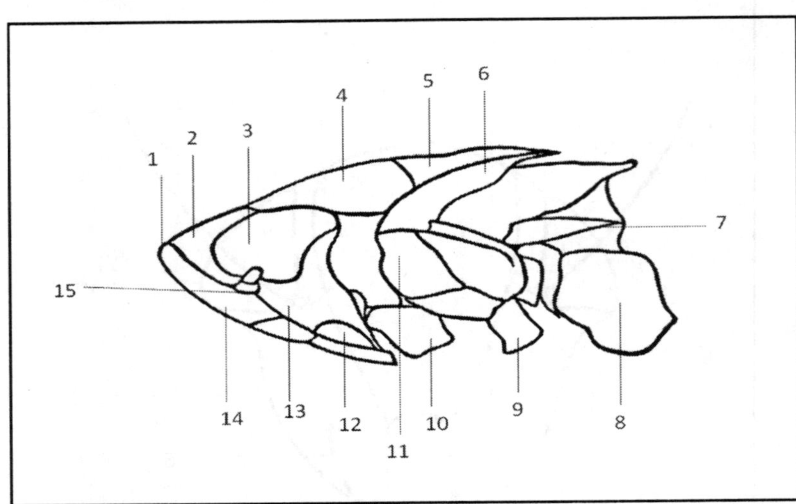

Fig. 4.5: **Lateral aspects of head and thorax of jassid:** 1 - **Ocellus,** 2 - **Vertex,** 3 - **Compound eye,** 4 - **Pronotum,** 5 - **Scutellum,** 6 - **Postnotum,** 7 - **Epimeron,** 8 - **Metacoxa,** 9 - **Mesocoxa,** 10 - **Procoxa,** 11 - **Anepisternum,** 12 - **Clypellus,** 13 - **Lorum,** 14 - **Episternum,** 15 - **Lateral frontal suture,** 16 - **Clypeus,** 17 - **Antenna**

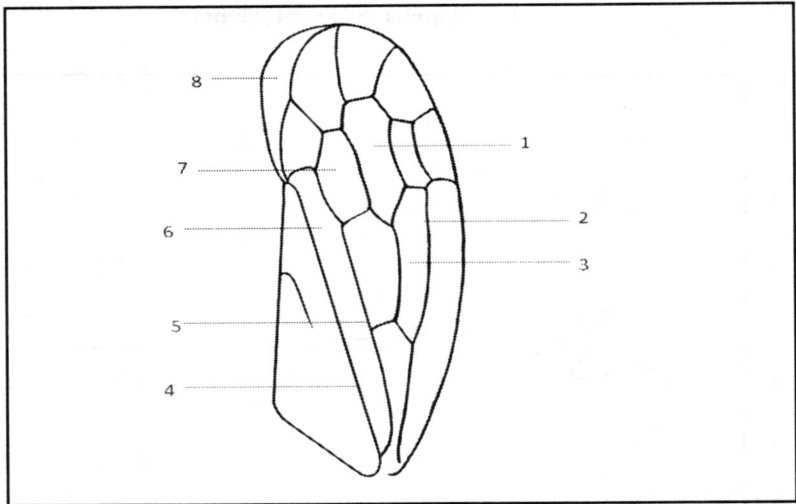

Fig. 4.6: **Forewing of jassid:** 1 - **Outer anteapical cell,** 2 - **Radius,** 3 - **Discal cells,** 4 - **Claval vein,** 5 - **Claval suture,** 6 - **Branchial cell,** 7 - **Central anteapical cell,** 8 - **Appendix**

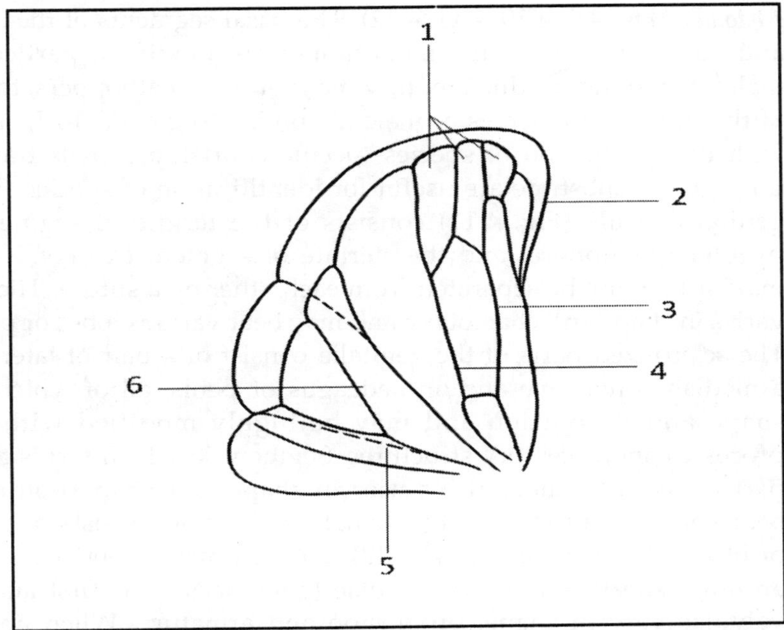

Fig. 4.7: **Hindwing of jassid:** 1 - **Apical cell,** 2 - **Costal margin,** 3 - **Media,** 4 - **Cubitus,** 5 - **Jugal fold,** 6 - **Postcubitus**

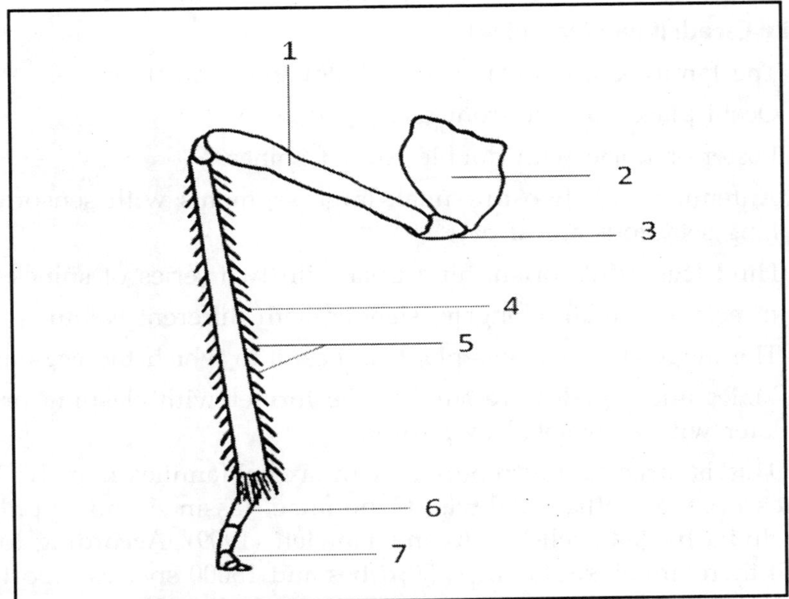

Fig.- 4.8: **Hindleg of jassid:** 1 - **Femar,** 2 - **Coxa,** 3 - **Trochantor,** 4- **Tibia,** 5 - **Setae,** 6 - **Tarsus,** 7 - **Claws**

- *Abdomen* (Fig. 4.9, 4.10, 4.11, 4.12): The basal segments of the abdomen and adjacent parts of the meta-thorax are modified, particularly in males, for sound production. In some groups of leafhoppers, the shapes of the internal apodemes of male abdominal segments I-III, associated with the production of species-specific courtship signals transmitted through the substrate are useful for identification of species. The male genital capsule (Fig. 4.11) consists of the tergite of segment IX or pygofer (pygophore) and the sternite of segment IX or valve, which may or may not be separated from each other by a suture. The pygofer varies in shape and chaetotaxy and may bear various lobes or processes. The sclerotized parts of the genitalia consist of a pair of lateral styles, a median connective and an aedeagus or penis, all of which vary in shape and proportion and may be highly modified with various processes and accessory structures. Segment X, which forms the major part of the anal tube, also varies in shape and proportion and may bear spines or processes. The female ovipositor consists of two pairs of blade-like structures (Fig. 4.12), the first and second valvulae, and an outer sheath, the third valvulae (gonoplacs). The first and second valvulae vary in shape, proportion and armature. When not in use, the ovipositor is partially enclosed by the enlarged ninth abdominal tergite, or pygofer. The seventh abdominal sternite vary in shape among species in some groups (Dietrich, 2005).

Family Cicadellidae (Jassidae)

The family Cicadellidae shows following characters:

1. Ocelli placed on the front margin of head.
2. Posterior tibiae with double row of spines.
3. Antennae with two proximal, large segments with sensorial with a long setaceous apical part.
4. Hind legs salutatorian, hind tibia with two series of spines.
5. Insects are small, elongate, slender with different colour.
6. The ovipositor lacerates plant tissues, into which the eggs are thrust.
7. Males and females are similar, the former with clasping organs, the later with a consoled ovipositor.

This is large family reported with six subfamilies namely: Ledrinae, Bythoscopinae, Tettigoniellinae, Gyponinae, Jassinae and Typhlocybinae from India by Maxwell-Lefroy and Howlett (1909). According to Dietrich (2005) there are 35 subfamilies, 50 tribes and 15000 species reported under this family from all over the world. From India 680 species have been reported (Ghosh *et al.* 2007).

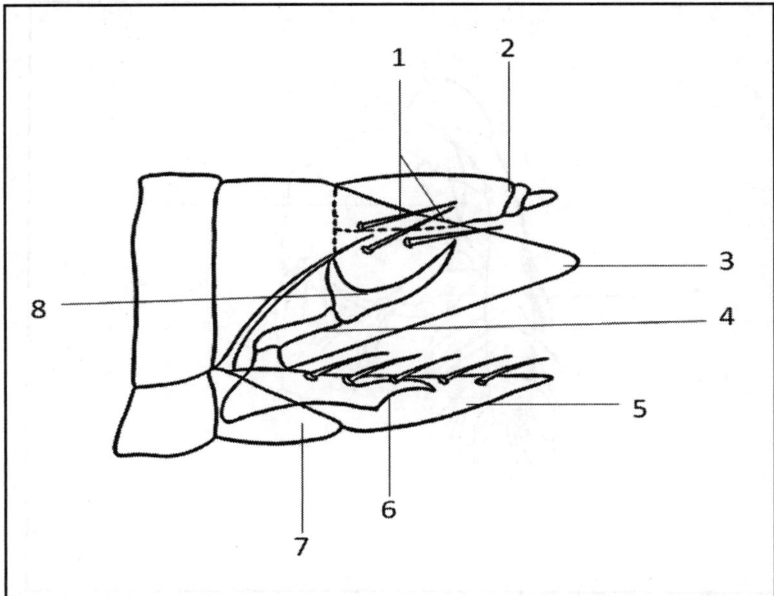

Fig. 4.9: **Apex of male abdomen of jassid:** 1 - **Macrosetae,** 2 - **Anal tube,** 3 - **Pygofer,** 4 - **Connective,** 5 - **Subgenital plate,** 6 - **Style,** 7 - **Valve,** 8 - **Aedeagus**

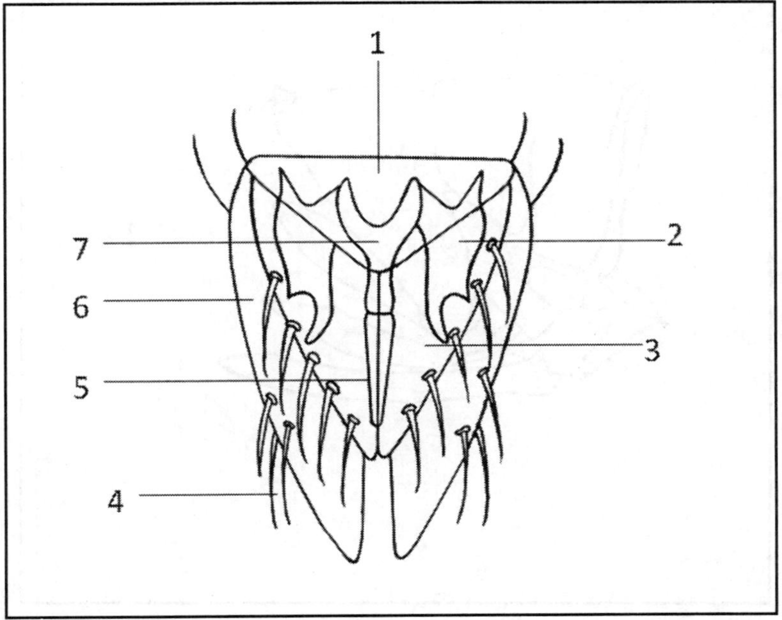

Fig. 4.10: **Apex of male abdomen of jassid:** 1 - **Valve,** 2 - **Style,** 3 - **Subgenital plate,** 4 - **Macrosetae,** 5 - **Aedeagus,** 6 - **Pygofer,** 7 - **Connective**

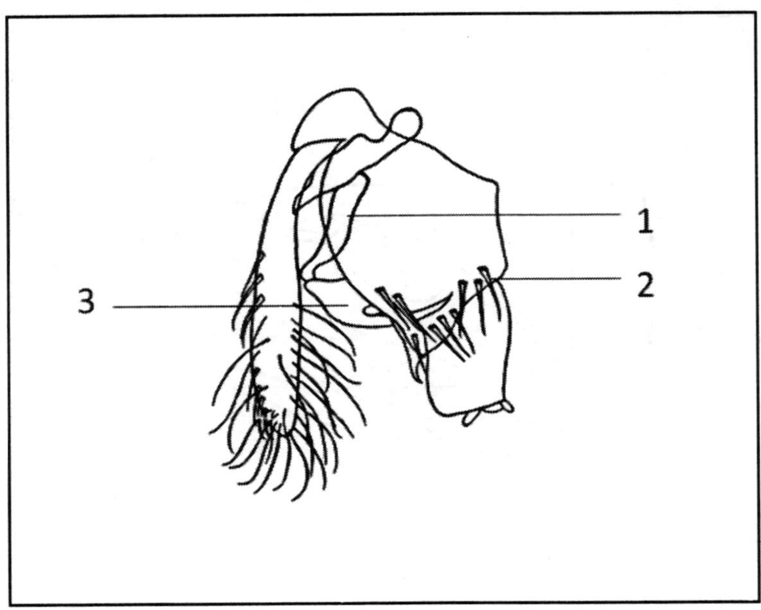

Fig. 4.11: **Male genital capsule of jassid:** 1 - **Connective,** 2 - **Macrosetae,** 3 - **Aedaegus**

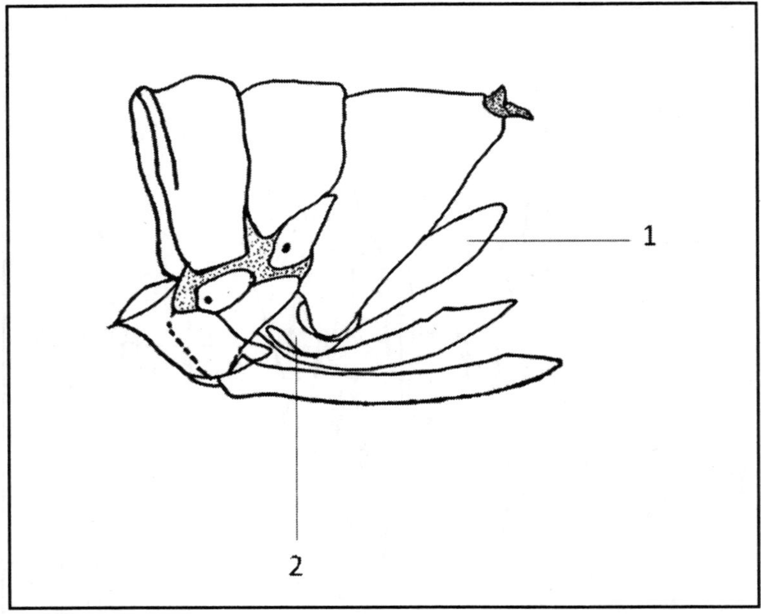

Fig. 4.12: **Apex of female abdomen of jassid:** 1 - **Valvula,** 2 - **Vulvifer**

Key to Subfamilies and tribes of Cicadellidae *(Dietrich, 2005)*

1. Hind tarsomere I pointed, without transverse row of rounded setae; forewing developed and without closed anteapical cells .... *Typhlocybinae*, 2

1′. Hind tarsomere I truncate distally, usually with transverse row of blunt setae, Forewing usually with one or more closed anteapical cell 8

2(1). Forewing always with appendix .... *Alebrini*

2′. Forewing generally without appendix 3

3(2′). Hind wing with submarginal vein present at wing apex 4

3′. Hind wing submarginal vein absent at the wing apex 6

4(3). Hind wing submarginal vein extended around wing apex and continuous with vein R2+3 .... *Dikraneurini*

4′. Hind wing vein R2+3 absent or in presence, not continuous with submarginal vein 5

5(4′). Hind wing with R4+5 and M1+2 free, connected by crossvein *Jorumini*

5′. Hind wing with R4+5 and M1+2 confluent distally .... *Empoascini*

6(3′). Hind wing vannal vein unbranched; forewing inner apical cell elongate, extended to apex; face with lorum well separated from margin of maxillary plate ventrally .... *Erythroneurini*

6′. Hind wing vannal vein branched forewing inner apical cell short, oblique, not extendedto apex; face with lorum extended to lower margin of maxillary plate 7

7(6′). Hind wing with distal segment of CuA absent, submarginal vein apparently connected directly to preapically .... *Zyginellini*

7′. Hind wing with distal segment present, submarginal vein apparently connected to CuAby crossvein .... *Typhlocybini*

8(1′). Mesanepisternum with horizontal keel; head and pronotum coarsely pitted; setae of hindtibial rows small and inconspicuous; head with maxillary plate and gena separated by distinct cleft ..... Ulopinae, 9

8′. Mesanepisternum not keeled, head and pronotum with or without coarse pits; hind tibia with well developed macrosetae; head with maxillary plate and gena fused, at most separated by suture 11

9(8). Body elongate, seed shaped; head more than 2 longer than pronotum .... *Cephalelini*

9′. Body robust, ovoid; head usually less than longer than pronotum 10

10(9′). Ocelli absent; forewing sexually dimorphic, that of male short and truncate, that of female emarginated apically .... *Monteithiini*

10′. Ocelli usually well-developed, on crown; forewings not sexually dimorphic .... *Ulopini*

11(8′). Hind femur with only 3 short, stout macrosetae grouped at apex proepisternum large, not concealed by gena .... *Ledrinae*, 12

11′. Hind femur without 3 short, stout macrosetae grouped at apex, if only three macrosetae present on femur, then one distinctly preapical, proepisternum concealed or exposed 15

12(11). Anterior margin of pronotum weakly produced, not extended as far as anteroomedial corners of eyes ocelli on crown distant from margin; head usually spatulate 13

12′. Anterior margin of pronotum produced to or anterad of anteromedial corners of eyes; ocelliposition variable, if on crown, not distant from margin; head usually not spatulate 14

13(12). Forewing appendix well developed, extended around wing apex . ... *Xerophloeini*

13′. Forewing appendix greatly reduced or absent .... *Ledrini*

14(12′). Rostrum elongate, extended to or beyond hind coxae; forewing anal veins confluent distally .... *Stenocotini*

14′. Rostrum not extended to hind coxae; forewing anal veins free ...... *Thymbrini*

15(11′). Ocelli absent, wings vestigial, overall habitus beetle like 16

15′. Ocelli on face, distinctly below margin of crown and not visible from above; hind femur macrosetal formula usually 2+1 17

15′. Ocelli on crown or on anterior margin of head and if crown not delimited and head broadly rounded in profile, or ocelli distinctly below sharply delimited crown margin, then hindwing veins confluent distally, or middle trochanter with stout ventral seta,..................... 28

16(15). Abdomen with prominent paired dorsal tubercles (Australia, Madagascar) .... *Euacanthellinae, Sagmatiini*

16′. Abdomen without paired dorsal tubercles .... *Megophthalminae, Evansiolini*

17(15′). Pronotum strongly produced, anterior margin unlimited anterad of eyes 18

17′. Pronotum not or weakly produced, anterior margin not extended anterad of eyes 21

18(17). Proepisternum large, not concealed by gena, hind wing vein R2+3 absent, submarginal vein not extended along costal margin basad of R4+5 Worldwide predictable .... *Macropsinae*

18′. Proepisternum small, entirely concealed by gena; hind wing vein R2+3 present, submarginal vein extended along costal margin basad of R4+5 19

19(18′). Head with lateral frontal sutures obsolete; hind tibia row AD with small cucullate setae between larger macrosetae; coloration pale with darker markings on head and pronotum .... *Neopsinae*

19′. Head with lateral frontal sutures well developed; hind tibia row AD with intercalary setae, when present, not cucullate; coloration black or reddish brown, without distinct markings .... *Nioniinae*, 20

20(19′). Forewing crossveins present, anal veins connected by crossvein; male with aedeagal shaft undivided, with single gonopore ..... *Magnentiini*

20′. Forewing crossveins usually absent, anal veins not connected by crossvein; male with aedeagal shaft divided, with two gonopores .... *Nioniini*

21(17′). Forewing distinctly and densely granulose; hind tibia macrosetal row PD with 0-1 more macrosetae than row AD; ovipositor with first valvula sculpturing not strigate .... *Megophthalminae*, 22

21′. Forewing glabrous; hind tibia macrosetal row PD with many more macrosetae than row AD; ovipositor with first valvula sculpturing strigate 24

22(21). Face and pronotum coarsely punctate; frontal sutures carinate .... *Megophthalmini*

22′. Face and pronotum not, or only sparsely punctate; frontal sutures when present not carinate 23

23(22′). Forewing venation reticulate; clypeal suture well developed, transverse .... *Adelungiini*

23′. Forewing venation not reticulate, clypeal suture arcuate, obsolete medially .... *Agalliini*

24(21′). Head with crown short but distinctly delimited, flat *Austroagalloidinae*

24′. Head with crown poorly delimited, convex, rounded to face..... 25

25(24′). Forewing with crossvein r-m1 elongate, connected between R2+3 and R4+5with three m-cu crossveins; hind femurin repose not reaching prothorax .... *Eurymelinae*, 26

25′. Forewing crossvein r-m1, if present, short, oblique, connected between R1 and R2+3, with two m-cu cross veins or if three in attendance, then crossvein present and membrane not opaquely sclerotized; hind femur in repose reaching prothorax ..... *Idiocerinae*

26(25). Head narrower than hind margin of pronotum; hind tibia row AD with macrosetae evenly distributed and subequal in size .... *Pogonoscopini*

26′. Head as wide as or wider than hind margin of pronotum; hind tibia row AD with distalsetae enlarged with spinose base 27

27(26′). Forewing opaquely sclerotized; male plates with accessory processes .... *Eurymelini*

27′. Forewing translucent; male plates without accessory processes ...... *Ipoini*

28(15′). Forewing with inner apical cell elongate, vein connected to submarginal vein near wing apex and if forewing reduced then crown elevated and shelf like mesad of eyes; crown connecting eyes less than twice as wide as median length; anterior margin of pronotum not extended anterd of eyes in dorsal view 29

28′. Forewing with inner apical cell shorter, distal segment of vein convergent toward commisural margin and connected to submarginal vein well based of wing apex, otherwise, not elevated and shelf like mesad of eyes, and/or anterior margin of pronotum extended anterad of eyes in dorsal view 50

29(28). Rostrum with distal segment longer than penultimate segment; antennal base in anterior view adjacent to anteroventral corner of eye, ledge absent or very weak; crown width between eyes usually less than eye width; front tibia with accessory row of setae connecting rows .... *Coelidiinae*

29′. Rostrum with distal segment little, if any, longer than penultimate segment; antennal base in anterior view near mid-height of eye, ledge well-developed; crown width among eyes greater than 1.5 eye width; front tibia without accessory row of setae between rows 37

30(29). Base of forewing concealed by pronotum; usually brachypterous .. .. *Tinobregmini*

30′. Base of forewing exposed; very rarely brachypterous 31

31(30′). Pronotum bicarinate laterally, crown with pair of arcuate longitudinal keels .... *Sandersellini*

31′. Pronotum unicarinate laterally, crown without keels 32

32(31′). Crown distinctly elevated above level of eyes, usually strongly produced anteriorly and with distinct striations convergent toward apex; male subgenital plate usually appearing two-segmented 33

32′. Crown softly or not prominent above level of eyes, weakly produced anteriorly and usually without distinct longitudinal striations; male plate not two-segmented 35

33(32). Aedeagus with a single shaft and symmetrical, combined to connective; subgenital plate sparsely setose (Afrotropical) .... *Hikangiini*

33′. Aedeagus bipendulate or asymmetrical, articulated to connective; plate profusely setose 34

34(33′). Aedeagus with two shafts (except *Neotharra*); style claw- or hooklike apically

34′. Aedeagus with single shaft; style not claw like, rarely hook like apically .... *Youngolidiini*

35(32′). Frontoclypeus with complete middle longitudinal carina.... *Teruliini*

35′. Frontoclypeus lacking or with partial median longitudinal carina.. 36

36(35′). Prothoracic tibia and femur flattened or deceptive .... *Gabritini*

36′. Prothoracic tibia and femur slender .... *Coelidiini*

37(29′). Forewing membrane clothed with setae otherwise scales; abdomen strongly depressed .... *Hylicinae*

37′. Forewing membrane without setae or scales; abdomen tectiform 38

38(37′). Hind femur with supernumerary setae 39

38′. Hind femur macrosetal formula 2+1+1 2+1 .... 41.

39(38). Anterior margin of head with, at most, a single transverse carina; hind wing veins R4+5 and M1+2 usually confluent apically ..... *Neocoelidiinae*

39′. Anterior margin of head with more than one transverse carinae otherwise with irregular striations; hind wing veins R4+5 and M1+2 free, connected by crossvein 40

40(39′). Frontoclypeus strongly inflated (eastern Palearctic and western Nearctic) .... *Evacanthinae, Pagaroniini*

40′. Frontoclypeus flat .... *Coelidiinae, Macroceratogoniini*

41(38). Pronotum extended to scutellar suture, coarsely punctate............... *Signoretiinae* (=Phlogisinae)

41′. Pronotum not extended to scutellar suture punctations indistinct or absent 42

42(41′). Forewing fully developed, vein absent; frontoclypeus with partial or complete median longitudinal carina; or if carina absent, frontoclypeus strongly flattened medially, or front femur with single enlarged ventral seta near midlength or equally .... *Evacanthinae*

42′. Forewing fully developed with vein r-m1 present or brachypterous; or, if forewingfully developed and r-m1 absent, then frontoclypeus without median carina and not strongly lattened medially, and front femur without single enlarged ventral seta near midlength 45

43(42′). Frontoclypeus with complete median carina .... *Evacanthini*

43′. Frontoclypeus with median carina incomplete or absent 44

44(43′). Pro - and mesothoracic tibiae flattened; crown notched anterad of eye, scape of antenna visible in dorsal view .... *Balbillini*

44′. Pro - and mesothoracic tibiae cylindrical; crown entire, conceal scape in dorsal view .... *Nirvanini*

45(42′). Hind wing submarginal vein on or very near wing margin apically 46

45′. Hind wing submarginal vein well separated from apical margin 48

46(45). Crown margin distinctly carinate; pronotum extended virtually to scutellar suture, particularly punctate .... *Makilingiinae*

46′. Crown margin not carinate; pronotum not extensive nearly to scutellar suture, puctures if present small and indistinct 47

47(46′). Forewing crossvein present, appendix inconspicuous; hind tarsus more than half length of tibia .... *Tinterominae*

47′. Forewing crossvein r-m1 absent, appendix well developed; hind tarsus less than half length of tibia .... *Mileewinae*

48(45′). Antennal ledge in dorsal view prominent; hind femur in repose not attaining postero-lateral margin of prothorax 49

48′. Antennal ledge in dorsal view not prominent; hind femur in repose usually attaining posterolateral margin of prothorax .... *Cicadellinae, Cicadellini*

49(48). Body cylindrical, crown margin not or indistinctly carinate .... *Cicadellinae, Proconiini.*

49′. Body strongly depressed, crown margin sharply carinate .... *Phereurhininae*

50(28′). Proepisternum large, not concealed by gena head in dorsal view little, if any, longer than wide; ocelli on crown well separated from margin 5

50′. Proepisternum small, concealed by genaor if proepisternum exposed, then head in dorsal view more than twice as long as wide and ocelli on or very near crown margin 52

51(50). Gena acutely emarginate otherwise with deep antennal grooves; hind femora without supernumerary macrosetae (Australia) .... *Euacanthellinae, Euacanthellini*

51′. Gena not acutely emarginate, without antennal grooves hind femur with supernumerary macrosetae (Holarctic) .... *Errhomeninae*

52(50′). Front tibia with distinct accessory longitudinal row of setae adjacent to row AV on anterior surface near base; male subgenital plates fully exposed, constricted basally, broadened distally (Neotropical) .... *Neobalinae*

52′. Front tibia without accessory row of setae adjacent to row AV on anterior surface (scattered setae may be present); male subgenital plates of various shapes, sometimes concealed by sternite VII 53

53(52′). Head with lateral frontal sutures partly or completely obsolete and not extended to ocelli; but head longer than wide in dorsal view then ocelli not on or slightly above crown margin; male valve and subgenital plates partly to completely concealed by enlarged abdominal sternite VII .... *Iassinae* 54

53′. Head with lateral frontal sutures well developed and extended to or very near ocelli; or, if lateral frontal sutures not extended to ocelli, then either head longer than wide in dorsal view and ocelli on or slightly above or below crown margin, or malevalve and subgenital plates not concealed by enlarged abdominal sternite VII, otherwise both 60

54(53). Hind wing veins R4+5 and M1+2 confluent near apex or if veins free, then head in profile broadly rounded, without distinctly delimited crown 55

54′. Hind wing veins R4+5 and M1+2 free, crown well delimited 58

55(54). Crown strongly depressed and produced, margin well delimited 56

55′. Crown convex, not or only weakly produced, rounded to face 57

56(55). Ocelli on or near margin of crown .... *Reuplemellini*

56′. Ocelli on crown, distant from margin .... *Platyjassini*

57(55′). Head distinctly bent at right angle across antennal ledges, crown verticaland forming continuous curve with strongly declivous pronotu .... *Trocnadini*

57′. Head with crown and face more or less evenly convex, pronotum usually weakly declivous .... *Iassini (Hyalojassini)*

58(54′). Ocelli on crown distant from margin .... *Scarini (Gyponini)*

58′. Ocelli on anterior margin of head 59

59(58′). Forewing with venation reticulate distally, inner apical cell narrow, acuminate .... *Krisnini*

59′. Forewing venation with, at most, 1-2 supernumerary crossveins, inner apical cell broad .... *Selenomorphini*

60(53′). Pronotum strongly produced, anterior margin extended anterad of eyes 61

60′. Pronotum not or weakly produced, anterior margin not extended anterad of eyes 62

61(60). Hind tibia macrosetal row AD with small cucullate setae interspersed between large setae; forewing membrane without conspicuous setae .... *Tartessinae*

61′. Hind tibia macro-setal row AD without cucullate intercalary setae; forewing membrane with conspicuous setae .... *Iassinae, Bythoniini*

62(60′). Front femur row AV with single stout seta near midlength; female with ovipositor distinctly arcuate ....*Aphrodinae, Xestocephalini*

62′. Front femur row AV with more than one stout seta or setae absent near midlength; female with ovipositor straight or somewhat recurred 63

63(62′). Forewing anal veins free, clavus without crossveins; male sub genital plates constricted basally, widest near or beyond midlength, valve with posterior margin not angulately produced; style slender, not broadly bilobed basally .... *Aphrodinae*, 64s

63′. Forewing with or without one or more cross veins in clavus, or anal veins partially confluent; male subgenital plates not constricted basally, widest near base and tapered toward apex, valve with lateral margin short and posterior margin usually distinctly produced and angulate medially, style usually broadly bilobed basally .... *Deltocephalinae*

64(63) Frontoclypeus in facial view at least 2×longer than wide; hind wing submarginal vein well developed .... *Portanini*

64′. Frontoclypeus in facial view little or no longer than wide; hind wing with submarginal vein obsolete apically ....*Aphrodini*

Key to Tribes and genera of Deltocephalinae

1. Front wings with 2 anteapical cells 2

- Fore wings with 3 anteapical cells cross vein present 4

2. Connective racket shaped with anterior arms close to each other/fused Slender aedeagus, with asymmetrical process .... *Paralimnini*

head with two black spots .... *Changwhania* Kwon

- Connective 'Y' shaped with anterior arms separated wide. Adeagus with shaft fused to base; 10th segment membranous ..... *Macrostelini* 3

3. Vertex of head with uniform length; hind basistarsus basally emarginated slender .... *Balclutha* Kirkaldy

- Vertex of head longer medially than next to eyes head and thoraxochraceous; two black dots on vertex. Hind basistarsus basally not emarginated .... *Cicadulina* China

4. Body depressed; head strongly produced; ocelli on crown near margin, very close to eyes .... Hecalinii.

Face and thorax green to yellowish green with Concentric parabolic orange fasciae on head and pronotum .... *Hecalus* Stål

- Body more or less cylindrical head not much produced. ocelli and antennal bases much closer to eyes than apex of crown 5

5. Male subgenital plate separate. Aedeagal shaft paired with pair gonopore. Shaft either completely divided or bifid apically .... *Opsiini* 6

- Male subgenital plate separate; Adeagal shaft single with one gonopore. Male connective articulated to aedeagus; Anterior arms of connective free distally 7

6. Forewing claval veins fused medially coloration creamy white with brown spots .... *Orosius* Distant

Forewing claval veins connected by cross vein colouration variable; fore wing maculate with well defined discal semicircular spot. Aedeagus has no ventral process .... *Hishimonus* Ishihara

7. Male connective linear fused to aedeagus .... *Deltocephalini*

Stout body.vertex more than twice as broad as long male plate fusedat the base linear male connective, fused to aedeagus ... *Deltocephalus* Burmeister

- Male connective Y shaped articulated with aedeagus 8

8. Male pygophore with dorsal margin sloping downwards; Ovipositor much elongated .... *Stenometopiini*

Male pygophore without a dorsal process .... *Doratulina* Melichar

- Male pygophore with dorsal margin more or less horizontal ovipositor not much elongate .... *Chiasmini*

9. Brown or ochraceous with black markings .... *Exitianus* Ball

Green colour with black markings .... *Nephotettix* Matsumura

Subfamily Deltocephalinae

Tribe Deltocephalini

Genus *Nephotettix* Matsumura

The genus *Nephotettix* was raised by Matsumura in 1908. From world 18 Species have been described from the world. The genus *Nephotettix* shows following characters.

1. Opaque green leafhoppers with black markings on head, face, pronotum, tegmen and other body parts.
2. Vertex sharply ridged.

Key to Species of the genus *Nephotettix*

1 Male 2
Female 8
2(1) Vertex distinctly pointed. 3
Vertex rounded 6
3(2) No marks on vertex .... *N. virescens*
Sub marginal black marking on head 4
4(3) Continuous sub marginal black bands .... *N. parvas*
Sub marginal band separated in the middle 5
5(4) Adeagus spines 4-5 pairs pygofer spines two groups, spine I large, 4-5 tiny spines as a group .... *N. virescens*
Adeagus spines, 3-4 pairs, pygofer spines two, spine I large, spine II tiny .... *N. sympatricus*
6(1) Anterior margin of pronotum and scutellum black.
Forewing black mark touches claval suture, ... *N. nigropictus*
Sub marginal band complete, 2 groups of pygofer spines
Adeagus spine 8-9 pairs-
Sub marginal band reduced to posterior to ocelli; one large black pygofer spine .... *N. malayanus*
7(1) Vertex pointed 8
Vertex rounded 10
8(7) No marks on vertex, forewing usually no marks. .... *N. virescens*
Sub marginal band present, either complete or separate at the middle. 9
9(8) Complete sub marginal band, apical third of forewing is black and rarely with black spot .... *N. parvus*
Sub marginal bands separated at the middle. Forewing entirely green. Face with transverse black marks .... *N. sympatricus*
10(7) No sub marginal black band, forewing entirely green;
Sub marginal band distict. Anterior margin of pronotum .... *N. malayanus*
Scutellum black usually apical third of forewing is black .... *N. nigropictus*

***Nephotettix virescens* (Distant, 1908)**
(Plate - 1: Figs. 4.13-4.19)

- *Male* (Fig. 4.13):
- *Head* (Fig. 4.14):

0.53mm long, 1.07mm broad, broader than long, yellow in colour, not rounded; crown (Fig. 4.14) 0.53mm long, 1.71mm broad, yellow,

Nephotettix parvus (Ishihara and Kawase) (Plate - 2: Figs. 4.20-4.26)

- *Male* (Fig. 4.20):
- *Head* (Fig. 4.21):

  0.38mm long, 1.15mm broad, yellow, broader than long, crown (Fig. 4.21) 0.38mm long, 0.76mm broad, yellow, pentagonal in shape; compound eye 0.57mm long, 0.19mm broad, black with irregular golden patches, interocular distance 0.76mm, ocelli two, pale, ocular distance 0.65mm.
- *Antenna* (Fig. 4.22) 1.5mm long, 0.11mm broad, yellowish brown, long threadlike; scape 0.15mm long, 0.11mm broad, yellowish; pedicel 0.19mm long, 0.07mm broad; flagellum 1.15mm long, 0.03mm broad, brown; rostrum 0.50mm long, brown.
- *Antennal formula* – S L/W = 1.36, P L/W = 2.71, F L/W = 38.33, A = 42.4/3 = 14.13
- *Thorax* (Fig. 4.21): 1.34mm long, 1.34mm broad, yellowish green; pronotum (Fig. 4.21) 0.57mm long, 1.34mm broad, yellowish green, not overlapping on scutellum (Fig. 4.21); mesonotum 0.38mm long, 0.96mm broad, yellowish brown; scutellum 0.38mm long, 0.38mm broad, greenish yellow. Wings fore wing (Fig. 4.23) 4.61mm long, 1.15mm broad, semitransparent, green at anterior side, black at posterior, not elytra like; hind wing (Fig. 4.59) 3.84mm long, 1.34mm broad, black, membranous, transparent. *Hind leg* (Fig. 4.25) 5.47mm long, 0.38mm broad, brownish; coxa 0.65mm long, 0.38mm broad, yellowish brown; trochanter 0.30mm long, 0.19mm broad, pale yellow; femur 1.46mm long, 0.36mm broad, pale yellow; tibia 2.30mm long, 0.23mm broad, yellow with spines; tarsus 0.76mm long, 0.11mm broad, brownish yellow; pre-tarsus 0.38mm long, 0.11mm broad, yellowish brown; meso-tarsus 0.19mm long, 0.11mm broad, brownish yellow; meta-tarsus 0.19mm long, 0.11mm broad, brown; claw with two hooks.
- *Abdomen* (Fig. 4.26): 2.65mm long, 1.07mm broad, black, dorsal surface black, ventral surface green, first segment 0.23mm long, 1.07mm broad; second segment 0.23mm long, 1.03mm broad; third segment 0.26mm long, 0.96mm broad; fourth segment 0.26mm long, 0.96mm broad; fifth segment 0.26mm long, 0.84mm broad; sixth segment 0.26mm long, 0.76mm broad; seventh segment 0.26mm long, 0.69mm broad; eighth segment 0.26mm long, 0.57mm broad.
- *Host Plants* : Rice *Oryzasativa* L., sugarcane *Saccharum officinarum* L., grasses.
- *Paratype*: 20 ♂, 22 ♀, Coll. Chandani Kamble, July to March, preserved in alcohol, labeled as above.
- *Distribution:* Western Maharashtra; 10 ♂, 05 ♀, Karvir (Kolhapur), 12-VII-2014; 03 ♂, 05 ♀, Shirala (Kolhapur), 23-XI-2013.

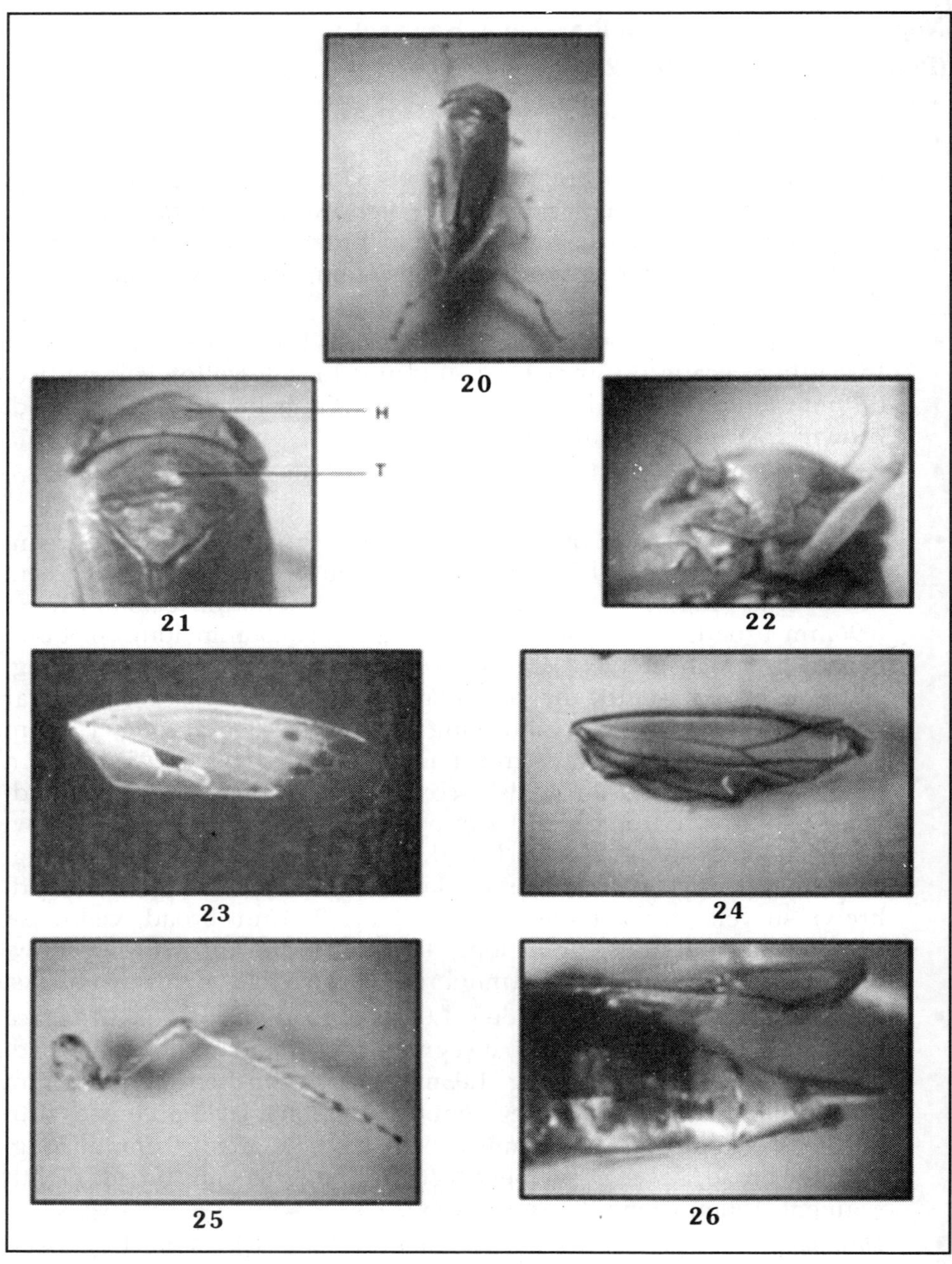

Plate - 2: ***N. parvus*:** Fig. 4.20: **Adult male,** Fig. 4.21: **Dorsal view head and thorax,** Fig. 4.22: **Ventral View head and thorax,** Fig. 4.23: **Forewing,** Fig. 4.24: **Hindwing,** Fig. 4.25: **Hindleg,** Fig. 4.26: **Abdomen**

Hecalus porrectus

(Plate - 3: Figs. 4.27-4.33)

- *Male* (Fig. 4.27):
- *Head* (Fig. 4.28):

  1.30mm long, 3.47mm broad, broader than long, pale colour, shiny, not rounded; crown (Fig. 4.28) 1.30mm long, 2.17mm broad, pale, pentagonal in shape. Compound eye 1.52mm long, 0.86mm broad, black, interocular distance 2.17mm, ocelli two, white, ocular distance 1.30mm.
- *Antenna* (Fig. 4.29) 2.60mm long, yellowish brown, long threadlike; scape 0.21mm long, 0.13mm broad, pale; pedicel 0.43mm long, 0.08mm broad; flagellum 1.95mm long, 0.04mm broad, brown; rostrum 0.43mm long, 0.08mm broad.
- *Antennal formula* – S L/W = 1.61, P L/W = 5.37, F L/W = 48.75, A = 55.73/3 = 18.57
- *Thorax* (Fig. 4.28): 3.04mm long, 3.47mm broad, brown; pronotum (Fig. 4.28) 1.52mm long, 3.47mm broad, on anterior margin blackish brown, posterior side blackish, in between anterior and posterior side golden yellow, not overlapping on scutellum (Fig. 4.28); scutellum anterior margin black; mesonotum 0.65mm long, 1.73mm broad, white at center, dark brown; scutellum 0.86mm long, 0.86mm broad, brownish white. *Wings*, fore wing (Fig. 4.30) 5.21mm long, 1.52mm broad, semitransparent, greenish brown colour, anterior side pale green, posterior side blackish touches to claval suture with whites rounded spots on forewing, not elytra like; hind wing (Fig. 4.31) 4.78mm long, 1.30mm broad, black, membranous, transparent. *Hind Leg* (Fig. 4.32) 6.92mm long, 0.34mm broad, brownish yellow; coxa 0.52mm long, 0.34mm broad, pale yellowish brown; trochanter 0.21mm long, 0.17mm broad, golden yellow; femur 1.95mm long, 0.34mm broad, pale yellow; tibia 3.26mm long, 0.21mm broad, golden brown with spines, black spot at base of each spine; tarsus 0.43mm long, 0.13mm broad, golden brown; pre-tarsus 0.21mm long, 0.08mm broad, golden brown; meso-tarsus 0.21mm long, 0.13mm broad, brown; meta-tarsus 0.13mm long, 0.13mm broad, brown; claw with two hooks.
- *Abdomen* (Fig. 4.33): 3.43mm long, 1.52mm broad, black, 1 to 8 segments contain black dorsally, 1 to 4 tergites with green at lateral side, black at middle; abdomen pale green from ventral side. First segment 0. 34mm long, 1.52mm broad; second segment 0.34mm long, 1.39mm broad; third segment 0.34mm long, 1.30mm broad; fourth segment 0.34mm long, 1.21mm broad; fifth segment 0.34mm long, 1.13mm broad; sixth segment 1.08mm long, 0.35mm broad; seventh segment 0.34mm long, 0.86mm broad; eighth segment 0.34mm long, 0.73mm broad.
- *Host Plants* : Rice *Oryzasativa* L., grasses.

- *Paratype* : 7 ♂, 8 ♀, Coll. Chandani Kamble, July to March, preserved in alcohol, labeled as above.
- *Distribution* : Western Maharashtra; 2 ♂, 3 ♀, Koyana (Satara), 03-X-2014; 05 ♂, 03 ♀, Kolhapur, 03 Sept. 2014.

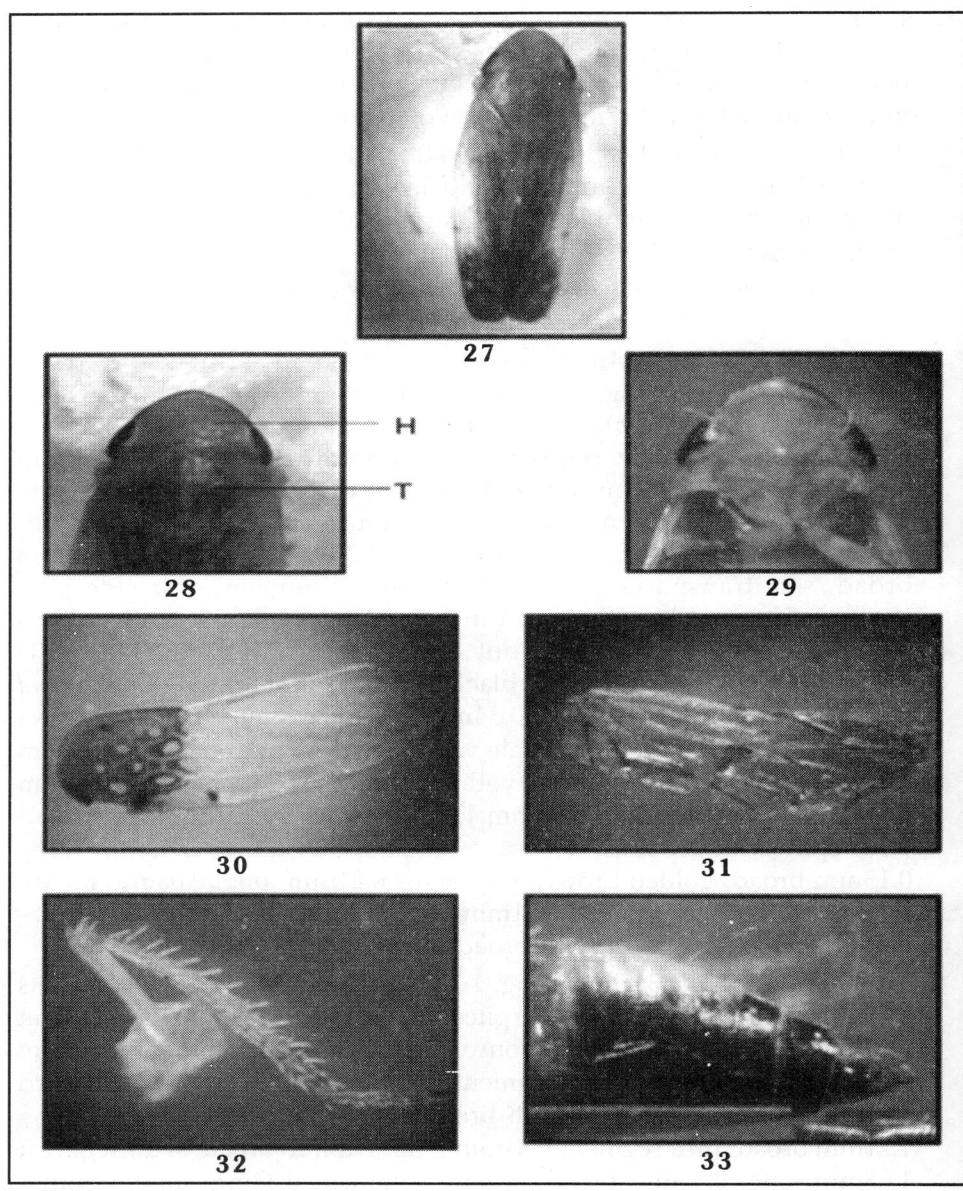

Plate - 3: ***H. porrectus*:** Fig. 4.27: **Adult male,** Fig. 4.28: **Dorsal view head and thorax,** Fig. 4.29: **Ventral view head and thorax,** Fig. 4.30: **Forewing,** Fig. 4.31: **Hindwing,** Fig. 4.32: **Hindleg,** Fig. 4.33: **Abdomen**

Genus Maiestas (Edwards)

Maiestas dorsalis _Motschulsky_

(Plate - 4: Figs. 4.34-4.40)

- *Male* (Fig. 4.34):
- *Head* (Fig. 4.35):

  0.5mm long, 1mm broad, broader than long, pale, black spots presents, not rounded; crown (Fig. 4.35) 0.5mm long, 1.75mm broad, pale with faint brown spots, pentagonal in shape, vertex ridged; compound eye 0.5mm long, 0.25mm broad, anterior side black, posterior side yellowish brown, distance 0.75mm, ocelli two, pale brown, ocular distance 0.25mm.
- *Antenna* (Fig. 4.36) 1.15mm long, 0.1mm broad, yellow, long thread like; scape 0.15mm long, 0.1mm broad, pale; pedicel 0.2mm long, 0.1mm broad; flagellum 0.8mm long, 0.05mm broad, yellowish brown.
- *Antennal formula* – S L/W = 1.5, P L/W = 2, F L/W = 16, A = 19.5/3 = 6.5
- *Thorax* (Fig. 4.35): 1.25mm long, 1.25mm broad, white at center, yellowish brown; pronotum (Fig. 4.35) 0.6mm long, 1.26mm broad, yellowish brown at anterior sides, two black spots presents on middle, irregular dark brown patches presents; mesonotum 0.3mm long, 1.75mm broad, white at center, anterior side brownish yellow, posterior sides pale; scutellum (Fig. 4.35) 0.35mm long, 0.35mm broad, pale whitish, shiny. *Wings*, fore wing (Fig. 4.37) 4.25mm long, 1mm broad, semitransparent, pale brown colour, vertical dark brown zig-zag structure presents not elytra like; hind wing (Fig. 4.38) 4mm long, 1.26mm broad, white, membranous, transparent. *Hind leg* (Fig. 4.39) 4.8mm long, 0.5mm broad, pale yellow; coxa 0.6mm long, 0.5mm broad, pale; trochanter 0.2mm long, 0.25mm broad, pale yellow; femur 1mm long, 0.4mm broad, golden yellow; tibia 2mm long, 0.3mm broad, yellowish brown with spines, black spot at base of each spine; tarsus 1mm long, 0.15mm broad, yellowish brown; pre-tarsus 0.5mm long, 0.15mm broad, brown. meso-tarsus 0.25mm long, 0.15mm broad, brownish yellow; meta-tarsus 0.25mm long, 0.1mm broad, yellowish brown.
- *Abdomen* (Fig. 4.40): 2.2mm long, 1mm broad, black, 1 to 8 segments contain dark brown patch dorsally, 1 to 4 tergites with black, remaining segments pale yellow. First segment 0.25mm long, 1mm broad; second segment 0.25mm long, 1mm broad; third segment 0.25mm long, 0.85mm broad; fourth segment 0.25mm long, 0.75mm broad; fifth segment 0.25mm long, 0.6mm broad; sixth segment 0.25mm long, 0.5mm broad; seventh segment 0.25mm long, 0.4mm broad; eighth segment 0.25mm long, 0.25mm broad; rostrum 0.28mm long, 0.3mm broad, pale. Ovipositor 0.30 mm long, coffee brown.
- *Host Plants* : Rice *Oryzasativa* L., grasses.

- *Paratype* : 5 ♂, 2 ♀, Coll. Chandani Kamble, July-March. preserved in alcohol.
- *Distribution* : 2 ♂, Sangli-Coll. Chandani Kamble, 09-VII-2014; 3 ♂, Kolhapur, 15-XI-2014; 1 ♀, Kolhapur, 15 Nov. 2014; 1 ♀, Sangli, 09-VII-2014.

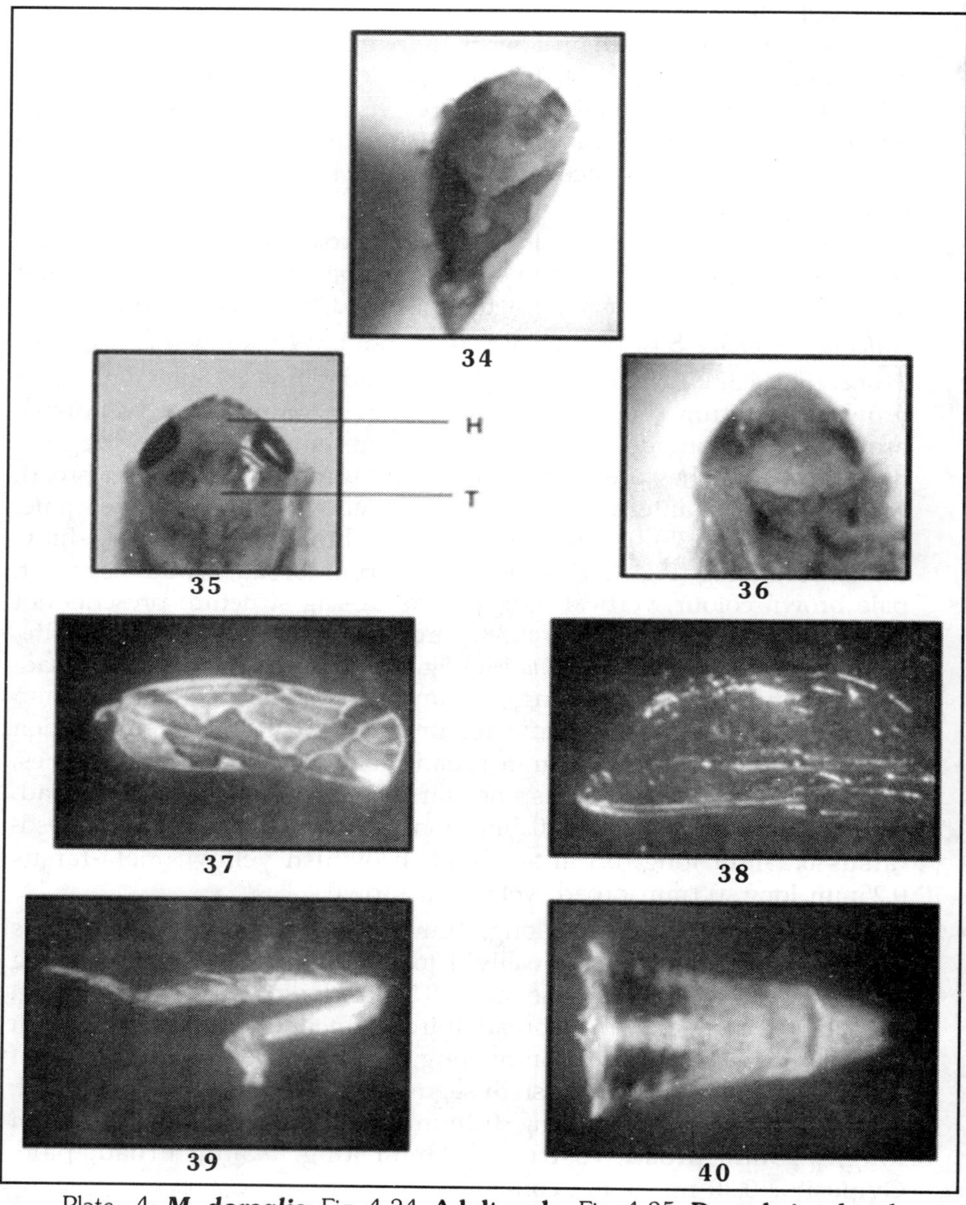

Plate - 4: ***M. dorsalis:*** Fig. 4.34: **Adult male,** Fig. 4.35: **Dorsal view head and thorax,** Fig. 4.36: **Ventral view head and thorax,** Fig. 4.37: **Forewing,** Fig. 4.38: **Hindwing,** Fig. 4.39: **Hindleg,** Fig. 4.40: **Abdomen**

Tribe Vartini

Genus *Varta* (Distant)

Key to Species of Genus *Varta* Distant

1. Aedeagal shaft sinuate curved at least in basal half, with an unpaired ventrally directed apical process 2

   Aedeagal shaft uniformly curved, terminated by a pair of slender different processes .... *V. bifida* sp. nov.

2. Pygophore with ventral sclerotized process measly curved, each process either crossing over or touching each other 3

   Pygophore with ventral sclerotized process posteriorly directed, their apices either dorsally or ventrally directed beyond middle 5

3. Aedeagal shaft with process curved first ventrally then caudally, long .... *V. rubrofasciata* Distant.

   Aedeagal shaft with process straight, short 4

4. Aedeagal shaft with process broad proximally, tapering distally to an acute point ventral sclerotized process of pygophore short, stout crossing over with its counterpart at mid length of aedeagal shaft .... *V. rubrostriata* (Horváth).

   Aedeagal shaft with process of uniform width, with a small tubercle on outer margin ventral pygophore process slender elongate, crossing over with its counter part near apex of aedeagal shaft .... *V. japonica* sp. nov.

5. Tenth segment with a pair of short toothlike projections on ventral margin; pygophore with sclerotized ventral process curved ventrally 6

   - Tenth segment with elongate processes on ventral margin; pygophore with sclerotized ventral process curved dorsally ... *V. longula* sp. nov.

6. Aedeagal shaft constricted and with a triangular projection at base, apex curved caudally, apophysis of style bidentate .... *V. sympatrica* sp. nov.

   - Aedeagal shaft without basal constriction and triangular projection, apex straight, apophysis of style not bidentate...... *V. rubrovittata* (Matsumura)

***Varta rubrofasciata* (Distant)**

(Plate - 5: Figs. 4.41-4.47)

- *Male* (Fig. 4.41):
- *Head* (Fig. 4.42):

  0.93mm long, 1.87mm broad, broader than long, brownish green, vertical saffron bands, not rounded; crown (Fig. 4.42) 0.93mm long, 1.93mm broad, brownish green, vertical saffron bands, pentagonal in shape. Compound eye 0.93mm long, 0.31mm broad, reddish brown, interocular distance 0.93mm, ocelli two, white, ocular distance 0.62mm.

- *Antenna* (Fig. 4.43) 3.43mm long, pale yellow, long threadlike; scape 0.18mm long, 0.18mm broad, pale yellow; pedicel 0.12mm long, 0.12mm broad; flagellum 3.12mm long, 0.06mm broad, brown.
- *Antennal formula* – S L/W = 1, P L/W = 1, F L/W = 52, A = 54.00/3=18
- *Thorax* (Fig. 4.42): 2.5mm long, 2.18mm broad, white at center, greenish brown vertical saffron bands. Pronotum (Fig. 4.42) 0.93mm long, 2.18mm broad, on anterior side pale yellow, posterior side greenish brown, not overlapping on scutellum (Fig. 4.42); mesonotum 0.93mm long, 1.56mm broad, brownish green; scutellum 0.62mm long, 1.25mm broad, brownish green, vertical saffron bands. *Wings*, Fore wing (Fig. 4.44) 9.3mm long, 2.18mm broad, semitransparent, saffron bands; hind wing (Fig. 4.45) 8.75mm long, 2.5mm broad, black, membranous, transparent. *Hind leg* (Fig. 4.46) 10.47mm long, 0.62mm broad, pale golden yellow; coxa 1.25mm long, 0.62mm broad, pale yellow; trochanter 0.5mm long, 0.31mm broad, pale yellow; femur 2.81mm long, 0.5mm broad, brownish yellow, on anterior side black patches; tibia 4.37mm long, 0.31mm broad, golden brown with spines, black spot at base of each spine; tarsus 1.36mm long, 0.18mm broad, pale brown, anterior side black, posterior pale brown; pre-tarsus 0.62mm long, 0.25mm broad, yellowish brown, meso-tarsus 0.43mm long, 0.18mm broad, brown; meta-tarsus 0.31mm long, 0.12mm broad, brown.
- *Abdomen* (Fig. 4.47): 3.68mm long, 2.37mm broad, black, 1 to 8 segments contain black dorsally, pale irregular patches present on 7 to 8 segments, first segment 0.43mm long, 2.18mm broad; second segment 0.5mm long, 2.37mm broad; third segment 0.5mm long, 2.18mm broad; fourth segment 0.5mm long, 2mm broad; fifth segment 0.5mm long, 1.68mm broad; sixth segment 0.5mm long, 1.37mm broad; seventh segment 0.5mm long, 1.25mm broad; eighth segment 0.5mm long, 0.93mm broad. Ovipositor 0.2mm long, brown.
- *Host Plants:* Sugarcane *Saccharum officinarum* L., Rice *Oryzasativa* L., Wheat *Triticum, aestivum* L., grasses.
- *Paratype*: ♂ 20, ♀ 10, Coll. Chandani Kamble, Sept. to Dec., preserved in alcohol.
- *Distribution*: Western Maharashtra; 5 ♂, 6 ♀, Kagal (Kolhapur), 15-X-2014; 3 ♂, 0 ♀, Karad (Satara), 07-XI-2014.

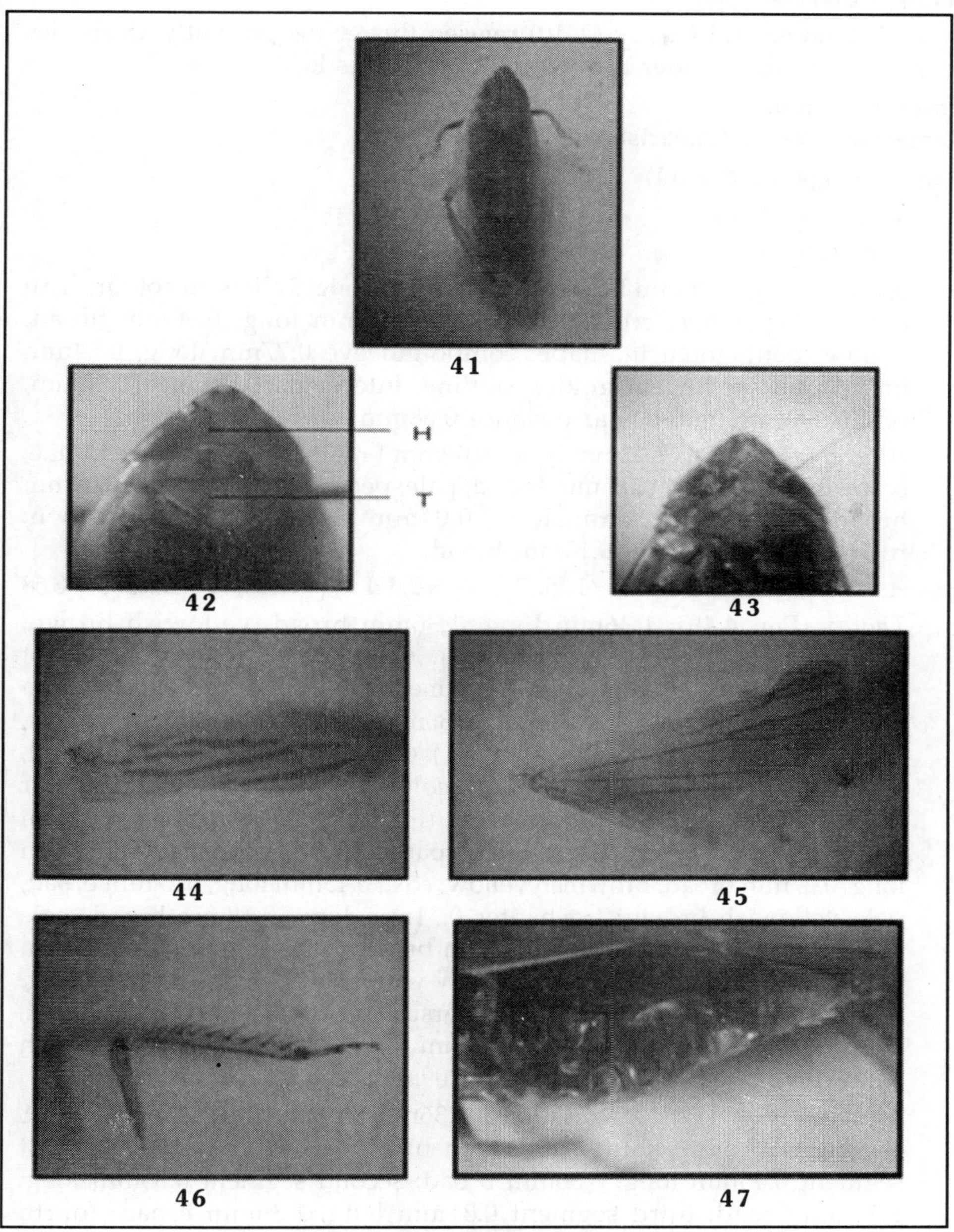

Plate - 5: ***V. rubrofasciata*:** Fig. 4.41: **Adult male,** Fig. 4.42: **Dorsal view head and thorax,** Fig. 4.43: **Ventral view head and thorax,** Fig. 4.44: **Forewing,** Fig. 4.45: **Hindwing,** Fig. 4.46: **Hindleg,** Fig. 4.47: **Abdomen**

Genus *Maiestas* (Delong)

Dominguez and Godoy (2010) revised this genus presently 48 species have been included under this genus with species key.

Maiestas menoni (Ramasubba Rao & Ramkrishnan) (Plate - 6: Figs. 4.48-4.54)

- *Male* (Fig. 4.48):
- *Head* (Fig. 4.49):

  0.45mm long, 1.36mm broad, broader than long, yellow in colour, with brownish patches; crown (Fig. 4.59) 0.45mm long, 0.90mm broad, yellow, pentagonal in shape; compound eye 0.77mm long, 0.54mm broad, red, yellowish golden outline, interocular distance 0.90mm, ocelli two, orange, ocular distance 0.68mm.
- *Antenna* (Fig. 4.50) 1.22mm long, 0.09mm broad, pale, long thread like; scape 0.14mm long, 0.09 mm broad, pale; pedicel 0.18mm long, 0.09mm broad; flagellum 0.90mm long, 0.04mm broad, yellowish brown; rostrum 0.36mm long, 0.14mm broad.
- *Antennal formula* – S L/W = 1.55, P L/W = 2, F L/W = 22.5, A = 26.05/3 = 8.68
- *Thorax* (Fig. 4.49): 1.36mm long, 1.36mm broad, yellowish brown; pronotum (Fig. 4.49) 0.68mm long, 1.36mm broad, yellow, shiny, not overlapping on scutellum (Fig. 4.49); mesonotum 0.31mm long, 1.72mm broad, brownish yellow; scutellum 0.36mm long, 0.45mm broad, yellow, shiny. *Wings*, fore wing (Fig. 4.51) 4.09mm long, 1.13mm broad, semitransparent, brownish yellow colour, brown rounded irregular structure, not elytra like; hind wing (Fig. 4.52) 3.86mm long, 1.36mm broad, black, membranous, semitransparent. *Hind leg* (Fig. 4.53) 5.78mm long, 0.27mm broad, brownish yellow; coxa 0.45mm long, 0.27mm broad, pale yellowish brown; trochanter 0.31mm long, 0.18mm broad, pale yellow; femur 1.36mm long, 0.27mm broad, pale yellow; tibia 2.72mm long, 0.18mm broad, brownish yellow with spines, tarsus 0.94mm long, 0.14mm broad, brown at base; pre-tarsus 0.54mm long, 0.14mm broad, yellowish brown, meso-tarsus 0.22mm long, 0.09mm broad, brownish yellow; meta-tarsus 0.18mm long, 0.09mm broad, yellowish brown.
- *Abdomen* (Fig. 4.54): 3.54mm long, 1.36mm broad, brown, shiny, 1 to 8 segments brown, shiny. abdomen brown from ventral side, first segment 0.45mm long, 0.36mm broad; second segment 0.36mm long, 1.27mm broad; third segment 0.31mm long, 1.36mm broad; fourth segment 0.31mm long, 1.22mm broad; fifth segment 0.31mm long, 1.13mm broad; sixth segment 0.31mm long, 0.90mm broad; seventh segment 0.68mm long, 0.45mm broad; eighth segment 0.45mm long, 0.45mm broad. Ovipositor 0.45mm long, brown.
- *Host Plants*: grasses.

- *Paratype*: ♂- 10, ♀- 12, Coll. Chandani Kamble, Aug. to Dec., preserved in alcohol.
- *Distribution*: 05 ♂, 06♀ Kolhapur, Coll. Chandani Kamble, 11-VIII-2014; 5 ♂, 1 ♀, Karad (Satara), 19-XI-2014.

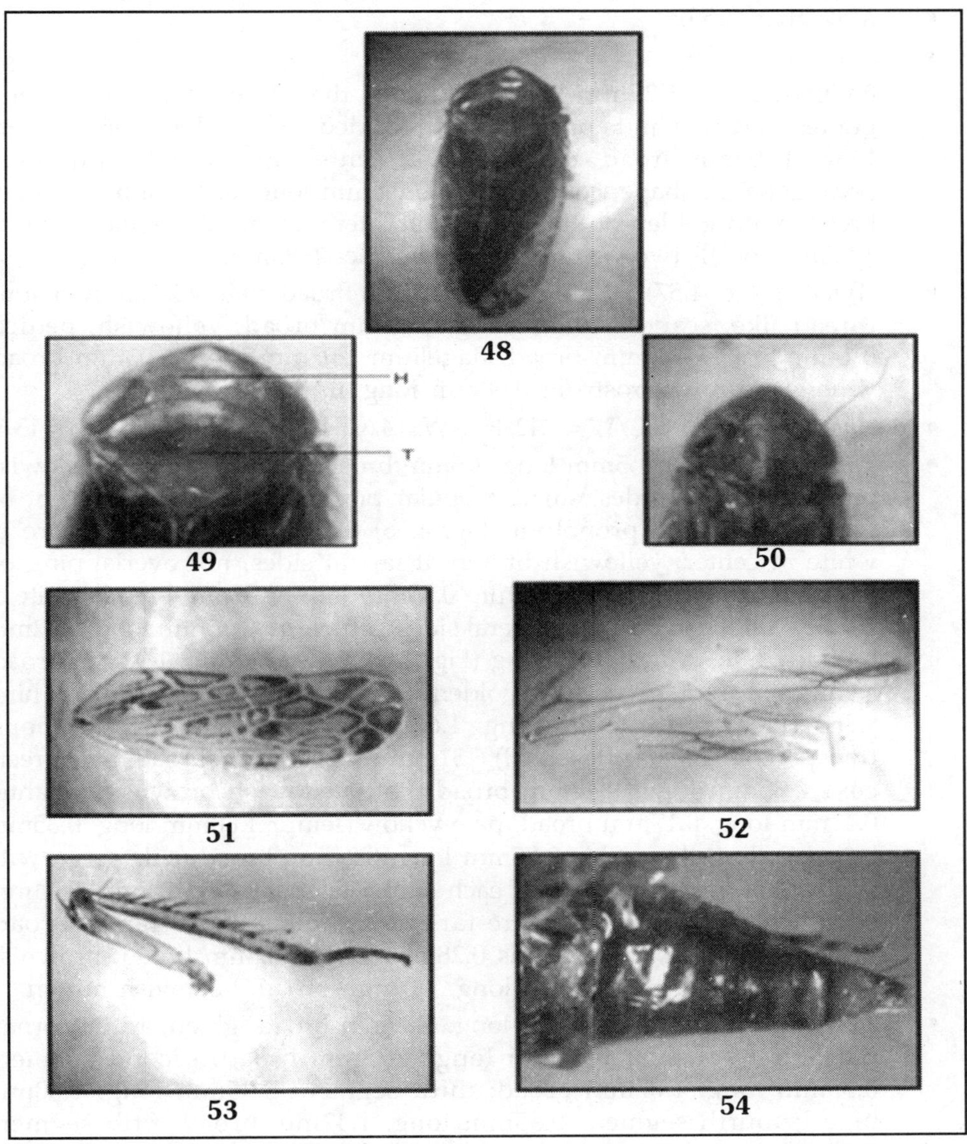

Plate - 6: ***M. menoni*:** Fig. 4.48: **Adult male,** Fig. 4.49: **Dorsal view head and thorax,** Fig. 4.50: **Ventral view head and thorax,** Fig. 4.51: **Forewing,** Fig. 4.52: **Hindwing,** Fig. 4.53: **Hindleg,** Fig. 4.54: **Abdomen**

Genus *Hecalus* Ball

Under this genus 33 species have been reported (NCBT, 2015)

***Hecalus cacuminal* Ball**

(Plate - 7: Figs. 4.55-4.61)

- *Male* (Fig. 4.55):
- *Head* (Fig. 4.56):

  0.60mm long, 1.25mm broad, broader than long, green in colour, golden vertical bands presents, not rounded; crown (Fig. 4.56) 0.60mm long, 1.07mm broad, pale green at center, green at lateral sides, pentagonal in shape; compound eye 0.5mm long, 0.25mm broad, dark brown with golden outline, brown at lateral side, interocular distance 1.07mm, ocelli two, white, ocular distance 0.35mm.
- *Antenna* (Fig. 4.57) 1.32mm long, 0.07mm broad, yellowish brown; long thread like, scape 0.10mm long, 0.07mm broad, yellowish; pedicel 0.14mm long, 0.03mm broad; flagellum 1.07mm long, 0.03mm broad, yellowish brown; rostrum 0.60mm long, 0.10mm broad.
- *Antennal formula* – S L/W = 1.42, P L/W = 4.6, F L/W = 35, A = 41.02/3 = 13.67
- *Thorax* (Fig. 4.56): 1.5mm long, 1.5mm broad, white at center, yellowish brown at lateral sides, small irregular pore like: structures present on middle of thorax; pronotum (Fig. 4.56) 0.78mm long, 1.57mm broad, white at center, yellowish brown at lateral sides, not overlapping on scutellum (Fig. 4.56); mesonotum 0.35mm long, 1.07mm broad, white at center, yellowish brown at lateral sides; scutellum 0.35mm long, 0.42mm broad, white. *Wings*, fore wing (Fig. 4.58) 3.92mm long, 1.92mm broad, semitransparent, green with golden vertical bands, not elytra like; hind wing (Fig. 4.59) 3.21mm long, 1.60mm broad, white, membranous, transparent. *Hind leg* (Fig. 4.60) 6.31mm long, 0.42mm broad, pale green; coxa 0.35mm long, 0.42mm broad, pale yellowish brown; trochanter 0.42mm long, 0.17mm broad, pale yellow; femur 1.60mm long, 0.35mm broad, pale yellow; tibia 2.85mm long, 0.21mm broad, pale green with spines, black spot at base of each spine; tarsus 1.09mm long, 0.14mm broad, brownish yellow; pre-tarsus 0.53mm long, 0.14mm broad, yellowish brown, meso-tarsus 0.28mm long, 0.07mm broad, brownish yellow; meta-tarsus 0.28mm long, 0.07mm broad, yellowish brown.
- *Abdomen* (Fig. 4.61): 2.92mm long, 0.89mm broad, green, at the corner, pale, first segment 0.35mm long, 1.78mm broad; second segment 0.35mm long, 1.67mm broad; third segment 0.35mm long, 1.60mm broad; fourth segment 0.35mm long, 1.42mm broad; fifth segment 0.35mm long, 1.25mm broad; sixth segment 0.35mm long, 1.14mm broad; seventh segment 0.35mm long, 0.96mm broad; eighth segment 0.35mm long, 0.89mm broad. Ovipositor 0.40 mm long, dark brown.
- *Host Plants*: Cashew nut (*Anacardiun accidentale* L.), grasses.

- *Paratype*: 3 ♂, 5 ♀, Coll- Chandani Kamble, Aug. to Jan. preserved in alcohol, labeled as above.
- *Distribution*: 3 ♂, 2 ♀, Ajara (Kolhapur), Coll. Chandani Kamble, 02-IX-2013; 01 ♂, Chandgad (Kolhapur), 18-XII-2014.

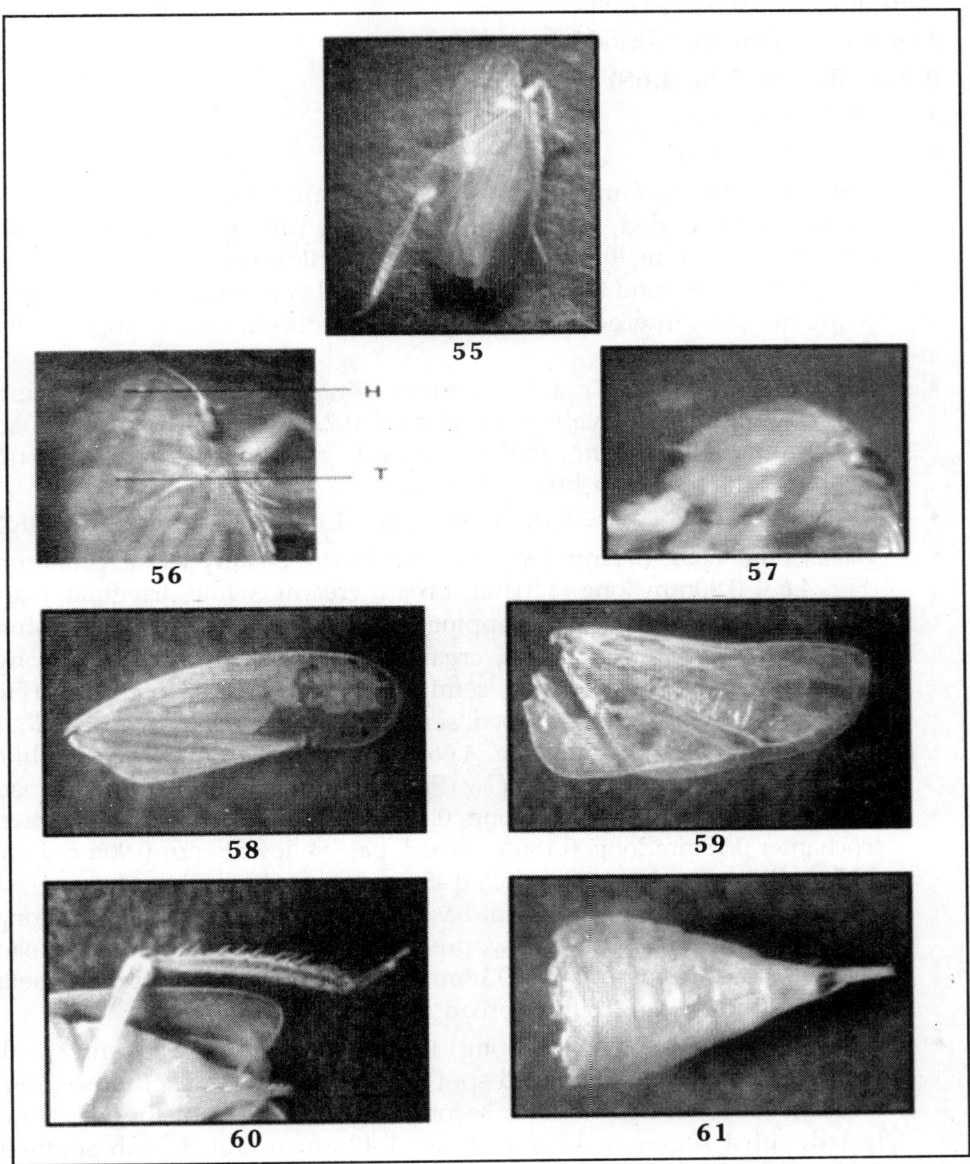

Plate - 7: ***H. cacuminal*:** Fig. 4.55: **Adult male,** Fig. 4.56: **Dorsal view head and thorax,** Fig. 4.57: **Ventral view head and thorax,** Fig. 4.58: **Forewing,** Fig. 4.59: **Hindwing,** Fig. 4.60: **Hindleg,** Fig. 4.61: **Abdomen**

Tribe Chiasmini

Genus *Exitianus* Ball

It contains 43 species reported from the world. Six species are found in Asia. It is characterised by having a transverse band on vertex. Males with apical setae on pygofer.

Exitianus plebeius (Kirkaldy)

(Plate - 8: Figs. 4.62-4.68)

- *Male* (Fig. 4.62):
- *Head* (Fig. 4.63):

  0.68mm long, 1.36mm broad, broader than long, creamy white in colour, not rounded, transverse black band present on vertex; crown (Fig. 4.63) 0.68mm long, 1.13mm broad, yellowish white, pentagonal in shape, compound eye 0.68mm long, 0.31mm broad, black, creamy white boarder, interocular distance 1.13mm, ocelli two, orange, ocular distance 0.90mm.
- *Antenna* (Fig. 4.64) 2.27mm long, brown; long thread like, scape 0.22mm long, 0.13mm broad, yellowish; pedicel 0.22mm long, 0.09mm broad; flagellum 1.81mm long, 0.04mm broad, yellowish brown; rostrum 0.28mm long, 0.13mm broad, brown.
- *Antennal formula* – S L/W = 1.69, P L/W = 2.44, F L/W = 45.25, A = 49.38/3 = 16.42
- *Thorax* (Fig. 4.63): 1.72mm long, 1.81mm broad, creamy white; pronotum (Fig. 4.63) 0.90mm long, 1.81mm broad, creamy white, irregular black spots at anterior side, not overlapping on scutellum (Fig. 4.63); mesonotum 0.31mm long, 1.36mm broad, creamy white; scutellum 0.5mm long, 0.45mm broad, creamy white, semitransparent. *Wings*, fore wing (Fig. 4.65) 5.45mm long, 1.13mm broad, semitransparent, pale brownish colour, not elytra like; hind wing (Fig. 4.66) 5mm long, 1.36mm broad, white, membranous, transparent. *Hind leg* (Fig. 4.67) 2.47mm long, 0.35mm broad, pale brownish; coxa 0.45mm long, 0.45mm broad, pale yellowish brown; trochanter 0.18mm long, 0.18mm broad, pale yellow; femur 0.90mm long, 0.27mm broad, pale yellow; tibia 0.45mm long, 0.18mm broad, brownish yellow with spines, black spot at base of each spine; tarsus 0.49mm long, 0.13mm broad, brownish yellow; pre-tarsus 0.18mm long, 0.13mm broad, yellowish brown. meso-tarsus 0.18mm long, 0.13mm broad, brown; meta-tarsus 0.13mm long, 0.09mm broad, yellowish brown.
- *Abdomen* (Fig. 4.68): 2.95mm long, 1.81mm broad, black at center, pale yellow at both sides, small red spot present at both sides; first segment 0.31mm long, 1.81mm broad; second segment 0.27mm long, 1.59mm broad; third segment 0.22mm long, 1.40mm broad; fourth segment 0.22mm long, 1.36mm broad; fifth segment 0.22mm long, 1.13mm broad; sixth segment 0.22mm long, 1.04mm broad; seventh segment 0.22mm long, 0.90mm broad; eighth segment 0.22mm long, 0.68mm broad. Ovipositor 0.30mm long, brown.

- *Host Plants*: Rice *Oryzasativa* L., Cotton genus *Gossypium* L., Wheat Tritium sp.
- *Paratype*: 5, ♂, 12 ♀, Coll. Chandani Kamble, Jan. to Nov., preserved in 70 per cent alcohol, labeled as above.
- *Distribution*: 2 ♂, 10 ♀, Ashta (Sangli) 17-VIII-2014; 3 ♂, 2 ♀, Kolhapur, 03-IX-2014, Kolhapur.

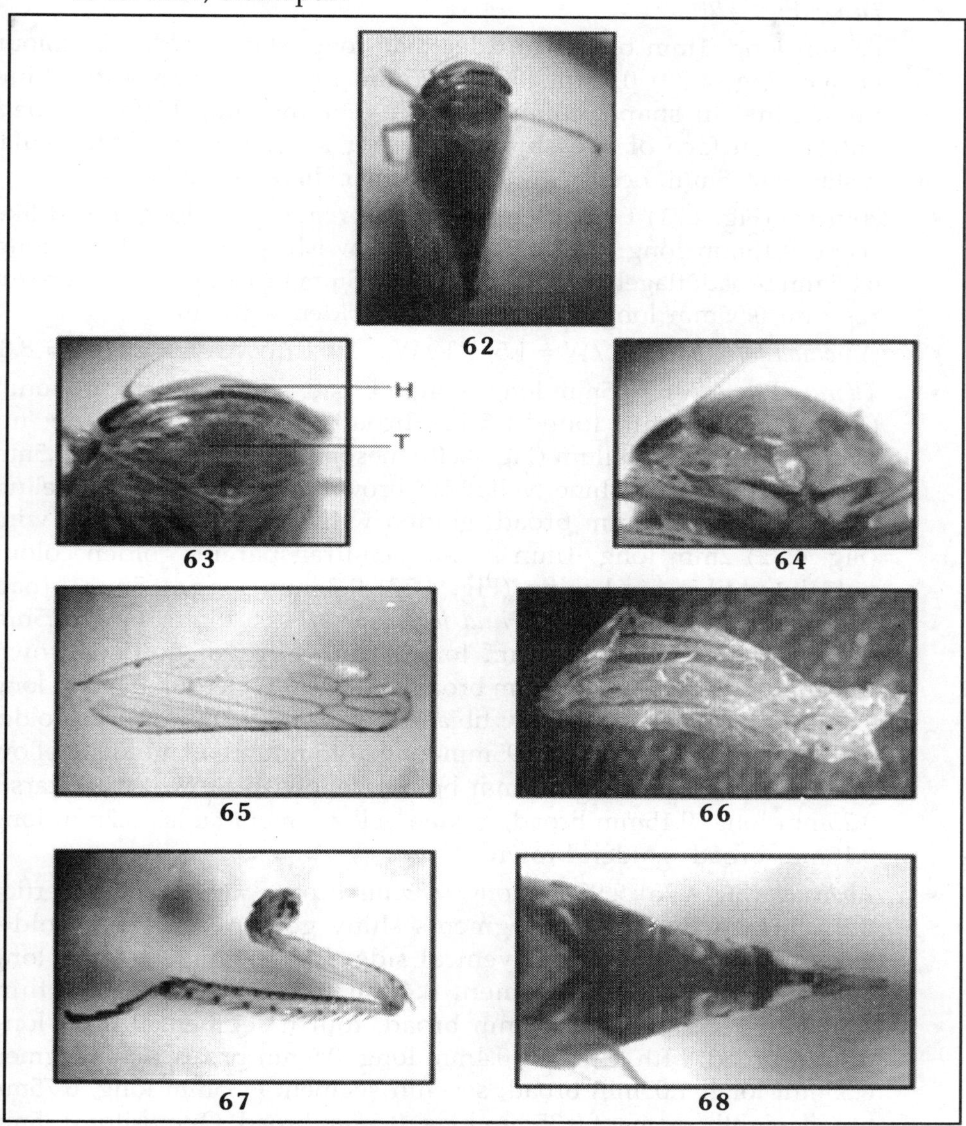

Plate - 8: ***E. indicus:*** 4.62 **Adult male,** Fig. 4.63: **Dorsal view head and thorax,** Fig. 4.64: **Ventral View head and thorax,** Fig. 4.65: **Forewing,** Fig. 4.66: **Hindwing,** Fig. 4.67: **Hindleg,** Fig. 4.68: **Abdomen**

Genus Paivanana Sahlberg

The genus was established by Sahlberg (1871).

Paivanana indra Distant

(Plate - 9: Figs. 4.69-4.75)

- *Male* (Fig. 4.69):
- *Head* (Fig. 4.70):

  0.5mm long, 1mm broad, broader than long, shiny golden in colour; crown (Fig. 4.70) 0.5mm long, 1.75mm broad, golden with shine, pentagonal in shape. compound eye 0.5mm long, 0.20mm broad, anterior surface of eye shiny, posterior surface black, interocular distance 0.75mm, ocelli two, black, ocular distance 0.35mm.
- *Antenna* (Fig. 4.71) 1.4mm long, 0.15mm broads, pale, long thread like; scape 0.15mm long, 0.1mm broad, yellowish; pedicel 0.15mm long, 0.05mm broad; flagellum 1.1mm long, 0.05mm broad, yellowish brown; rostrum 0.55mm long, 0.15mm broad, golden with shine.
- *Antennal formula* – S L/W = 1.5, P L/W = 3 F L/W 22, A = 26.5/3 = 8.83
- *Thorax* (Fig. 4.70): 0.85mm long, 1.5mm broad, shiny golden; pronotum (Fig. 4.70) 0.35mm long, 1.5mm broad, golden with shine, not overlapping on scutellum (Fig. 4.70); mesonotum 0.25mm long, 0.5mm broad, golden with shine, yellowish brown at lateral sides; scutellum 0.25mm long, 0.25mm broad, golden with shine. *Wings*, fore wing (Fig. 4.72) 2mm long, 1mm broad, semitransparent, golden colour, not elytra like; hind wing (Fig. 4.73) 0.75mm long, 0.5mm broad, membranous, transparent. *Hind leg* (Fig. 4.74) 5.75mm long, 0.5mm broad, golden; coxa 0.75mm long, 0.5mm broad, golden brown; trochanter 0.3mm long, 0.2mm broad, pale yellow; femur 1.25mm long, 0.3mm broad, golden yellow; tibia 2.5mm long, 0.2mm broad, golden yellow with spines; tarsus 0.95mm long, 0.15mm broad, golden yellow; pre-tarsus 0.5 mm long, 0.2mm broad, yellowish brown. meso-tarsus 0.25mm long, 0.15mm broad, golden yellow; meta-tarsus 0.2mm long, 0.15mm broad, golden brown.
- *Abdomen* (Fig. 4.75): 2.92mm long, 0.89mm broad, golden, shiny, vertical thick brown lines,1 to 8 segments shiny golden, abdomen golden without brown lines from ventral side. first segment 0.4mm long, 1.6mm broad; second segment 0.4mm long, 1.6mm broad; third segment 0.4mm long, 1.55mm broad; fourth segment 0.4mm long, 0.5mm broad; fifth segment 0.4mm long, 0.5mm broad; sixth segment 0.35mm long, 1.05mm broad; seventh segment 0.35mm long, 0.75mm broad; eighth segment 0.35mm long, 0.5mm broad. Ovipositor 0.35mm long, black.
- *Host Plants*: Unknown

- *Paratype* : 7 ♂, 3 ♀, Coll. Chandani Kamble, Aug. to Dec., preserved in 70 per cent alcohol, labeled as above.
- *Distribution* : 5 ♂, 2♀ Amba Ghats 25-VIII-2015, 02 ♂, 01♀ Ajara (Kolhapur), 10- IX- 2014.

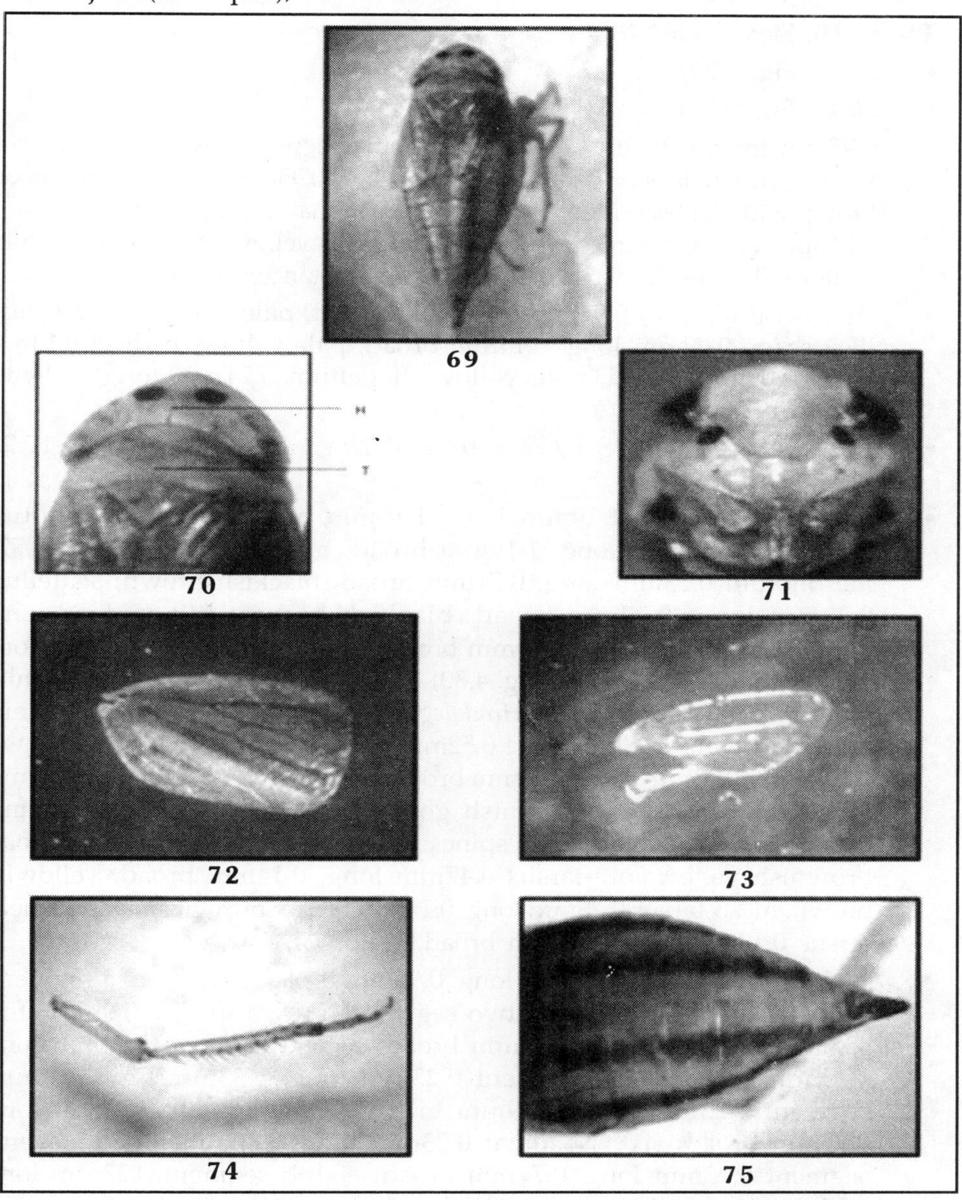

Plate - 9: ***P. indra*:** Fig. 4.69: **Adult male,** Fig. 4.70: **Dorsal view head and thorax,** Fig. 4.71: **Ventral view head and thorax,** Fig. 4.72: **Forewing,** Fig. 4.73: **Hindwing,** Fig. 4.74: **Hindleg,** Fig. 4.75: **Abdomen**

Tribe Scaphytopiini

Genus *Grammacephalus* Ball

38 species have been reported.

***Grammacephalus* sp.**

(Plate - 10: Figs. 4.76-4.82)

- *Male* (Fig. 4.76):
- *Head* (Fig. 4.77):

  0.95mm long, 0.95mm broad, broader than long, brown in colour, two vertical brown lines presents; crown (Fig. 4.77) 0.95mm long, 0.71mm broad, brown with yellow irregular patches, pentagonal in shape. Compound eye 0.71mm long, 0.47mm broad, wine red with yellow margin, interocular distance 0.71mm, ocelli two, white, ocular distance 0.47mm.
- *Antenna* (Fig. 4.78) 0.95mm long, 0.14 broad, pale yellow, long thread like; scape 0.09mm long, 0.14mm broad, pale yellow; pedicel 0.14mm long, 0.09mm broad, pale yellow; flagellum 0.71mm long, 0.04mm broad, brown.
- *Antennal formula* – S L/W = 0.64, P L/W = 1.55, F L/W = 17.75, A = 19.94/3 = 6.64
- *Thorax* (Fig. 4.77): 1.19mm long, 1.19mm broad, brown. pronotum (Fig. 4.77) 0.47mm long, 1.19mm broad, blackish brown (Fig. 4.77); mesonotum 0.23mm long, 0.71mm broad, blackish brown; scutellum 0.23mm long, 0.23mm broad, blackish brown. *Wings*, fore wing (Fig. 4.79) 4.28mm long, 1.42mm broad, semitransparent, brown colour, not elytra like; hind wing (Fig. 4.80) 4.04mm long, 1.66mm broad, white, membranous, transparent. *Hind leg* (Fig. 4.81) 6.01mm long, 0.33mm broad, brownish golden; coxa 0.52mm long, 0.33mm broad, pale brown; trochanter 0.33mm long, 0.23mm broad, brownish golden; femur 1.42mm long, 0.33mm broad, brownish golden; tibia 2.85mm long, 0.32mm broad, brownish golden with spines; tarsus 0.89mm long, 0.14mm broad, brownish yellow; pre-tarsus 0.47mm long, 0.14mm broad, yellowish brown. meso-tarsus 0.23mm long, 0.14mm broad, brownish yellow; meta-tarsus 0.19mm long, 0.09mm broad, yellowish brown.
- *Abdomen* (Fig. 4.82): 2.85mm long, 0.95mm broad, black, 1 to 8 segments contain black dorsally, last two segments brownish black, shiny, first segment 0.23mm long, 1.42mm broad; second segment 0.23mm long, 1.42mm broad; third segment 0.23mm long, 1.33mm broad; fourth segment 0.23mm long, 1.19mm broad; fifth segment 0.23mm long, 0.95mm broad; sixth segment 0.23mm long, 0.80mm broad; seventh segment 0.23mm long, 0.71mm broad; eighth segment 0.23mm long, 0.57mm broad. Pygofer 0.5 mm long, grayish.
- *Host Plants* : Barley *Hordeum vulgare* L., Jowar *Sorghum vulgare* L., grasses.

- *Paratype* : 10 ♂, 17 ♀, Coll. Chandani Kamble, Aug. to Jan., preserved in 70 per cent alcohol.
- *Distribution* : 6 ♂, 3 ♀, Amba (Kolhapur,), 1-VIII-2014; 4 ♂, 0 ♀, Chandgad (Kolhapur), 03-XI-2014.

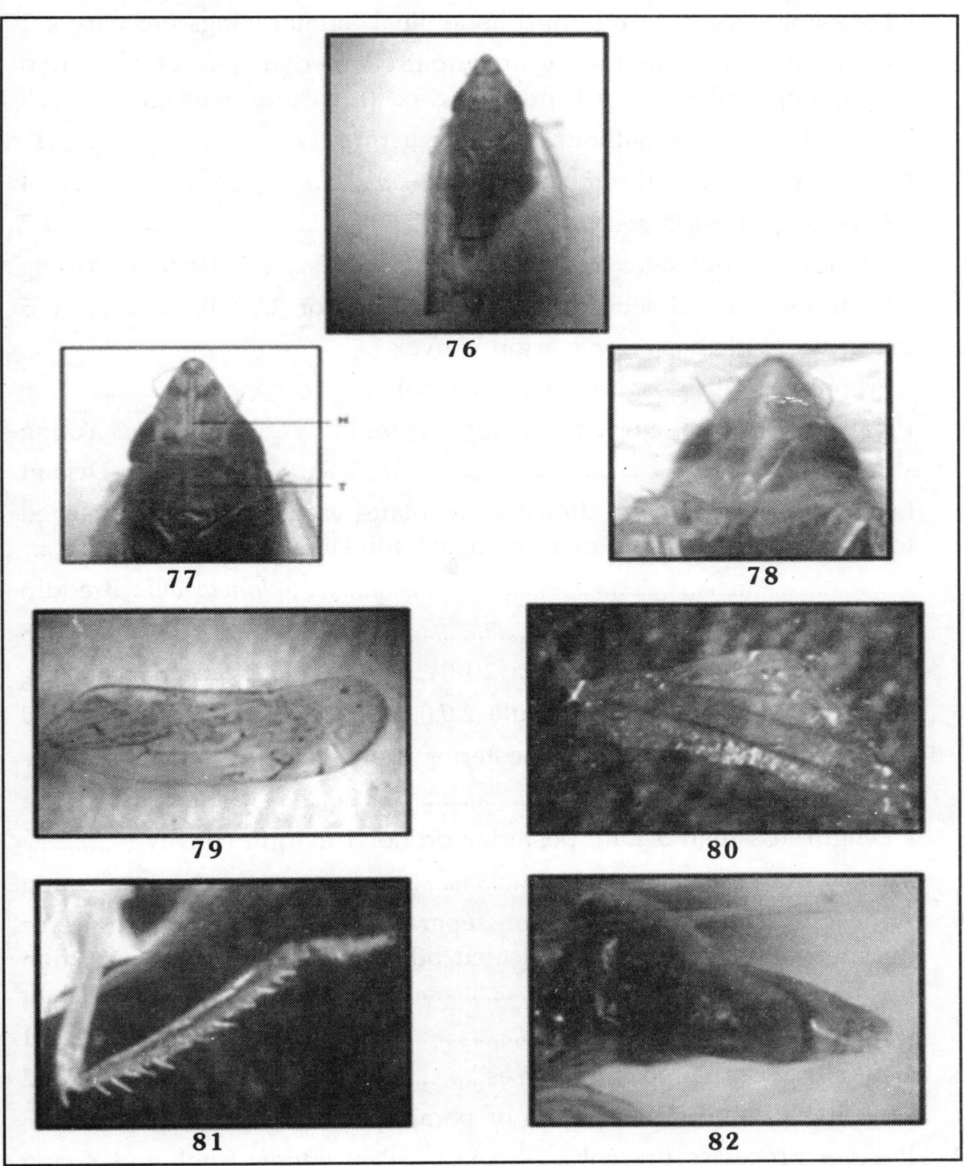

Plate - 10: ***Scaphytopius* sp.:** Fig. 4.76: **Adult male,** Fig. 4.77: **Dorsal view head and thorax,** Fig. 4.78: **Ventral view head and thorax,** Fig. 4.79: **Forewing,** Fig. 4.80: **Hindwing,** Fig. 4.81: **Hindleg,** Fig. 4.82: **Abdomen**

Subfamily: Cicadellinae

Key to the genera of cicadellinae

1. Forewing only reaching the second abdominal tergite, wings rudimentary .... *Oniroxis* China
   - Forewing exceeding the third abdominal tergite, wings ordinary ... 2
2. Genital structures including an unpaired median paraphysis often articulating with but not firmly attached to base of aedeagus 3
   - Genital structures without such a structure 10
3. Pygofer processes present 4
   - Pygofer processes absent 7
4. Posterior femoral setal formula 2:1:0 .... *Paratkina* Young
   - Posterior femoral setal formula 2:0:0, 2:1:1, or 2:1:1:1 5
5. Pronotum with posterior margin convex.
   - Pronotum with posterior margin rectilinear or concave 6
6. Preatrium distinct, curved strongly ventrad .... *Anatkina* Young
   - Preatrium absent .... *Atkinsoniella* Distant
7. Pronotum constricted in dorsal view; plates each with apex narrowed to a small point or to a more elongate spinelike process .... *Sphinctogonia* Breddin
   - Pronotum not as above 8
8. Posterior femoral setal formula 2:1:0 .... *Stenatkina* Young
   - Posterior femoral setal formula 2:0:0, 2:1:1, or 2:1:1:1 9
9. Length greater than 15 mm; posterior pronotal margin convex .... *Gunungidia* Young
   - Length less than 5 mm; posterior pronotal margin convave .... *Nanatka* Young
10. Aedeagus with its basal portion separated from shaft by a suture or by lateral notches; or not indicated otherwise than by a constriction in caudal view .... *Kolla* Distant
    - Aedeagus not as above 11
11. Genitalia with paired paraphyses 12
    - Genitalia without paraphysis or paraphyses 13
12. Pygofer processes present .... *Paracicadella* Kuoh and Zhang
    - Pygofer processes absent .... *Cicadella* Latreille

13. Forewing with a reduced clavus, a wide appendix and lacking vein .. 14

- Forewing with a clavus of normal scope, a tapered appendix and with vein present 15

14. Vertex with a fine essential longitudinal carination and an oblique carination on each side of anterior area; forewing moderately broad .... *Mileewa* Distant

- Vertex without any carination; forewing elongate .... *Ujna* Distant

15. Head with the cephalic process longly produced, antennal ledges thickened .... *Namsangia* Distant

- Head without the cephalic process, antennal ledges obscure 16

16. Styles short, not or barely exceeding apex of connective 17

- Styles well beyond apex of connective 21

17. Pygofer processes present 18

- Pygofer processes absent 20

18. Pygofer processes arising apically and short; aedeagus with paired processes at base of shaft .... *Aspidia* Yang and Zhang

- Pygofer processes arising basiventrally and long; aedeagus without paired processes 19

19. Crown pale yellow with orange spots, anterior margin paraboloid in dorsal view; clypellus concave apically .... *Anagonalia* Young

- Crown heavily marked with black, gray, or castaneous, anterior margin very broadly convex in dorsal view; clypellus convex apically .... *Erragonalia* Young

20. Apodemes of abdominal sternum II well developed .. *Cofana* Melichar

- Apodemes of abdominal sternum II absent *Miscana* Yang and Zhang

21. Forewing with base of third apical cell more proximal basal than base of fourth apical cell .... *Bothrogonia* Melichar

- Forewing with bottom of third apical cell more distal than base of fourth apical cell 22

22. Pygofer processes arising posteroventrally .... *Seasogonia* Young

- Pygofer processes arising basiventrally 23

23. Length 6 mm or less, pygofer lacking macrosetae, subgenital plates long and narrow, style with rounded apex .... Processina gen. nov.

- Length greater than 9.5mm, pygofer with discal or anteapical macrosetae, subgenital plates triangular, style with gradually tapered apex .... *Bharagonalia* Young

Tribe Cicadellini

Genus *Cofana* Melichar

It is found in grass habitat and in rice field and from Bamboo ecosystems. Under this genus 24 species have been reported (Krishnankutty and Viraktamath, 1908; Young *et al.* 2015). This genus is characterized by lacking veins R 2+3 in forewing (young, 1986). Seven species are reported from India.

Key to species of genus *Cofana*

1. Head with transocular width less than greatest width of pronotum 2
   - Head with transocular width equal to or greater than greatest width of pronotum 3
2. Forewing with inner anteapical cell closed basally ...... albida. (Walker)
   - Forewing with inner anteapical cell open basally .... eburnea (Walker)
3. Crown with paired discal spots or with a discal transverse marking .... maai, new species
   - Crown with one discal spot or a longitudinal line otherwise without discal marking 4
4. Head without a median apical black spot 5
   - Head with a median apical black spot 9
5. Length of male 9.2mm or more; of female 10mm or more 6
   - Length of male 5.3-8.0mm; of female 5.3-9.4mm 7
6. Crown and pronotum dark, marked with yellow ...... separata, new species
   - Crown and pronotum usually unmarked .. hoogstraali, new species.
7. Head with a median pale spot at transition from crown to face 8
   - Head without such a spot .... unimaculatu (Signoret).
8. Pronotum and scutellum with a conspicuous dark line .... polaris, new species.
   - Pronotum and scutellum unmarked .... sotoi, new species.
9. Large specimens, length usually 10mm or more; female abdominal sternum VII truncate apically but slightly convex medially .... suhviresccns (Stal).
   - Without above combination of characters; length almost always less than 10mm 10
10. Crown with a median posterior longitudinal dark marking that continues as a median pronotal dark stripe without interruption ... 11
    - Crown not so marked, with a broader median discal spot 12

11. Lateral pronotal margins dark, in dorsal view ..... perkinsi (Kirkaldy)

    - Lateral pronotal margins not dark-bordered in dorsal view jedarfa, ... new species

12. Head produced and triangular; specimens smaller (length of male 5.4-5.9mm; of female 6.0-6.6mm); head with median length interocular width or more, among a median pronotal line continuing onto scutellum .... *lineata* (Distant)

    - Head less produced, more broadly rounded at apex, specimens bigger (length at least 6.3mm in male; 7.7mm in female), head with median length less in relation to interocular width; with or without median pronotal line that continues onto scutellum 13

13. Forewing with middle anteapical cell open basally; male with a pair of short apical aedeagal processes .... yasumatsui, new species.

    - Forewing with middle anteapical cell usually closed basally; male without aedeagal processes 14

14. Pronotum with 3 parallel brown longitudinal lines on disk, all extending onto scutellum; aedeagal shaft broad in lateral view ...... lata, new species

    - Pronotum with only one line extending onto scutellum, otherwise none, aedeagal shaft cylindrical, not broader in lateral than in ventral view 15

15. Specimens more robust; female abdominal sternum VII with posterior margin slightly undulate, but broadly convex .... *spectra* (Distant)

    - Specimens more slender; female abdominal sternum VII narrowed and truncate or emarginated apically 16

16. Head with median discal spot usually larger; often with a median pronotal dark stripe extending onto scutellum; female abdominal sternum VII narrowed and truncate apically .... *nigrilinea* (Stal)

    - Head with median discal spot usually smaller; without such a pronotal stripe; female abdominal sternum VII narrowed and emarginate apically .... *medleri*, new species

Cofana subvirescence (Walker)

(Plate - 11 Figs. 4.83-4.89)

- *Male* (Fig. 4.83):
- *Head* (Fig. 4.84):

  1.11mm long, 2.22mm broad, broader than long, yellowish brown in colour, not rounded; head with transocular with less than greatest width of pronotum, crown (Fig. 4.84) 1.11mm long, 1.85mm broad, yellowish brown, at center black oval spot, pentagonal in shape; compound eye 0.74mm long, 0.37mm broad, black, interocular distance 1.85mm, ocelli two, blackish brown, ocular distance 1.11mm.

- *Antenna* (Fig. 4.85) 1.40mm long, 0.11mm broad, pale yellow, long thread like; scape 0.11mm long, 0.11mm broad, brownish yellow; pedicel 0.18mm long, 0.07mm broad; flagellum 1.11mm long, 0.03mm broad, pale brown; rostrum 0.92mm long, 0.11mm broad, brown.
- *Antennal formula* – S L/W = 1, P L/W = 2.57, F L/W = 37, A = 40.57/3 = 13.52
- *Thorax* (Fig. 4.84): 2.59mm long, 2.22mm broad, white at center, greenish black; pronotum (Fig. 4.84) 1.11mm long, 2.22mm broad, anterior side pale green, posterior blackish green, not overlapping on scutellum (Fig. 4.84) but reaching to it; mesonotum 0.74mm long, 1.48mm broad, golden white; scutellum 0.74mm long, 0.74mm broad, golden white. *Wings*, fore wing (Fig. 4.86) 8.88mm long, 2.22mm broad, transparent, pale green colour, not elytra like, with inner antiapical cell closed basally; hind wing (Fig. 4.87) 8.51mm long, 2.96mm broad, black, membranous, semitransparent. *Hind leg* (Fig. 4.88) 11.49mm long, 1.13mm broad, pale brown; coxa 0.48mm long, 0.11mm broad, pale brown; trochanter 0.74mm long, 0.29mm broad, pale brown; femur 2.22mm long, 0.25mm broad, pale brown; tibia 6.11mm long, 0.22mm broad, pale brown with spines; tarsus 1.13mm long, 0.14mm broad, brown; pre-tarsus 0.55mm long, 0.14mm broad, brown; meso-tarsus 0.29mm long, 0.18mm broad, brown; meta-tarsus 0.29mm long, 0.14mm broad, brown.
- *Abdomen* (Fig. 4.89): 7.40mm long, 2.40mm broad, black, 1 to 6 segments contain black, 7 to 8 segments pale brown, first segment 0.74mm long, 2.22mm broad; second segment 0.74mm long, 2.40mm broad; third segment 0.74mm long, 2.40mm broad; fourth segment 0.74mm long, 2.22mm broad; fifth segment 0.74mm long, 2.03mm broad; sixth segment 0.74mm long, 1.85mm broad; seventh segment 0.74mm long, 1.66mm broad; eighth segment 0.74mm long, 1.29mm broad. Ovipositor 0.80mm long, pale yellow.
- *Host Plants:* Sugarcane *Saccharum officinarum* L., Paddy *Oryzasativa* L., grasses.
- *Paratype* : 30 ♂, 20 ♀, Coll. Chandani Kamble, July to March, preserved in alcohol
- *Distribution*: 20 ♂, 12 ♀, Hatkanangale (Kolhapur), Coll. Chandani Kamble, 21-VII-2014; 10 ♂, 08 ♀ Kadegaon (Sangli), 30-IX-2015.

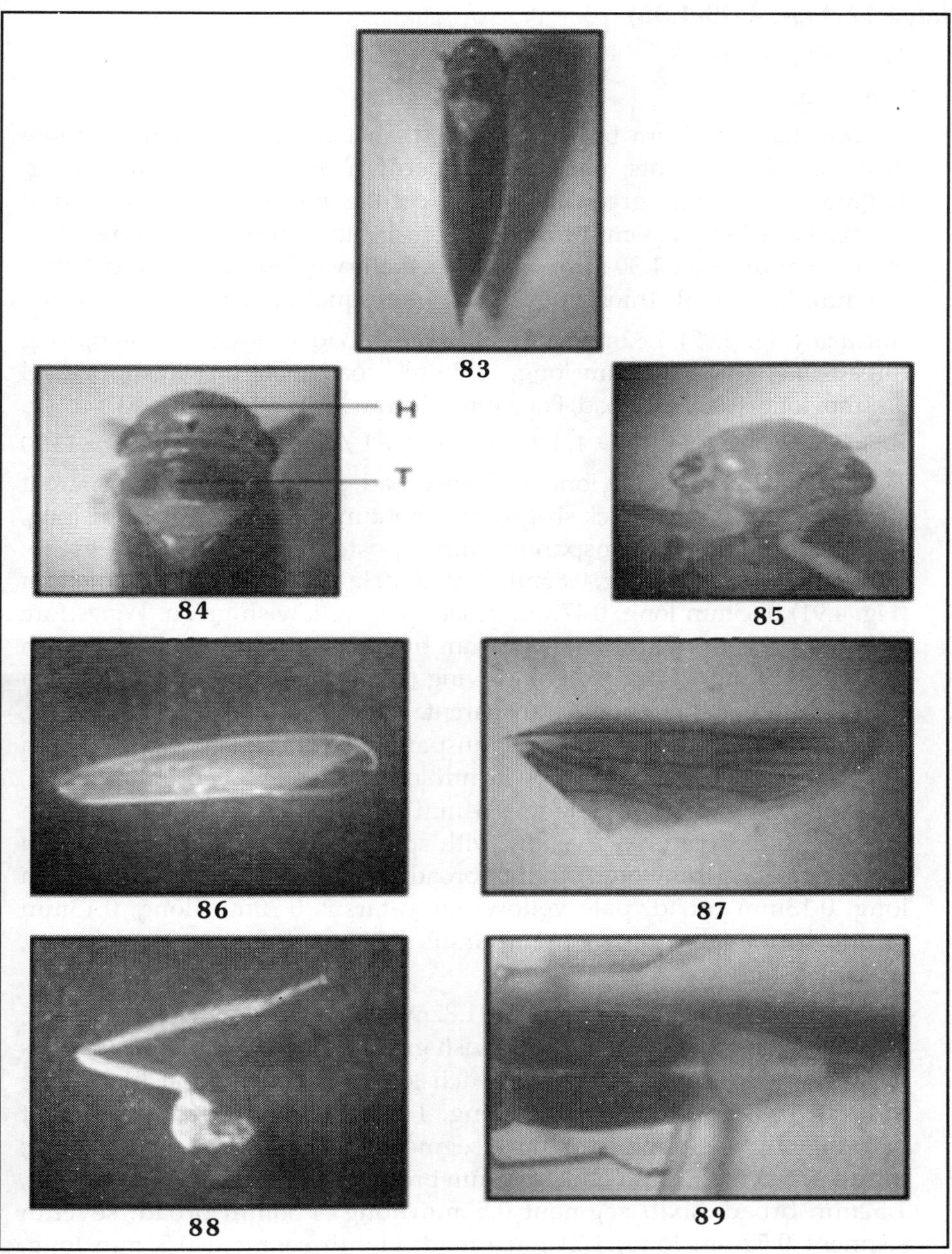

Plate - 11: ***C. albida:*** Fig. 4.83: **Adult male,** Fig. 4.84: **Dorsal view head and thorax,** Fig. 4.85: **Ventral view head and thorax,** Fig. 4.86: **Forewing,** Fig. 4.87: **Hindwing,** Fig. 4.87: **Hindleg,** Fig. 4.89: **Abdomen**

Cofana unimaculata Young
(Plate - 12: Figs. 4.90-4.96)

- *Male* (Fig. 4.90):
- *Head* (Fig. 4.91):

  0.86mm long, 1.73mm broad, broader than long, pale greenish yellow in colour, black spots, not rounded; crown (Fig. 4.91) 0.86mm long, 1.30mm broad, pale greenish yellow, pentagonal in shape. compound eye 0.78mm long, 0.43mm broad, greenish black, brown at lateral side, interocular distance 1.30 mm, ocelli two, watery coloured, ocular distance 0.86mm, head with transocular width not equal to with of pronotum.
- *Antenna* (Fig. 4.92) 1.82mm long, 0.13mm broad yellowish brown, long thread like; scape 0.13mm long, 0.13mm broad, pale brownish; pedicel 0.17mm long, 0.08mm broad; flagellum 1.52mm long, 0.04mm broad, brown.
- *Antennal formula* – S L/W = 1, P L/W = 2.12, F L/W = 38, A = 41.12/3 = 13.70
- *Thorax* (Fig. 4.91): 2.08mm long, 1.82mm broad, pale green, semitransparent shiny, posterior part blackish green; pronotum (Fig. 4.91) 1.28mm long, 1.82mm broad, semitransparent shiny, posterior part blackish green; mesonotum 0.34mm long, 0.86mm broad, pale yellowish green; scutellum (Fig. 4.91) 0.65mm long, 0.47mm broad, pale yellowish green. *Wings* fore wing (Fig. 4.93) 6.52mm long, 1.52mm broad, semitransparent, brownish green colour, not elytra like; hind wing (Fig. 4.94) 6.08mm long, 1.73mm broad, white, membranous, transparent. *Hind leg* (Fig. 4.95) 8.1mm long, 0.52mm broad, pale yellow, semitransparent; coxa 0.78mm long, 0.52mm broad, pale yellow; trochanter 0.52mm long, pale yellow, 0.26mm broad, pale yellow; femur 2.39mm long, 0.34mm broad, pale yellow; tibia 3.47mm long, 0.71mm broad, pale yellow with spines, black spot at base of each spine; tarsus 0.94mm long, 0.13mm broad, pale yellow; pre-tarsus 0.43mm long, 0.13mm broad, pale yellow; meso-tarsus 0.30mm long, 0.13mm broad, brownish yellow; meta-tarsus 0.21mm long, 0.13mm broad, yellowish brown.
- *Abdomen* (Fig. 4.96): 6.52mm long, 1.82mm broad, pale yellowish green, 1 to 6 segments contain pale yellowish green dorsally, last two segments whitish green, at the centre of each segment, horizontal black line present, first segment 0.52mm long, 1.82mm broad; second segment 0.52mm long, 1.73mm broad; third segment 0.52mm long, 1.73mm broad; fourth segment 0.52mm long, 1.65mm broad; fifth segment 0.52mm long, 1.52mm broad; sixth segment 0.52mm long, 1.30mm broad; seventh segment 0.52mm long, 1.21mm broad; eighth segment 0.52mm long, 0.95mm broad. Ovipositor 0.60mm long, pale yellow, shiny.
- *Host Plants :* Soyabean *Glycinemax* (L.), Paddy *Oryzasativa* L., Sugarcane *Saccharum officinarum* L., grasses.

- *Paratype*: 5 p ♂, 10 ♀, Coll. Chandani Kamble, June to Feb., Preserved in alcohol, labeled as above.
- *Distribution*: Western Maharashtra, 2 ♂, 05 ♀, Gadhahinglaj (Kolhapur), 06-VI-2014; 3 ♂, 05 ♀, Miraj (Sangli), 23-XI-2015.

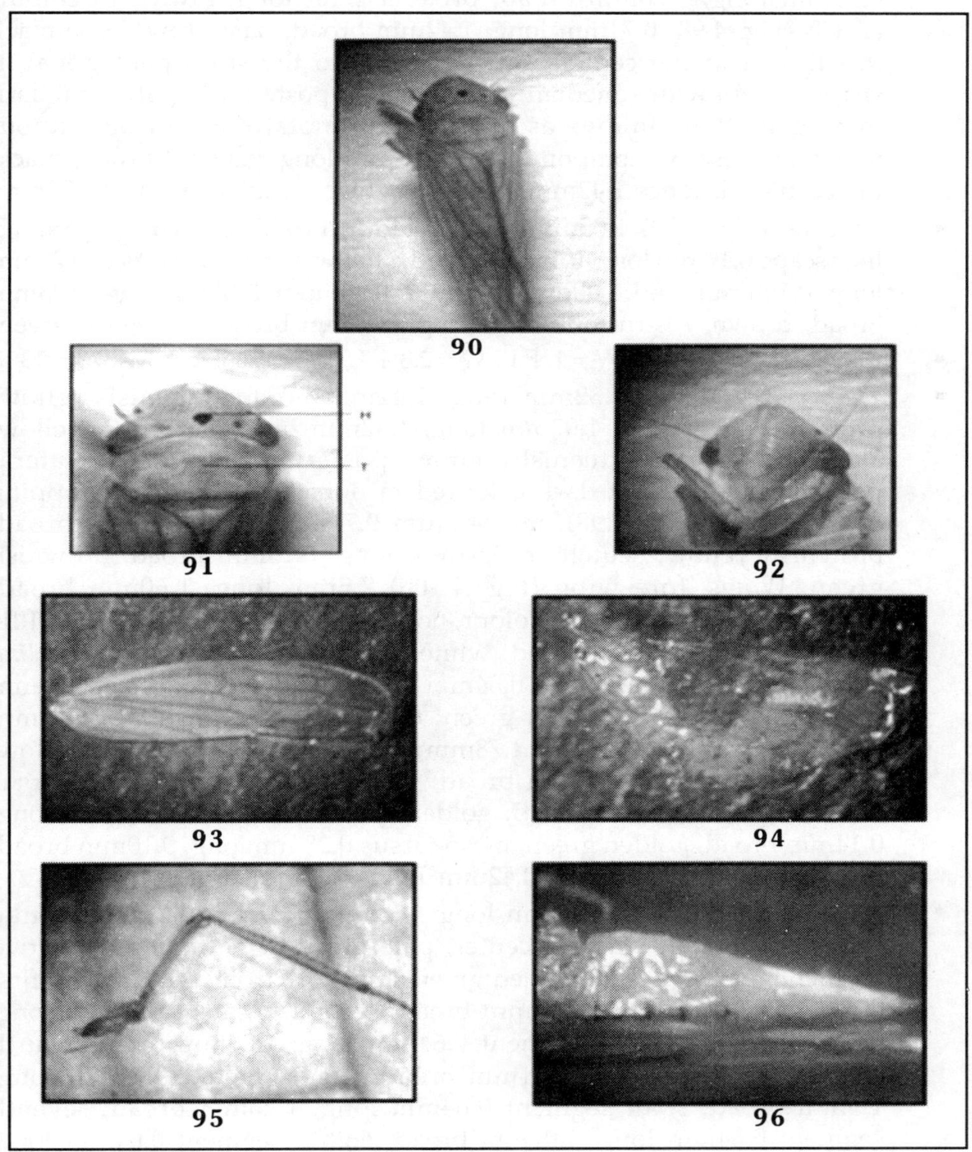

Plate - 12: ***C. unimaculata*:** Fig. 4.90: **Adult male,** Fig. 4.91: **Dorsal view head and thorax,** Fig. 4.92: **Ventral view head and thorax,** Fig. 4.93: **Forewing,** Fig. 4.94: **Hindwing,** Fig. 4.95: **Hindleg,** Fig. 4.96: **Abdomen**

***Cofana jedarfa* Young**
(Plate - 13: Figs. 4.97-4.103)

- *Male* (Fig. 4.97):
- *Head* (Fig. 4.98):
  0.71mm long, 1.78mm broad, broader than long, brown in colour; crown (Fig. 4.98) 0.71mm long, 1.42mm broad, pale brown, one black discal spot at the center and two small to the sides pentagonal in shape, crown with a median with a median posterior longitudinal dark markig that continuous as a median pronotal dark stripe without interption disc ps. compound eye 0.71mm long, 0.35mm broad, black, interocular distance 1.42mm, ocelli two, black, ocular distance 0.71mm.
- *Antenna* (Fig. 4.99) 1.05mm long, 0.14mm broad, brown long thread like; scape 0.14mm long, 0.14mm broad, yellowish brown; pedicel 0.28mm long, 0.10mm broad, yellowish brown; flagellum 1.07mm long, 0.03mm broad, brown; rostrum 0.64mm long, 0.10mm broad, yellowish green.
- *Antennal formula* – S L/W = 1, P L/W = 2.8, F L/W = 35.66, A = 39.46/3 = 13.15
- *Thorax* (Fig. 4.98): 2.32mm long, 1.42mm broad, greenish yellow; pronotum (Fig. 4.98) 1.07mm long, 1.42mm broad, greenish yellow, anterior side pale greenish yellow, posterior pale yellow, lateral pronotal margins not dark coloured in dorsal view, not overlapping on scutellum (Fig. 4.98); mesonotum 0.71mm long, 1.07mm broad, brownish yellow; scutellum 0.53mm long, 0.25mm broad, brownish green. *Wings*, fore wing (Fig. 4.100) 7.5mm long, 1.60mm broad, semitransparent, brownish colour, not elytra like; hind wing (Fig. 4.101) 7.14mm long, 1.78mm broad, white, membranous, transparent. *Hind leg* (Fig. 4.102) 7.86mm long, 0.64mm broad, golden green; coxa 0.89mm long, 0.5mm broad, golden green; trochanter 0.53mm long, 0.28mm broad, golden green; femur 1.78mm long, 0.39mm broad, pale yellow; tibia 3.75mm long, 0.25mm broad, golden green with spines; tarsus 0.91mm long, 0.14mm broad, golden green; pre-tarsus 0.21mm long, 0.14mm broad, golden green, meso-tarsus 0.28mm long, 0.10mm broad, golden green; meta-tarsus 0.42mm long, 0.10mm broad, brown.
- *Abdomen* (Fig. 4.103): 6.92mm long, 1.92mm broad, pale green, 1 to 6 segments contain black at center, pale green at both sides, last two segments pale green, abdomen greenish yellow from ventral side. first segment 0.64mm long, 1.92mm broad; second segment 0.64mm long, 1.85 mm broad; third segment 0.64mm long, 1.78mm broad; fourth segment 0.64mm long, 1.71mm broad; fifth segment 0.64mm long, 1.5mm broad; sixth segment 0.64mm long, 1.25mm broad; seventh segment 0.64mm long, 1.07mm broad; eighth segment 0.64mm long, 0.89mm broad. Ovipositor 0.70mm long, pale yellow.
- *Host Plants* : Sugarcane *Saccharum officinarum* L., rice *Oryzasativa* L., Wheat *Triticum* sp., grasses.

- *Paratype* : 15 ♂, 17 ♀, Coll. Chandani Kamble, March to Dec. Preserved in alcohol, labeled as above.
- *Distribution* : Western Maharashtra, 10 ♂, 9 ♀, Chandgad (Kolhapur), Coll. Chandani Kamble, 30-III-2014; 5 ♂, 8 ♀, Satara, 12-VIII-2014.

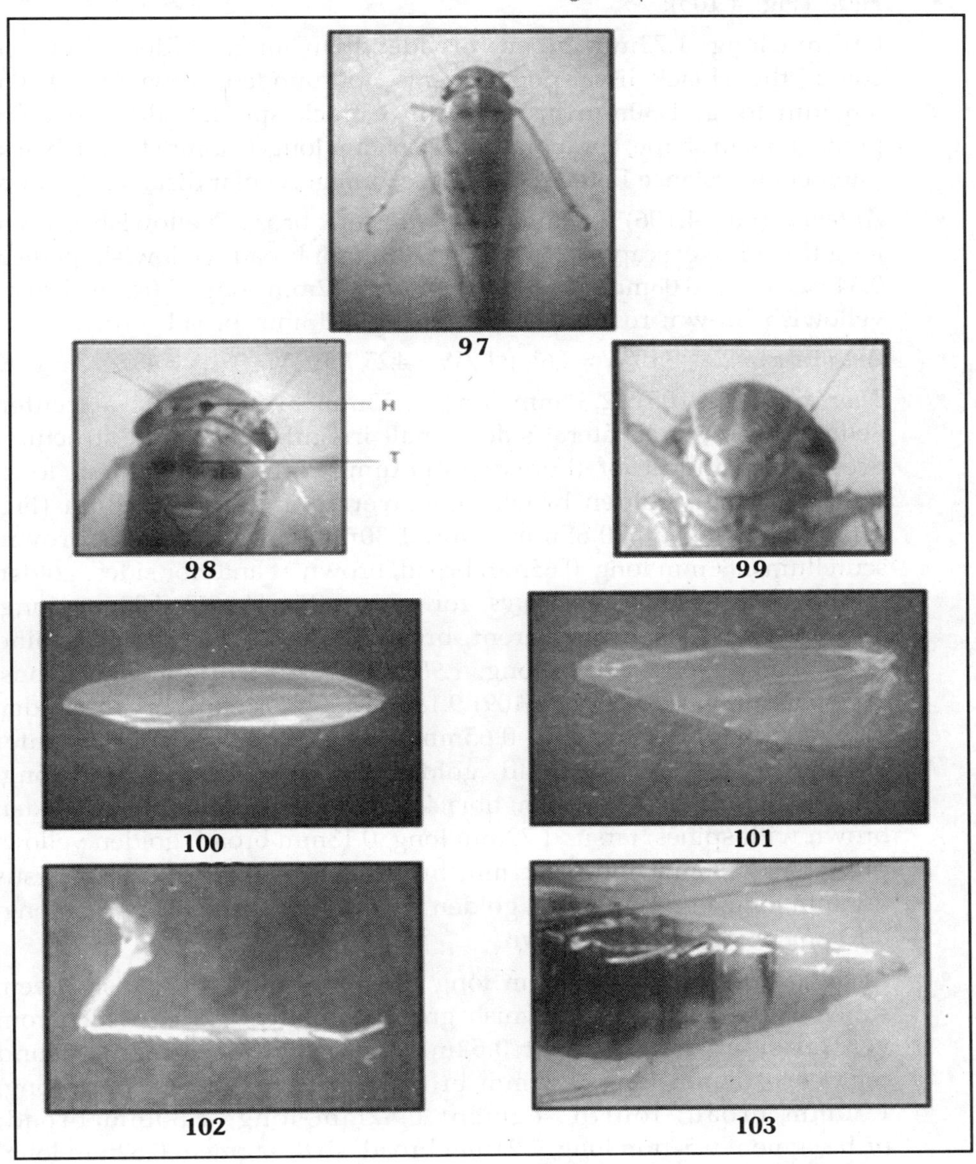

Plate - 13: ***C. jedarfa*:** Fig. 4.97: **Adult male,** Fig. 4.98: **Dorsal view head and thorax,** Fig. 4.99: **Ventral view head and thorax,** Fig. 4.100: **Forewing,** Fig. 4.101: **Hindwing,** Fig. 4.102: **Hindleg,** Fig. 4.103: **Abdomen**

Cofana oryzae sp. Nov.

(Plate - 14: Figs. 4.104-4.110)

- *Male* (Fig. 4.104):
- *Head* (Fig. 4.105):

  0.65mm long, 1.73mm broad, broader than long, golden brown in colour, three black discalspots presents, not rounded; crown (Fig. 4.105) 0.65mm long, 1.30mm broad with 3 black spots, golden brown, pentagonal in shape; compound eye 0.65mm long, 0.43mm broad, black, interocular distance 1.30mm, ocelli two, orange, ocular distance 0.86mm.
- *Antenna* (Fig. 4.106) 2.08mm long, 0.13mm broad, yellowish brown, long thread like; scape 0.21mm long, 0.13mm broad, yellowish; pedicel 0.34mm long, 0.08mm broad; flagellum 1.52mm long, 0.04mm broad, yellowish brown; rostrum 0.65mm long, 0.13mm broad, brown.
- *Antennal formula* – S L/W = 1.61, P L/W = 4.25, F L/W = 38, A = 43.86/3 = 14.62
- *Thorax* (Fig. 4.105): 2.39mm long, 1.73mm broad, white at center, yellowish brown at lateral sides, small irregular pore like: structures present on middle of thorax; pronotum (Fig. 4.105) 0.86mm long, 1.73mm broad, golden brown, not overlapping on scutellum (Fig. 4.105); mesonotum 0.65mm long, 1.30mm broad, golden brown; scutellum 0.86mm long, 0.65mm broad, brown at anterior sides, golden white at posterior side. *Wings,* fore wing (Fig. 4.107) 7.82mm long, 1.73mm broad, semitransparent, brown, shiny, not elytra like; hind wing (Fig. 4.108) 7.39mm long, 1.95mm broad, white, membranous, transparent. *Hind leg* (Fig. 4.109) 9.18mm long, 0.65mm broad, golden brown; coxa 0.60mm long, 0.65mm broad, pale brown; trochanter 0.43mm long, 0.34mm broad, golden brown; femur 2.17mm long, 0.43mm broad, golden brown; tibia 4.3mm long, 0.30mm broad, golden brown with spines; tarsus 1.72mm long, 0.13mm broad, golden yellow; pre-tarsus 0.86mm long, 0.21mm broad, golden yellow; meso-tarsus 0.43mm long, 0.13mm broad, golden yellow; meta-tarsus 0.34 mm long, 0.13mm broad, golden brown.
- *Abdomen* (Fig. 4.110): 6.08mm long, 1.52mm broad, brownish green, shiny, 1 to 8 segments brownish green; abdomen golden white from ventral side, first segment 0.52mm long, 1.52mm broad; second segment 0.52mm long, 1.39mm broad; third segment 0.52mm long, 1.30mm broad; fourth segment 0.52mm long, 1.30mm broad; fifth segment 0.52mm long, 1.21mm broad; sixth segment 0.52mm long, 1.08mm broad; seventh segment 0.52mm long, 0.95mm broad; eighth segment 0.52mm long, 0.86mm broad. Pygofer 0.50mm long, pale yellow with macrosetae.

- *Host plants:* grasses.
- *Holotype* : ♂, India, Maharashtra, Panhala (Kolhapur), Coll. Chandani Kamble. 10-X-2014, Antenna, wings, hindlegs, on slide labeled as above, rest part preserved in alcohol, labeled as above.
- *Paratype*: 5 ♂, 6 ♀, Coll. Chandani Kamble, Oct. to Feb.preserved in alcohol, labeled as above.
- *Distribution*: 3 ♂, 3 ♀, Panhala, Coll. Chandani Kamble, 10-X-2014; 2 ♂, 3 ♀, Tasgaon (Sangli), 07-II-2015.

Remarks

These speices runs close to *C. jedarfa* by having lateral margins of pronotum not dark bordered/banded. However, it differ from above species by having following characters.

1. 3 district discal spots on crown.
2. Antennal formula.
3. Pronotum with two black spots.
4. Body colour golden.

Genus *Scaphoideus* Uhler (1889)

The genus *Scaphoideus* is characterised by having body colour brown or yellowish brown, mottled with dark brown, orange or yellow patterns, streaks and spots, beads or lines; head equal or narrower than pronotum; crown with bluntly pointed anterior margin; tegmina with well developed appendix, aedeagus with tubular shaft, elongate; seventh sternite (female) twice as long as sixth sternite. Under this genus five species have been reported from India. A new species *Scaphoideus indica* sp.n has been described for the first time from India.

Key to species of genus *Scaphoideus*

1. Vertex of head with an almost solid unbroken transverse black fascia across eyes .... *baeticus* (Distant)

   - Coloration of vertex variable but not as above, if the transverse fascia is black, it is broken into a number of connected longitudinal spindle-shaped stripes 2

2. Vertex with a series of four to six longitudinal spindle-shaped brown stripes 3

   - Markings on vertex not as above 4

3. Hind margin of female seventh sternum sinuate with a concave median area; vertex of head with elongate spindle-shaped stripes; male with apophysis of style exceeding subgenital plate, aedeagus with an apical and a subapical pair of long processes .... *stigmaticus* Distant

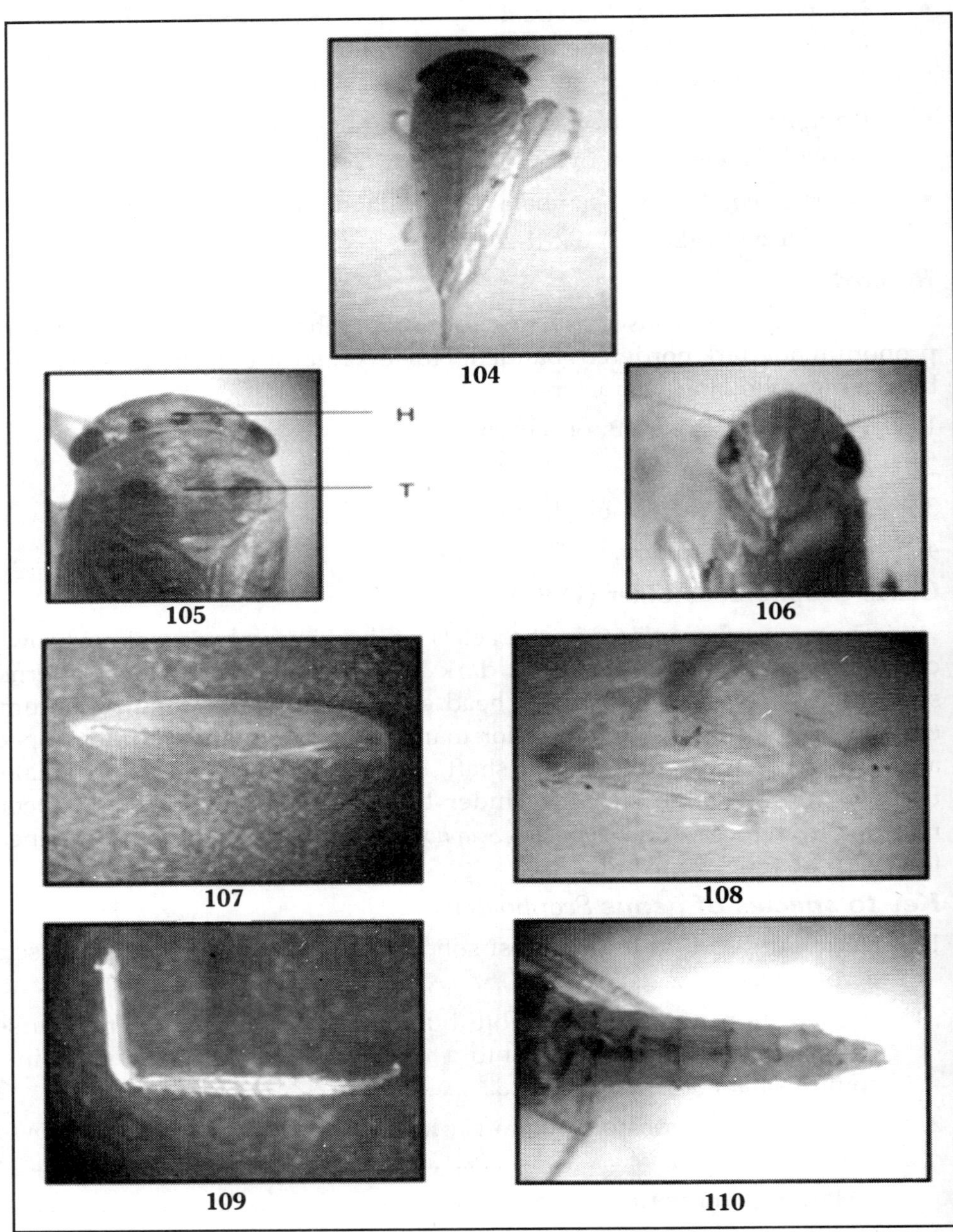

Plate - 14: ***C. oryzae:*** Fig. 4.104: **Adult male,** Fig. 4.105: **Dorsal view head and thorax,** Fig. 4.106: **Ventral view head and thorax,** Fig. 4.107: **Forewing, Fig**. 4.108: **Hindwing,** Fig. 4.109: **Hindleg,** Fig. 4.110: **Abdomen**

- Hind margin of female seventh sternum concave with a median notched lobe; vertex with short spindle-shaped stripes, apophysis of style not exceeding subgenital plate; aedeagus with a pair of apical short processes .... *assamensis* Distant

4. Male subgenital plate deeply bilobed or with a notch on mesal margin before Apex, apophysis of style slender, about half as long as total length or longer 5

   - Male subgenital plate not bilobed or with a notch on mesal margin before apex; apophysis of style stout, usually less than half as long as its length 7

5. Male subgenital plate deeply bilobed; paraphyses separate from base, symmetrical,of equal length; aedeagus not S-shaped 6

   - Subgenital plate with a notch on mesal margin before apex paraphysis slender, fused for proximal 0.75 length then separated, unequal in length; aedeagus S-shaped .... *inequalis* sp. nov.

6. Male pygophore with a ventral process; face ochraceous with dark brown bands or markings ....*S. elegantulus* Melichar

   - Male pygophore without a ventral process; face chocolate brown .... *jogensis* sp. nov.

7. Vertex, pronotum, and scutellum with a median longitudinal yellowish or whitish broad stripe extending on-to folded front wings, overlain on it with one or two narrower orange or red longitudinal stripes 8

   - Vertex with a transverse band between eyes sometimes indistinct, red, orange, black or brown; no longitudinal stripe extending from head to front wings, pronotum either with two transverse red or brown bands or with a series of 5-7 longitudinal short stripes 11

8. Paraphyses fused at their proximal 0.66; large stout species measuring over 6.00 mm in length .... *insignis* (Distant)

   - Paraphyses separate for most of their length; aedeagal process when present apical; smaller species not exceeding 4.50mm 9

9. Aedeagal shaft with a pair of short processes at midlength; paraphyses diverging right from proximal end, more or less of uniform width in their proximal 0.8 length then tapered, dorsal margin of male pygophore bilobed .... *bifidus* sp. nov.

   - Aedeagal shaft with apical processes; paraphyses either not divergent or divergent beyond basal 0.5 length, uneven in width; dorsal margin of male pygophore entire 10

10. Paraphyses closely oppressed over their entire length, female seventh sternum straight, with a median concavity .... *katraini* Rao and Ramakrishnan

    - Paraphyses divergent in their distal half ; hind margin of female seventh sternum broadly produced medially .... *kirti* sp. nov.

11. Paraphyses with spicules 12
- Paraphyses smooth, without spicules 13
12. Aedeagal shaft with a pair of basal processes extending entire length of shaft .... *sculptus* sp. nov.
- Aedeagal shaft without basal processes but dorsal apodeme with a hooked process .... *sculptellus* sp. nov.
13. Vertex with an apical round black spot; transverse band across eyes black and darkbrown; aedeagus slender, tubular, strongly curved with well-developed dorsal apodeme .... *russus* Distant
- Vertex without round black apical spot, transverse band across eyes brown, red or orange aedeagus short and stout 14
14. Paraphyses forming a 'horse-shoe' pronotum and scutellum with longitudinal brown stripes 15
- Paraphyses elongate, may be twisted at apex but not horse-shoe shaped, pronotum with transverse stripes some times indistict 16
15. Paraphyses bluntly pointed at apex .... *morosus* Melichar
- Paraphyses sharply pointed at apex*harlani* Kitbamroong and Freytag
16. Subgenital plate with numerous long hairlike setae, their length as long as or longer than subgenital plate; paraphyses fused at their basal half .... *hirsutus* sp. nov.
- Subgenital plate with shorter, fewer hairlike setae, their length 0.2 to 0.1 as long as subgenital plate; paraphyses not as above 17
17. Male pygophore with proximal spinelike process on dorsal margin 18
- Male pygophore without a proximal spinelike process on dorsal margin 20
18. Male pygophore with dorsal spine strongly curved meso-ventrally ... . *karachiensis* Ahmed, Murthaza and Malik
- Male pygophore with dorsal spine straight, directed caudally 19
19. Male pygophore with dorsal spine short, not more than 0.2 as long as pygophore lobe, caudo-ventral angle angularly produced, paraphyses divergent caudally aedeagal shaft shorter and stouter, of uniform width in lateral aspect for its 0.75 length ...... *sabourensis* Rao and Ramakrishnan
- Male pygophore with dorsal spine long, more than 0.5 as long as pygophore lobe, caudo-ventral angle produced ventrally into a spine, paraphyses convergent caudally; aedeagal shaft longer, gradually narrowed distally .... *zhangi* sp. nov.
20. Head, thorax and proximal 0.33 of fore wings chocolate brown contrasted with ochraceous rest of body; paraphyses slender, needlelike 21
- Coloration of head, thorax and abdomen not as above; paraphyses stout, not needle like 22

21. Aedeagus rather S-shaped, shaft without processes ....*varna* sp. nov.
- Aedeagus not S-shaped, shaft with a pair of apical processes ....
bicoloratus sp. nov.

22. Aedeagal shaft with shorter or longer processes 23
- Aedeagal shaft without processes, may be keeled 27

23. Paraphyses parallel to each other, acutely pointed at apex; at 0.33 from apex expanded into a small triangular area; aedeagus with apical pair of spine like processes .... *ornatus* Melichar
- Paraphyses not as above, aedeagus either with two or four processes
.... 24

24. Aedeagal shaft with a pair of apical and a subapical pair of processes, paraphyses strongly sinuate .... *vaticus* sp. nov.
- Aedeagal shaft with subapical pair of processes; paraphyses not strongly sinuate 25

25. Paraphyses strongly divergent beyond basal 0.33 aedeagal shaft with a pair of strong dorsal keel, each with a recurved process ....
illustris Rao and Emiliyamma
- Paraphyses either convergent or strongly asymmetrically curved; aedeagus without keels 26

26. Aedeagal shaft in caudal view appearing trilobed paraphyses symmetrical, each shaft of even width except near apex ....*trilobatus* sp. nov.
- Aedeagal shaft with a pair of lateral process at midlength; paraphyses strongly asymmetrical... *asymmetricus* sp. nov.

27. Paraphyses widely separated at base, each shaft slightly to strongly twisted at apical 28
- Paraphyses close together at base, not twisted 29

28. Aedeagal shaft slender in lateral aspect, constricted at midlength in caudal aspect each shaft of paraphyses strongly twisted at apical 0.25
.... *coloratus* Rao
- Aedeagal shaft stout in lateral aspect, gradually narrowed distally in caudal aspect; each shaft of paraphyses slightly twisted at apical 0.33 .... *decorates* Rao and Emiliyamma

29. Paraphyses convergent aedeagal shaft in lateral aspect rather fusiform *lamellaris* sp. nov.
- Paraphyses divergent aedeagal shaft not fusiform in lateral aspect .. 30

30. Aedeagal shaft of uniform width in lateral aspect; paraphyses straight, not curved in lateral aspect .... *spiculatus* sp. nov.
- Aedeagal shaft broadest at base and abruptly narrowed; paraphyses in lateral aspect curved dorsally in distal half ....*malaisei* sp. nov.

Scaphoideus indica sp. nov.

(Plate - 15: Figs. 4.111-4.117)

- *Male* (Fig. 4.111):
- *Head* (Fig. 4.112):

  0.53mm long, 1.5mm broad, broader than long, white in colour, black spots presents, not rounded; crown (Fig. 4.112) 0.53mm long, 1.07mm broad, white, pentagonal in shape. Compound eye 0.53mm long, 0.35mm broad, black, brown at lateral side, interocular distance 0.71mm, ocelli two, orange, ocular distance 0.50mm.
- *Antenna* (Fig. 4.113) 2.5mm long, yellowish brown; long threadlike, scape 0.10mm long, 0.007mm broad, yellowish; pedicel 0.14mm long, 0.035mm broad; flagellum 1.78mm long, 0.00035mm broad, yellowish brown.
- *Antennal formula* – S L/W = 14.28, P L/W = 40, F L/W = 5085, A = 51.3/93 = 17.13
- *Thorax* (Fig. 1.112): 1.5mm long, 1.42mm broad, white at center, yellowish brown at lateral sides, small irregular pore like structures present on middle of thorax; pronotum (Fig. 4.112) 0.71mm long, 1.42mm broad, white at center, yellowish brown at lateral sides, not overlapping on scutellum (Fig. 4.112); mesonotum 0.39mm long, 1.07mm broad, white at center, yellowish brown at lateral sides; scutellum 0.32mm long, 0.35mm broad, white. *Wings,* fore wing (Fig. 4.114) 5mm long, 1.25mm broad, semitransparent, brownish colour, not elytra like; hind wing (Fig. 4.115) 4.82mm long, 0.5mm broad, white, membranous, transparent. *Hind leg* (Fig. 4.116) 5mm long, 0.35mm broad, brownish yellow; coxa 1.78mm long, 0.89mm broad, pale yellowish brown; trochanter 0.35mm long, 0.01mm broad, pale yellow; femur 1.07mm long, 0.21mm broad, pale yellow; tibia 2.85mm long, 0.21mm broad, brownish yellow with spines, black spot at base of each spine; tarsus 1.24mm long, 0.01mm broad, brownish yellow; pre-tarsus 0.71mm long, 0.01mm broad, yellowish brown, meso-tarsus 0.21mm long, 0.01mm broad, brownish yellow; meta-tarsus 0.32mm long, 0.01mm broad, yellowish brown.
- *Abdomen* (Fig. 4.117): 2.92mm long, 0.89mm broad, white at lateral sides, 1 to 8 segments contain dark brown patch dorsally, 1 to 4 tergites with black spots; abdomen whitish from ventral side, first segment 0.89mm long, 0.35mm broad; second segment 0.71mm long, 0.35mm broad; third segment 0.64mm long, 0.35mm broad; fourth segment 0.60mm long, 0.35mm broad; fifth segment 0.53mm long, 0.35mm broad; sixth segment 0.35mm long, 0.35mm broad; seventh segment 0.28mm long, 0.35mm broad; eighth segment 0.21mm long, 0.35mm

broad. *Genitalia*: plate triangular with spine like: macro-setae pygofer variously modified, bluntly pointed posterior side, tapered gradually.

- *Host Plants* : Grapes (*Vitis vinifera* L.), grasses, it such the cell sap from leaves, flowering and fruiting bodies of host plants.
- *Holotype* : ♂, India, Maharashtra, Peth Vadgaon, Kolhapur. Coll. Chandani Kamble. 14-VIII- 2014, Antenna, wings, legs, genitalia on slide labeled as above, rest part preserved in alcohol, labeled as above.
- *Paratype :* ♂- 5, ♀- 2,Coll. Chandani Kamble, July. to Dec., pinned insects labeled as above.
- *Distribution* : Western Maharashtra; 2 ♂, 1 ♀, Peth Vadgaon (Kolhapur), 14-X-2014; 3 ♂, 1 ♀, Kolhapur, 03-XI-2014.

Remarks

This species runs close to *S. insignis* Distant (Praveen, *et al.* 2014) by having following characters:

1. General appearance.
2. Intermediate and posterior tibiae spotted with black.

However, it differs from above species by having following characters:

1. Head, pronotum and scutellum not uniformly light brown. Lateral transverse area brownish and mid portion whitish.
2. No small marginal spot on vertex.
3. Body beneath the legs not pale ocheraceous.
4. *Antennal formula* - S L/W = 14.28, P L/W = 40, F L/W = 50.85, A = 51.39/3 = 17.13

Genus *Kolla* Matsumura

This genus contains 3 species. (OBIS Australia, 2015)

Kolla paulula Signoret

(Plate - 16: Figs. 4.118-4.124)

- *Male* (Fig. 4.118):
- *Head* (Fig. 4.124):

  0.95mm long, 1.90mm broad, broader than long, yellowish golden with shine, black spots presents, not rounded; crown (Fig. 4.119) 0.95mm long, 1.42mm broad, golden with shine, three black spots, pentagonal in shape. compound eye 0.76mm long, 0.28mm broad, black, interocular distance 1.42mm, ocelli two, brown, ocular distance 0.71mm.

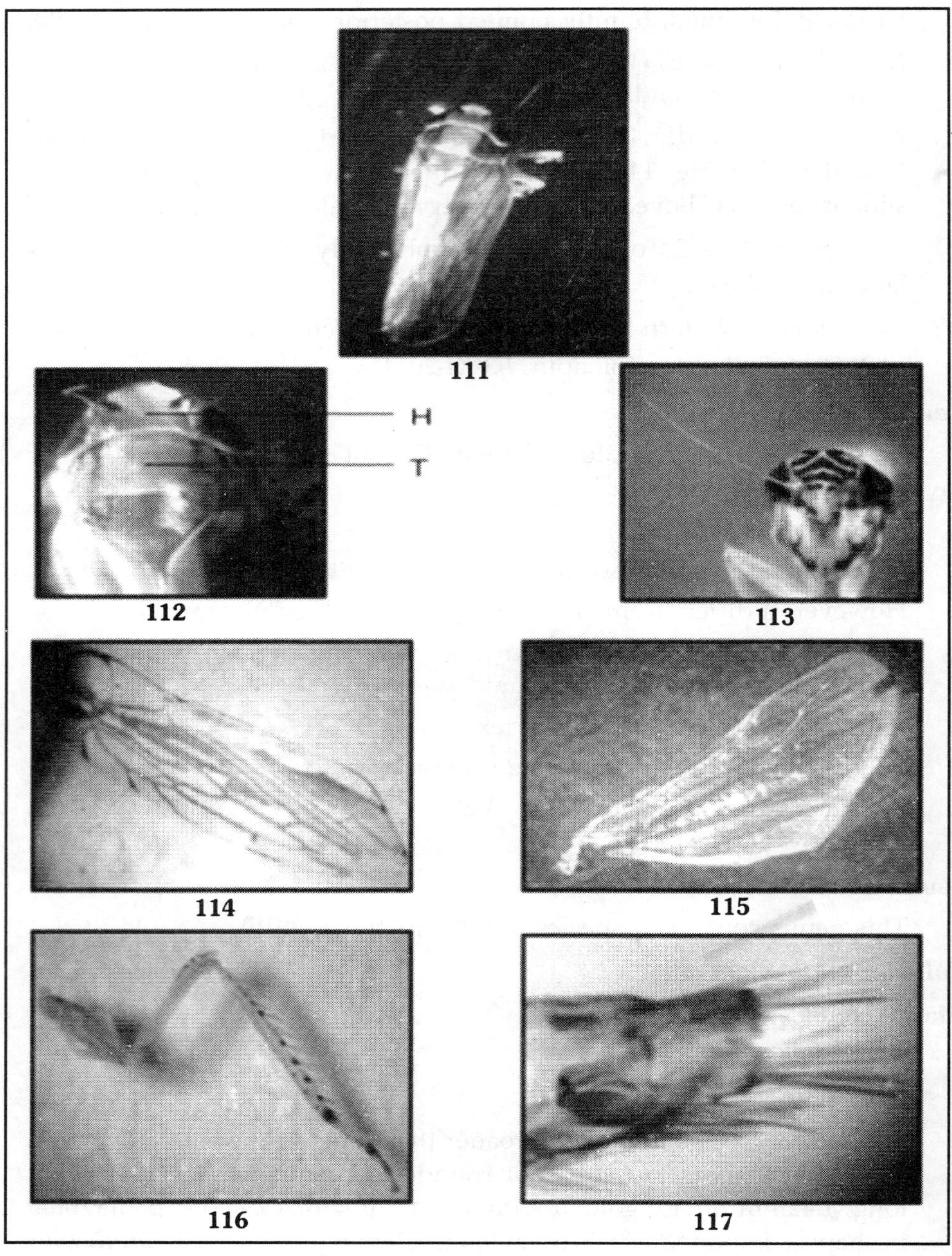

Plate - 15: ***S. indica sp. n.*:** Fig. 4.111: **Adult male,** Fig. 4.112: **Dorsal view head and thorax,** Fig. 4.113: **Ventral view head and thorax,** Fig. 4.114: **Forewing,** Fig. 4.115: **Hindwing,** Fig. 4.116: **Hindleg,** Fig. 4.117: **Abdomen**

- *Antenna* (Fig. 4.120) 1.66mm long, 0.14mm broad, pale, long thread like; scape 0.14mm long, 0.14mm broad, pale; pedicel 0.19mm long, 0.09mm broad, pale; flagellum 1.33mm long, 0.04mm broad, brown; rostrum 0.71mm long, 0.14mm broad.
- *Antennal formula* – S L/W = 1, P L/W = 2.1, F L/W = 33.25, A = 36.25/3 = 12.08
- *Thorax* (Fig. 4.119): 2.38mm long, 1.90mm broad, golden brown; pronotum (Fig. 4.119) 0.95mm long, 1.90mm broad, golden, shiny on anterior side, brown at posterior; mesonotum 0.71mm long, 1.42mm broad, brown at anterior sides, golden at posterior side, shiny; scutellum (Fig. 4.119) 0.71mm long, 0.71mm broad, golden with shine. *Wings*, Fore wing (Fig. 4.122) 5mm long, 1.42mm broad, semitransparent, coffee brown at one side, another side transparent white, not elytra like; hind wing (Fig. 4.121) 4.76mm long, 1.66mm broad, whitish brown, membranous, semitransparent. *Hind leg* (Fig. 4.123) 5.32mm long, 0.38mm broad, pale yellow; coxa 0.57mm long, 0.38mm broad, pale; trochanter 0.38mm long, 0.19mm broad, pale yellow; femur 1.66mm long, 0.23mm broad, pale yellow; tibia 2.14mm long, 0.19mm broad, brownish yellow with spines; tarsus 0.57mm long, 0.14mm broad, pale, brown at the base; pre-tarsus 0.19mm long, 0.14mm broad, yellowish brown; meso-tarsus 0.19mm long, 0.14mm broad, brownish yellow; meta-tarsus 0.19mm long, 0.14mm broad, yellowish brown.
- *Abdomen* (Fig. 4.124): 3.52mm long, 1.42mm broad, coffee brown, 1 to 2 segments contain pale yellow, 3 to 4 pale brown, remaining segment dark brown at center and pale brown at both sides. First segment 0.38mm long, 1.42mm broad; second segment 0.38mm long, 1.28mm broad; third segment 0.38mm long, 1.19mm broad; fourth segment 1.04mm long, 0.35mm broad; fifth segment 0.38mm long, 0.85mm broad; sixth segment 0.38mm long, 0.71mm broad; seventh segment 0.38mm long, 0.57mm broad; eighth segment 0.38mm long, 0.47mm broad. Ovipositor 0.40mm long, pale brown.
- *Host Plants*: Pumpkin *Cucurbita pepo* L., grasses.
- *Paratype* : 10 ♂, 05 ♀, Coll. Chandani Kamble, Sept. to Dec., preserved in alcohol, labeled as above.
- *Distribution*: 5 ♂, 2 ♀, Kolhapur, 23-IX-2014; 5 ♂, 3♀ Sangli, 15-XI-2014.

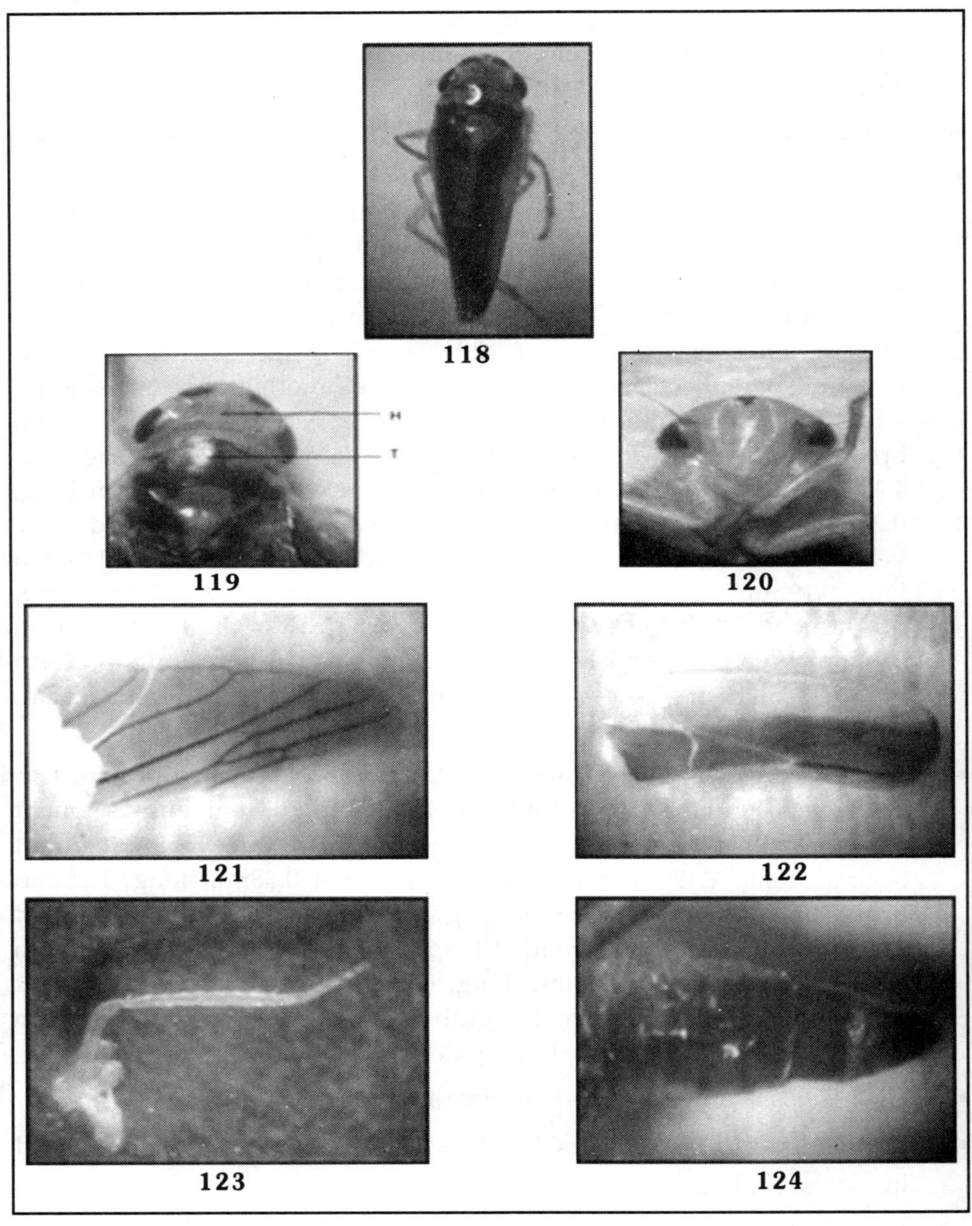

Plate - 16: ***K. paulule:*** Fig. 4.118: **Adult male,** Fig. 4.119: **Dorsal view head and thorax,** Fig. 4.120: **Ventral view head and thorax,** Fig. 4.121: **Hindwing,** Fig. 4.122: **Forewing,** Fig. 4.123: **Hindleg,** Fig. 4.124: **Abdomen**

Subfamily Typhlocybinae

Key to Tribes of the Subfamily Typhlocybinae

Fore wing with distinct appendix (Two well-defined ocelli present on junction among vertex and face, inside sutures marking boundaries of frontoclypeus.

1. Hind wing with peripheric vein extending around near apex and recurved to meet subcostal vein approximately at level of cross-veins between sub costal and median veins .... *Alebrini*

   Fore wing without distinct appendix (Ocelli often absent; if present, on junction between vertex and face, between lines of sutures making boundaries of frontoclypeus and corresponding eyes) 2

2. Internal apical vein of fore wing curved, reaching inner margin nearer apex of clavus thanapex of wing. (Peripheric vein of hind wing not extending beyond medianvein; anal vein of hind wing forked. External apical vein and medianapical vein of fore wing arising from common stem) .... *Typhlocybini*

   Internal apical vein of fore wing straight, terminating almost at apex of wing, parallel (or almost so) with median apical vein 3

3. Peripheric vein of hind wing not extending beyond median vein; anal vein of hind wing simple, not forked. Length of external apical cell offore wing at most half that of subexternal cell. (In male, paramere terminating in two or more point or rather sharply truncate, with more or less well developed laminar projection of stem .... *Erythroneurini*

   Peripheric vein of hind wing extending beyond median vein to near apex of wing, either ending there or recurved parallel to costal margin; anal vein of hind wing forked .Length of external apical cell of fore wing more than half that of sub external apical cell. (In male, paramere either without laminar projection of stem or ending in a single blunted point. In the latter case, the laminar outgrowth may also exhibit a pointed appearance 4

4. Peripheric vein of hind wing ending at apex of subcostal vein, which is mortally coalescent with radial vein; median vein simple throughout. (Species always greenish, but this colour often fades after death except on legs) .... *Empoascini*

   Peripheric vein of hind wing extending round apex and parallel to costal border, meeting subcostal vein about half-way along; median vein branched apically .... *Dikraneurini*

Tribe Empoascini

Genus *Amrasca* Ghauri

Ghauri (1967) gave autogenerated description of this genus. Qin and Zhang (2008) and Ramkrishan and Menon (1972) studied this genus.

***Amrasca bigutulla biguttula* Ishida**

(Plate - 17: Figs. 4.125-4.131)

- *Male* (Fig. 4.125):
- *Head* (Fig. 4.126):

  0.35mm long, 0.5mm broad, broader than long, pale yellow colour, not rounded; crown (Fig. 4.126) 0.24mm long, 0.35mm broad, yellow, two black spots presents, pentagonal in shape; compound eye 0.5mm long, 0.25mm broad, brown, interocular distance 0.5mm, ocelli two, brown, ocular distance 0.2mm.
- *Antenna* (Fig. 4.127) 1.15mm long, 1mm broad, yellow, long thread like; scape 0.1mm long, 0.1mm broad, pale yellow; pedicel 0.15mm long, 0.05mm broad, pale yellow; flagellum 0.9mm long, 0.05mm broad, brown; rostrum 0.6mm long, 0.1mm broad, brown.
- *Antennal formula* – S L/W = 1, P L/W = 3, F L/W = 18, A = 22.00/3 = 7.33
- *Thorax* (Fig. 4.126): 1mm long, 1mm broad, pale yellow; pronotum (Fig. 4.126) 0.5mm long, 1mm broad, pale yellow, mesonotum 0.25mm long, 0.5mm broad, brown; scutellum (Fig. 4.126); 0.25mm long, 0.25mm broad, brown. *Wings*, fore wing (Fig. 4.128) 3mm long, 0.75mm broad, semitransparent, yellowish green colour, on posterior side one black spot present at middle, not elytra like; hind wing (Fig. 4.129) 2.75mm long, 1mm broad, white, membranous, transparent. *Hind leg* (Fig. 4.130) 3.7mm long, 0.2mm broad, golden yellow; coxa 0.35mm long, 0.2mm broad, pale golden yellow; trochanter 0.2mm long, 0.15mm broad, pale pale golden yellow; femur 0.75mm long, 0.2mm broad, pale pale golden yellow; tibia 1.5mm long, 0.15mm broad, brownish yellow with spines, black spot at base of each spine; tarsus 0.8mm long, 0.15mm broad, yellowish brown; pre-tarsus 0.35mm long, 0.15mm broad, yellowish brown; meso-tarsus 0.2mm long, 0.1mm broad, yellowish brown; meta-tarsus 0.75mm long, 0.1mm broad, yellowish brown.
- *Abdomen* (Fig. 4.131): 1.65mm long, 0.9mm broad, greenish yellow, 1 to 8 segments contain brownish yellow, shiny, tip of abdomen brown dorsally, 1 to 4 tergites with black spots. abdomen whitish from ventral side. first segment 0.2mm long, 0.9mm broad; second segment 0.15mm long, 0.9mm broad; third segment 0.15mm long, 0.8mm broad; fourth

segment 0.15mm long, 0.75mm broad; fifth segment 0.15mm long, 0.7mm broad; sixth segment 0.15mm long, 0.6mm broad; seventh segment 0.15mm long, 0.5mm broad; eighth segment 0.15mm long, 0.35mm broad. Ovipositor 0.20 mm long, pale yellow, shiny.

- *Host Plants*: Cotton genus *Gossypium*, soybean *Glycinemax* (L.), mung Bean *Vigna rediata* L., brinjal *Solanum melongena* L., okra *Abelmoschus esculentus* (L.), sunflower *Abelmoschus esculentus* (L.),Cowpea *Vignasinensis* L., pigeon pea *Cajanus cajan* (L.), china rose *Hibiscus rosasinensis* L., durva grasses.
- *Paratype*: ♂ - 30, ♀ - 40, Coll. Chandani Kamble, June to March, preserved in alcohol, labeled as above.
- *Distribution*: 20 ♂, 15 ♀ Gadhinglaj (Kolhapur),17-XI-2013; 15 ♂, 10 ♀, Satara, 03-X-2014.

Subfamily Aphrodinae

Genus *Anoscopus*

***Anoscopus albifrons* Linnaeus**

(Plate - 18: Figs. 4.132-4.138)

- *Male* (Fig. 4.132):
- *Head* (Fig. 4.133):

  0.53mm long, 1.5mm broad, broader than long, dark brown in colour, small pores presents, not rounded; crown (Fig. 4.133) 0.53mm long, 1.07mm broad, brown, pentagonal in shape. Compound eye 0.53mm long, 0.35mm broad, black, brown at lateral side, interocular distance 0.71mm, ocelli two, pale, ocular distance 0.50mm.
- *Antenna* (Fig. 4.134) 2.5mm long, yellowish brown, long threadlike; scape 0.10mm long, 0.007mm broad, yellowish brown; pedicel 0.14mm long, 0.035mm broad, yellowish brown; flagellum 1.78mm long, 0.00035mm broad, brown.
- *Antennal formula* – S L/W = 14.28, P L/W = 40, F L/W = 5085, A = 51.39/3 = 17.13
- *Thorax* (Fig. 4.133): 1.5mm long, 1.42mm broad, brown with pores. pronotum (Fig. 4.133) 0.71mm long, 1.42mm broad, brown; mesonotum 0.39mm long, 1.07mm broad, brown; scutellum (Fig. 4.133) 0.32mm long, 0.35mm broad, white. *Wings* fore wing (Fig. 4.135) 5mm long, 1.25mm broad, brown colour, not elytra like; hind wing (Fig. 4.136) 4.82mm long, 0.5mm broad, white, membranous, transparent. *Hind leg* (Fig. 4.137) 5mm long, 0.35mm broad, brown; coxa 1.78mm

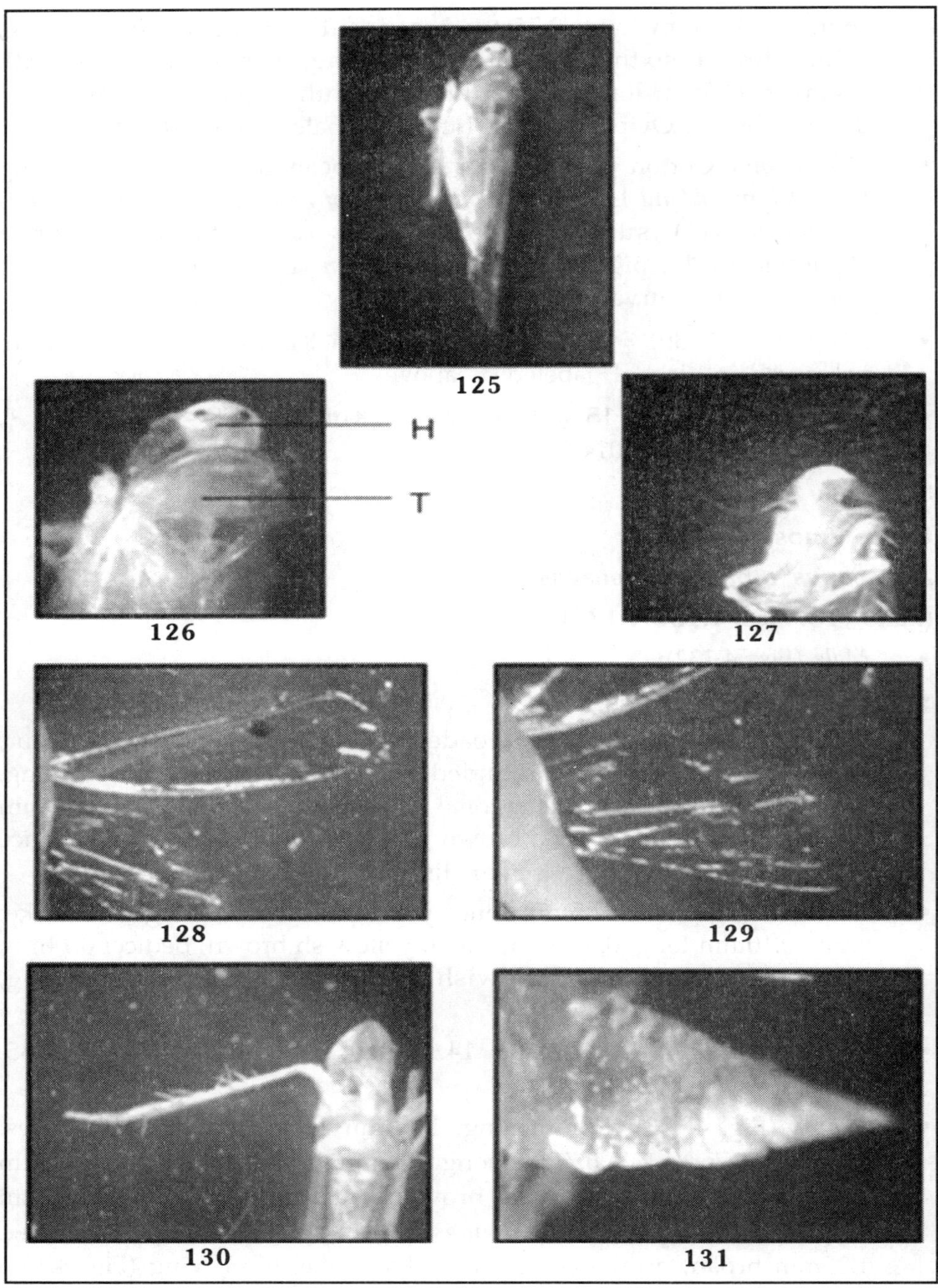

Plate - 17: ***A. biguttula biguttula*:** Fig. 4.125: **Adult male,** Fig. 4.126: **Dorsal view head and thorax,** Fig. 4.127: **Ventral view head and thorax,** Fig. 4.128: **Forewing,** Fig. 4.129: **Hindwing,** Fig. 4.130: **Hindleg,** Fig. 4.131: **Abdomen**

ong, 0.89mm broad, pale yellowish brown; trochanter 0.35mm long, 0.01mm broad, pale yellow; femur 1.07mm long, 0.21mm broad, pale yellow; tibia 2.85mm long, 0.21mm broad, brown with spines; tarsus 1.24mm long, 0.01mm broad, brown; pre-tarsus 0.71mm long, 0.01mm broad, brown. meso-tarsus 0.21mm long, 0.01mm broad, brownish yellow; meta-tarsus 0.32mm long, 0.01mm broad, brown.

- *Abdomen* (Fig. 4.138): 2.92mm long, 0.89mm broad, black, 1 to 8 segments contain black dorsally, at dorso-lateral sides brown. First segment 0.89mm long, 0.35mm broad; second segment 0.71mm long, 0.35mm broad; third segment 0.64mm long, 0.35mm broad; fourth segment 0.60mm long, 0.35mm broad; fifth segment 0.53mm long, 0.35mm broad; sixth segment 0.35mm long, 0.35mm broad; seventh segment 0.28mm long, 0.35mm broad; eighth segment 0.21mm long, 0.35 mm broad. Pygofer 0.6 mm long, black.
- *Host Plants* : Unknown.
- *Paratype* : 3 ♂, 1 ♀, Coll. Chandani Kamble, Aug. to Dec., preserved in 70 per cent alcohol, labeled as above.
- *Distribution* : Western Maharashtra, 2 ♂, 1 ♀, Gaganbawda (Kolhapur), 1-IX-2014; 1 ♂, 0 ♀, Chandgad, 03-XI-2014.

Ptyelus subfasciata (Frog hopper)

(Plate - 19: Figs. 4.139-4.145)

- *Male* (Fig. 4.139):
- *Head* (Fig. 4.140):

  0.8mm long, 1.4mm broad, broader than long, yellowish brown in colour, vertical pale brown lines presents, not rounded; crown (Fig. 4.140) 0.6mm long, 1mm broad, yellowish brown in colour, vertical pale brown lines presents, pentagonal in shape. Compound eye 0.6mm long, 0.4mm broad, greenish white, interocular distance 0.6mm, ocelli two, brown, ocular distance 0.4mm.
- *Antenna* (Fig. 4.141) 0.84mm long, 0.08 broad, yellowish brown, long thread like; scape 0.08mm long, 0.08mm broad, brown; pedicel 0.12mm long, 0.08mm broad; flagellum 0.64mm long, 0.04mm broad, brown; rostrum brown, 0.6mm long, 0.12mm broad.
- *Antennal formula* – S L/W = 1, P L/W = 1.5, F L/W = 16, A = 18.5/3 = 6.16

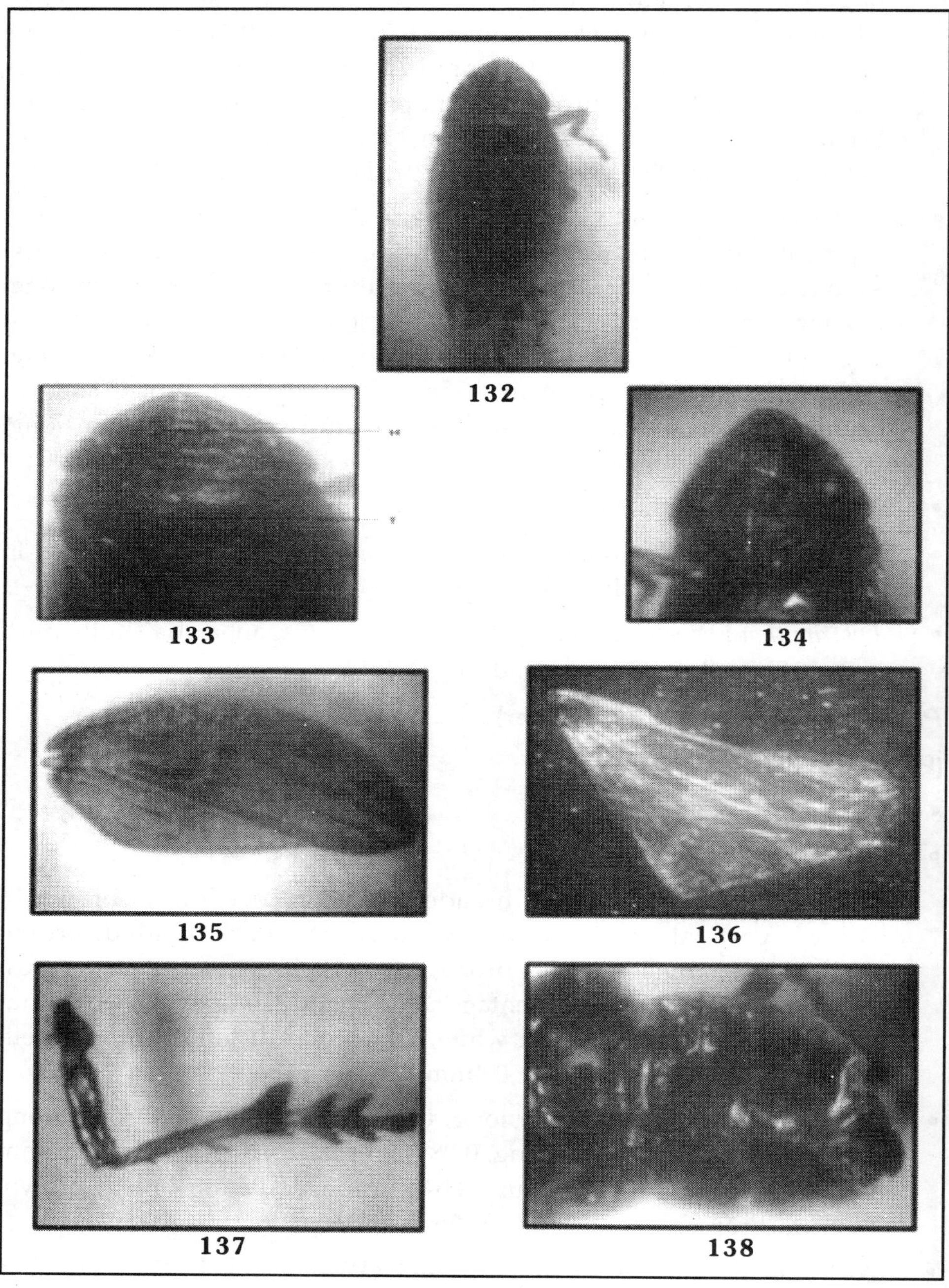

Plate - 18: ***A. albifrons:*** Fig. 4.132: **Adult male,** Fig. 4.133: **Dorsal view head and thorax,** Fig. 4.134: **Ventral view head and thorax,** Fig. 4.135: **Forewing,** Fig. 4.136: **Hindwing,** Fig. 4.137: **Hindleg,** Fig. 4.138: **Abdomen**

- *Thorax* (Fig. 4.140): 1.6mm long, 1.6mm broad, pale brown, vertical dark coffee brown bands present, pronotum (Fig. 4.140) 0.8mm long, 1.6mm broad, pale brown, vertical dark coffee brown bands present, small hair like projections, (Fig. 4.140); mesonotum 0.4mm long, 1.6mm broad, pale brown with dark coffee brown bands; scutellum 0.4mm long, 0.4mm broad, pale brown with dark coffee brown bands. *Wings*, fore wing (Fig. 4.177) 4.8mm long, 1.6mm broad, semitransparent, white, horizontal brown bands, hair like projection, not elytra like; hind wing (Fig. 4.143) 4.4mm long, 1.8mm broad, white, membranous, transparent. *Hind leg* (Fig. 4.144) 4.36mm long, 0.24mm broad, yellowish brown; coxa 0.24mm long, 0.2mm broad, black; trochanter 1.2mm long, 0.24mm broad, brown; femur 1.8mm long, 0.16mm broad, yellowish brown; tibia 2.85mm long, 0.16mm broad, yellowish brown with spines, small hair like: projection; tarsus 1.24mm long, 0.01mm broad, anterior side pale, black at posterior side; pre-tarsus 0.4mm long, 0.16mm broad, anterior side pale, black at posterior side. meso-tarsus 0.2mm long, 0.2mm broad, anterior side pale, black at posterior side; meta-tarsus 0.12mm long, 0.32mm broad, anterior side pale, black at posterior side.
- *Abdomen* (Fig. 4.145): 1.84mm long, 1.28mm broad, black, 1 to 8 segments contain black dorsally; abdomen black from ventral side, posterior side of each segment brown, first segment 0.2mm long, 1.2mm broad; second segment 0.2mm long, 1.28mm broad; third segment 0.2mm long, 1.28mm broad; fourth segment 0.2mm long, 1.2mm broad; fifth segment 0.16mm long, 1.2mm broad; sixth segment 0.35mm long, 1mm broad; seventh segment 0.16mm long, 0.8mm broad; eighth segment 0.16mm long, 0.6mm broad.
- *Host Plants*: Forest area, grasses.
- *Holotype* : ♂, India, Maharashtra, Ajara (Kolhapur) Coll. Chandani Kamble, 09-VIII-2014, Antenna, wings, legs, on slide labeled as above, rest part preserved in 70 per cent alcohol, labeled as above.
- *Paratype* : 06 ♂, 04 females Oct. to Feb. preserved in alcohol.
- *Distribution* : 3 ♂, 4 ♀, Ajara (Kolhapur), 14-X-2014; 2 ♂, 1 ♀, Shirala (Sangli) 03-XI-2014.

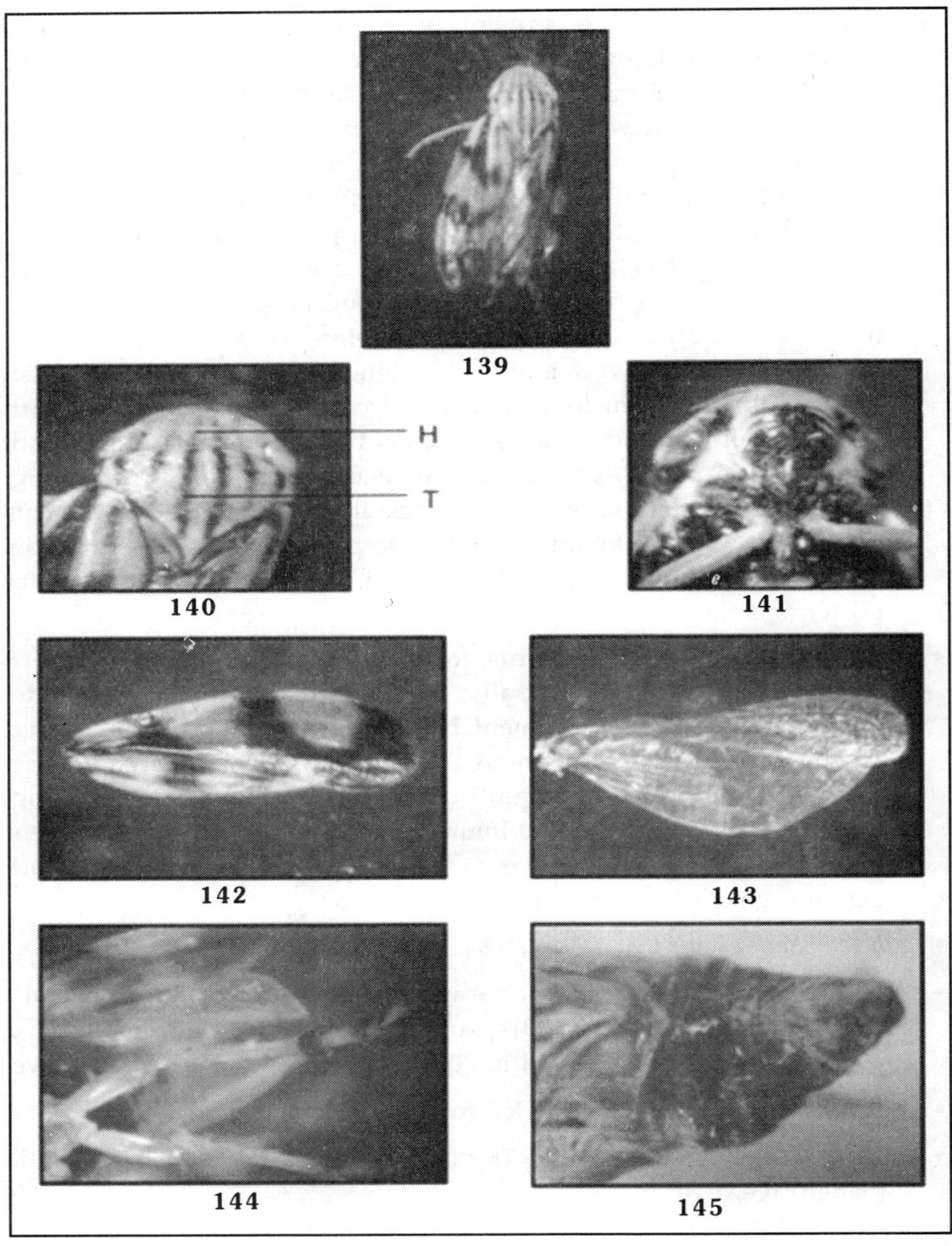

Plate - 19: ***P. subfasciata*:** Fig. 4.139: **Adult male,** Fig. 4.140: **Dorsal view head and thorax,** Fig. 4.141: **Ventral view head and thorax,** Fig. 4.142: **Forewing,** Fig. 4.143: **Hindwing,** Fig. 4.144: **Hindleg,** Fig. 4.145: **Abdomen**

Subfamily Scaphoideini

Mimotettix Species

(Plate - 20: Figs. 4.146-4.152)

- *Male* (Fig. 4.146):
- *Head* (Fig. 4.147):

  0.52mm long, 1.57mm broad, broader than long, blackish brown; crown (Fig. 4.147) 0.52mm long, 1.05mm broad, coffee brown, pentagonal in shape. Compound eye 1.05mm long, 0.52mm broad, black with brown margin, interocular distance 1.05mm, ocelli two, white, ocular distance 0.52mm.
- *Antenna* (Fig. 4.148) 1.26mm long, 0.15mm broad, pale yellowish brown, long threadlike; scape 0.15mm long, 0.15mm broad, yellowish brown; pedicel 0.21mm long, 0.10mm broad, yellowish brown; flagellum 0.89mm long, 0.05mm broad, brown; rostrum 1.05mm long, 0.15mm broad, brown.
- *Antennal formula* – S L/W = 1, P L/W = 2.1, F L/W = 17.8, A = 20.9/3 = 6.96
- *Thorax* (Fig. 4.147): 2.10mm long, 2.10mm broad, black; pronotum (Fig. 4.147) 1.05mm long, 2.10mm broad, anterior side pale yellowish brown, posterior side brownish black, not overlapping on scutellum (Fig. 4.147); mesonotum 0.52mm long, 1.31mm broad, coffee brown; scutellum 0.52mm long, 0.52mm broad, coffee brown. *Wings*, Fore wing (Fig. 4.149) 5.26mm long, 1.57mm broad, semitransparent, brownish colour, not elytra like: hind wing (Fig. 4.150) 5mm long, 1.84mm broad, white, membranous, transparent. *Hind leg* (Fig. 4.157) 7.07mm long, 0.42mm broad, coffee brown; coxa 0.52mm long, 0.42mm broad, pale brown; trochanter 0.42mm long, 0.31mm broad, pale brown; femur 2.10mm long, 0.36mm broad, pale brown; tibia 3.15mm long, 0.26mm broad, brown with spines, black spot at base of each spine; tarsus 0.88mm long, 0.21mm broad, brownish yellow; pre-tarsus 0.36mm long, 0.21mm broad, yellowish brown. meso-tarsus 0.26mm long, 0.15mm broad, brownish yellow; meta-tarsus 0.26mm long, 0.15mm broad, yellowish brown.
- *Abdomen* (Fig. 4.152): 3.42mm long, 2.21mm broad, black, 1 to 8 segments contain black, at the both sides of segments pale yellow. Abdomen brown from ventral side, first segment 0.31mm long, 2.21mm broad; second segment 0.26mm long, 2.10mm broad; third segment 0.26mm long, 2mm broad; fourth segment 0.26mm long, 2mm broad; fifth segment 0.26mm long, 1.84mm broad; sixth segment 0.26mm long, 1.84mm broad; seventh segment 0.26mm long, 1.78mm broad; eighth segment 0.26mm long, 1.68mm broad. Ovipositor 0.30 mm long, pale yellow.
- *Host Plants* : Unknown.

- *Paratype* : ♂ 05, ♀, 02 Coll. Chandani Kamble, July. to Nov., preserved in 70 per cent alcohol, labeled as above.
- *Distribution* : 03 ♂, 1 ♀, Gaganbawda (Kolhapur), 14-VII-2014; 3 ♂, 1 ♀, Shirala (Sangli), 03-XI-2014.

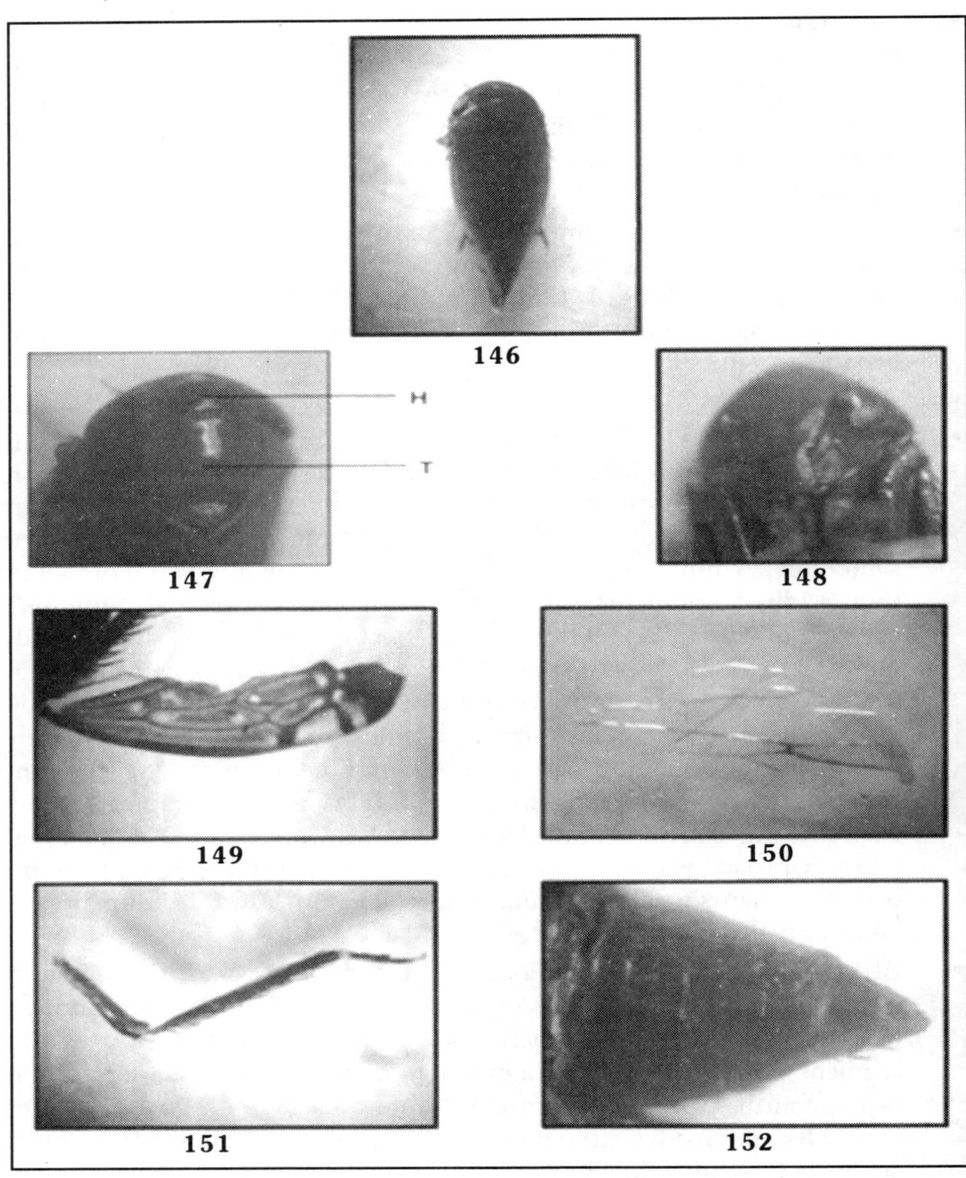

Plate - 20: ***Mimottettix sp.***: Fig. 4.146: **Adult male,** Fig. 4.147: **Dorsal view head and thorax,** Fig. 4.148: **Ventral view head and thorax,** Fig. 4.149: **Forewing,** Fig. 4.150: **Hindwing,** Fig. 4.151: **Hindleg,** Fig. 4.152: **Abdomen**

Tribe EHecalini

Hecalus sp.

(Plate - 21: Figs. 4.153-4.159)

- *Male* (Fig. 4.153):
- *Head* (Fig. 4.154):

  0.95mm long, 1.90mm broad, broader than long, yellowish golden with shine, black spots presents, not rounded, crown (Fig. 4.154) 0.95mm long, 1.42mm broad, golden with shine, three black spots, pentagonal in shape; compound eye 0.76mm long, 0.28mm broad, black, interocular distance 1.42mm, ocelli two, brown, ocellar distance 0.71mm.
- *Antenna* (Fig. 4.155) 1.66mm long, 0.14mm broad, pale; long thread like, scape 0.14mm long, 0.14mm broad, pale; pedicel 0.19mm long, 0.09mm broad, pale; flagellum 1.33mm long, 0.04mm broad, brown; rostrum 0.71mm long, 0.14mm broad.
- *Antennal formula* – S L/W = 1, P L/W = 2.1, F L/W = 33.25, A = 36.25/3 = 12.08
- *Thorax* (Fig. 4.154): 2.38mm long, 1.90mm broad, golden brown; pronotum (Fig. 4.154) 0.95mm long, 1.90mm broad, golden, shiny on anterior side, brown at posterior; mesonotum 0.71mm long, 1.42mm broad, brown at anterior sides, golden at posterior side, shiny; scutellum (Fig. 4.154) 0.71mm long, 0.71mm broad, golden with shine. *Wings*, fore wing (Fig. 4.156) 5mm long, 1.42mm broad, semitransparent, coffee brown at one side, another side transparent white, not elytra like: hind wing (Fig. 4.157) 4.76mm long, 1.66mm broad, whitish brown, membranous, semitransparent. *Hind leg* (Fig. 4.158) 5.32mm long, 0.38mm broad, pale yellow; coxa 0.57mm long, 0.38mm broad, pale; trochanter 0.38mm long, 0.19mm broad, pale yellow; femur 1.66mm long, 0.23mm broad, pale yellow; tibia 2.14mm long, 0.19mm broad, brownish yellow with spines; tarsus 0.57mm long, 0.14mm broad, pale, brown at the base; pre-tarsus 0.19mm long, 0.14mm broad, yellowish brown. meso-tarsus 0.19mm long, 0.14mm broad, brownish yellow; meta-tarsus 0.19mm long, 0.14mm broad, yellowish brown.
- *Abdomen* (Fig. 4.159): 3.52mm long, 1.42mm broad, coffee brown, 1 to 2 segments contain pale yellow, 3 to 4 pale brown, remaining segment dark brown at center and pale brown at both sides. First segment 0.38mm long, 1.42mm broad, second segment 0.38mm long, 1.28mm broad, third segment 0.38mm long, 1.19mm broad, fourth segment 1.04mm long, 0.35mm broad, fifth segment 0.38mm long, 0.85mm broad, sixth segment 0.38mm long, 0.71mm broad, seventh segment 0.38mm long, 0.57mm broad, eighth segment 0.38mm long, 0.47mm broad. Ovipositor 0.45mm long, pale yellow.
- *Host Plants*: Soyabean *Glycine max*, Sunflower *Abelmoschus esculentus* (L.), grasses.

- *Holotype* : ♂, India, Maharashtra, Kolhapur. Coll. Chandani Kamble. 15-I-2015; antenna, wings, legs, on slide labeled as above, rest part preserved 70 per cent alcohol as above.
- *Paratype* : ♂ - 03, ♀ - 02, Coll. Chandani Kamble, March to Nov., preserved in alcohol.
- *Distribution* : 02 ♂, 1 ♀, Kolhapur, 15-I-2015; 01 ♂, Sangli, 1 ♀, 03-XI-2014.

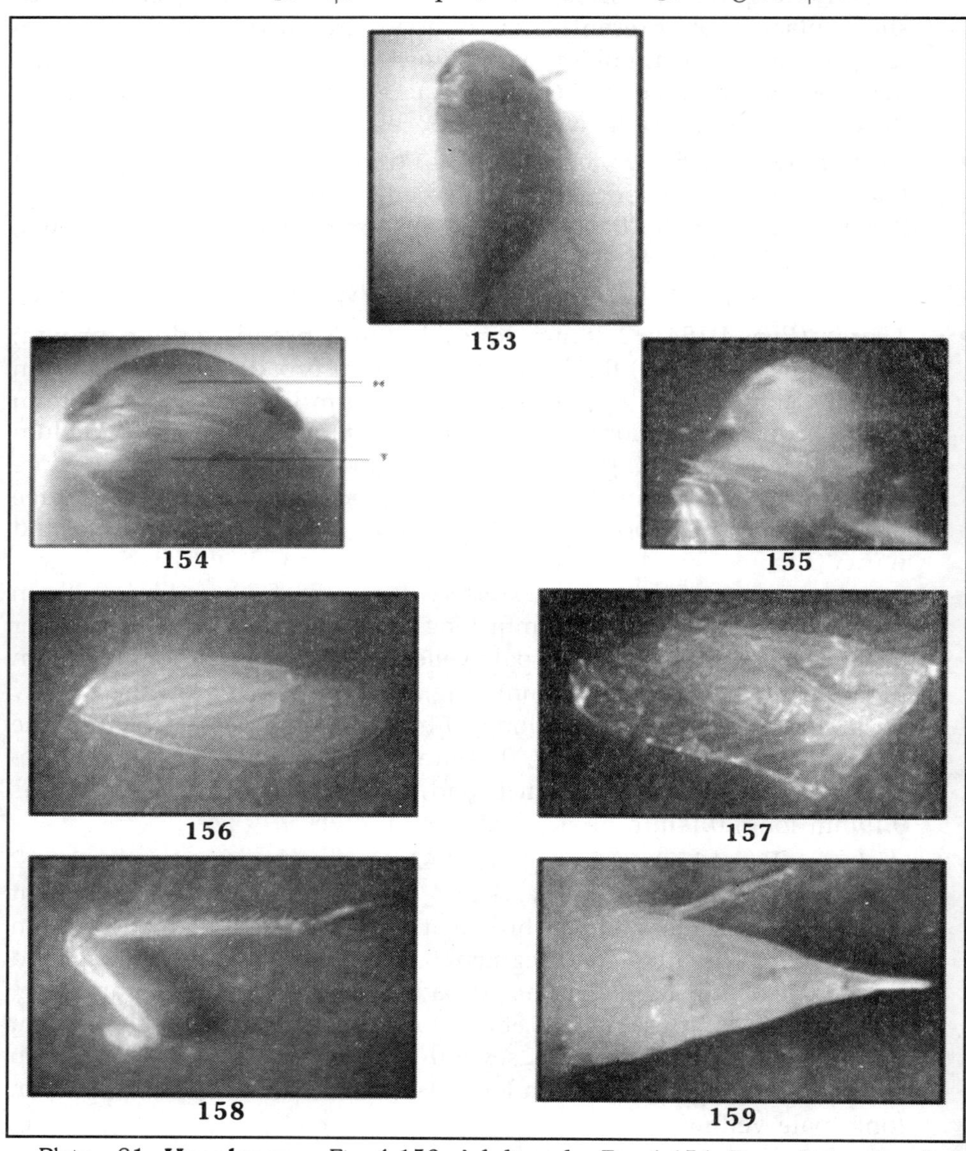

Plate – 21: ***Hecalus* sp. :** Fig. 4.153: **Adult male,** Fig. 4.154: **Dorsal view head and thorax,** Fig. 4.155: **Ventral view head and thorax,** Fig. 4.156: **Forewing,** Fig. 4.157: **Hindwing,** Fig. 4.158: **Hindleg,** Fig. 4.159: **Abdomen**

Genus *Amrasca* sp.

(Plate - 22: Figs. 4.160-4.166)

- *Male* (Fig. 4.160):
- *Head* (Fig. 4.161):

  0.44mm long, 1.2mm broad, broader than long, golden; crown (Fig. 4.161) 0.44mm long, 0.8mm broad, golden, pentagonal in shape, compound eye 0.48mm long, 0.24mm broad, yellowish green, interocular distance 0.8mm, ocelli two, white, ocular distance 0.6mm.
- *Antenna* (Fig. 4.162) 1.4mm long, brown, long thread like; scape 1.4mm long, 0.12mm broad, yellowish; pedicel 0.08mm long, 0.08mm broad; flagellum 1.2mm long, 0.04mm broad, brown; rostrum 0.6mm long, 0.08mm broad, golden brown.
- *Antennal formula* – S L/W = 1, P L/W = 1, F L/W = 30, A = 32.00/3 = 10.66
- *Thorax* (Fig. 4.161): 1.6mm long, 1.4mm broad, white at center, golden brown. pronotum (Fig. 4.161) 0.8mm long, 1.4mm broad, golden white, not overlapping on scutellum (Fig. 4.161); mesonotum 0.32mm long, 1.8mm broad, golden brown; scutellum 0.48mm long, 0.4mm broad, golden white. *Wings* fore wing (Fig. 4.163) 4.4mm long, 1.2mm broad, transparent, golden brown colour, not elytra like; hind wing (Fig. 4.164) 4mm long, 1.4mm broad, white, membranous, transparent. *Hind leg* (Fig. 4.165) 6mm long, 0.32smm broad, golden brown with shine; coxa 0.48mm long, 0.32mm broad, pale golden brown; trochanter 0.24mm long, 0.2mm broad, golden yellow, two spines; femur 1.6mm long, 0.28mm broad, golden yellow; tibia 2.8mm long, 0.2mm broad, golden brown with spines, black spot at base of each spine; tarsus 0.88mm long, 0.12mm broad, brownish yellow; pre-tarsus 0.4mm long, 0.2mm broad, golden brown. meso-tarsus 0.2mm long, 0.12mm broad, golden yellow; meta-tarsus 0.28mm long, 0.12mm broad, golden brown.
- *Abdomen* (Fig. 4.166): 2.92mm long, 0.89mm broad, golden white, 1 to 8 segments contain golden white dorsally; abdomen golden from ventral side. first segment 0.28mm long, 1.2mm broad; second segment 0.28mm long, 1.2mm broad; third segment 0.28mm long, 1.08mm broad; fourth segment 0.28mm long, 1mm broad; fifth segment 0.28mm long, 1mm broad; sixth segment 0.28mm long, 0.88mm broad; seventh segment 0.28mm long, 0.8mm broad; eighth segment 0.28mm long, 0.8mm broad. Ovipositor 0.22mm long, pale golden yellow.
- *Host Plants*: Pigeon pea *Cajanus cajan* (L.), Sunflower *Abelmoschus esculentus* (L.), cotton genus *Gossypium*, soybean *Glycine max*, grasses.
- *Holotype* : ♂, India, Maharashtra, Kagal (Kolhapur), Coll. Chandani Kamble. 9-XII-2013, antenna, wings, legs, on slide labeled as above, rest part preserved in 70 per cent alcohol, labeled as above.

- *Paratype* : ♂- 11, ♀- 9, Coll. Chandani Kamble, Aug. to March., preserved in alcohol.
- *Distribution* : 3 ♂, 5 ♀, Shirol (Kolhapur), 19-II-2015; 3 ♂, 6 ♀, Patan (Satara), 20-VIII-2014.

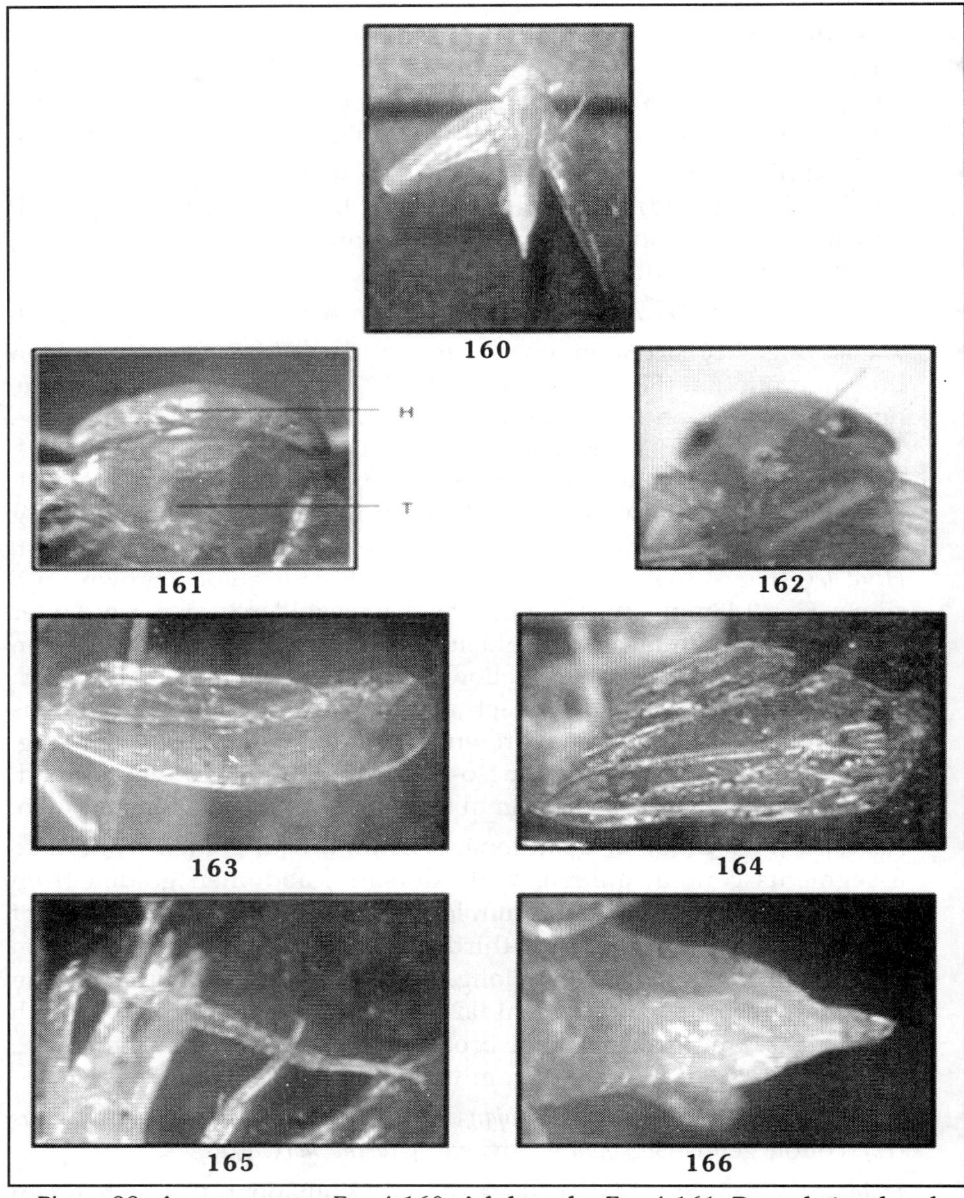

Plate - 22: ***Amrasca sp.* :** Fig. 4.160: **Adult male,** Fig. 4.161: **Dorsal view head and thorax,** Fig. 4.162: **Ventral view head and thorax,** Fig. 4.163: **Forewing,** Fig. 4.164: **Hindwing,** Fig. 4.165: **Hindleg,** Fig. 4.166: **Abdomen**

Tribe Opsini

***Masiripius lugubris* (Distant)**

(Plate - 23: Figs. 4.167-173)

- *Male* (Fig. 4.167):
- *Head* (Fig. 4.168):
  0.65mm long, 1.30mm broad, blackish brown in colour, brown spots presents, not rounded; crown (Fig. 4.168) 0.65mm long, 0.65mm broad, brownish yellow, small black spots, pentagonal in shape. Compound eye 0.65mm long, 0.43mm broad, black, interocular distance 0.65mm, ocelli two, brown, ocular distance 0.43 mm.
- *Antenna* (Fig. 4.169) 0.95mm long, 0.13mm broad, yellowish brown, long threadlike; scape 0.13mm long, 0.08mm broad, yellowish brown; pedicel 0.8mm long, 0.04mm broad, pale yellowish brown; flagellum 0.73mm long, 0.04mm broad, brown; rostrum 0.43mm long, 0.13mm broad, golden brown.
- *Antennal formula* – S L/W = 1.62, P L/W = 2, F L/W = 18.25, A = 21.87/3 = 7.29
- *Thorax* (Fig. 4.168): 1.17mm long, 1.30mm broad, yellowish brown; pronotum (Fig. 4.168) 0.65mm long, 1.30mm broad, grey with black spot; mesonotum 0.21mm long, 0.43mm broad, brownish yellow; scutellum (Fig. 4.168) 0.30mm long, 0.21mm broad, yellowish brown with black spot. *Wings* fore wing (Fig. 4.170) 4.13mm long, 1.08mm broad, semitransparent, pale brown colour, dark brown spots presents, not elytra like; hind wing (Fig. 4.171) 3.91mm long, 1.30 mm broad, white, membranous, transparent. *Hind leg* (Fig. 4.172) 4.93mm long, 0.30mm broad, golden brown with black spot; coxa 0.43mm long, 0.30mm broad, golden brown with black spots; trochanter 0.21mm long, 0.17mm broad, golden brown with black spots; femur 1.22mm long, 0.26mm broad, golden brown with black spots; tibia 2.39mm long, 0.21mm broad, golden yellow, black spot at base of each spine; tarsus 0.68mm long, 0.13mm broad, brownish yellow; pre-tarsus 0.30mm long, 0.13mm broad, golden yellow; meso-tarsus 0.21mm long, 0.13mm broad, golden yellow; meta-tarsus 0.17mm long, 0.08mm broad, golden yellow.
- *Abdomen* (Fig. 4.173): 2.17mm long, 1.30mm broad, black, 1 to 8 segments contain black with shine; abdomen black from ventral side. first segment 0.21mm long, 1.30mm broad; second segment 0.21mm long, 0.86mm broad; third segment 0.21mm long, 1.21mm broad; fourth segment 0.21mm long, 1.21mm broad; fifth segment 0.21mm long, 1.08mm broad; sixth segment 0.21mm long, 0.95mm broad; seventh segment 0.21mm long, 0.78mm broad; eighth segment 0.21mm long, 0.65mm broad. Pygofer 0.25mm long, pale yellow.
- *Host Plants* : Vegetables.
- *Holotype* : ♂, India, Maharashtra, Radhanagari (Kolhapur). Coll. Chandani Kamble. 5-XI-2014, Antenna, wings, legs, on slide labeled as above, rest part preserved in 70 per cent alcohol, labeled as above.

- *Paratype* : 3 ♂, 2 ♀, Coll. Chandani Kamble, Sept. to Nov. preserved in 70 per cent alcohol.
- *Distribution* : Western Maharashtra, 2 ♂, 0 ♀, Radhanagari (Kolhapur), 14 Oct. 2014; 1 ♂, 2 ♀, Kolhapur, 05-XI-2014.

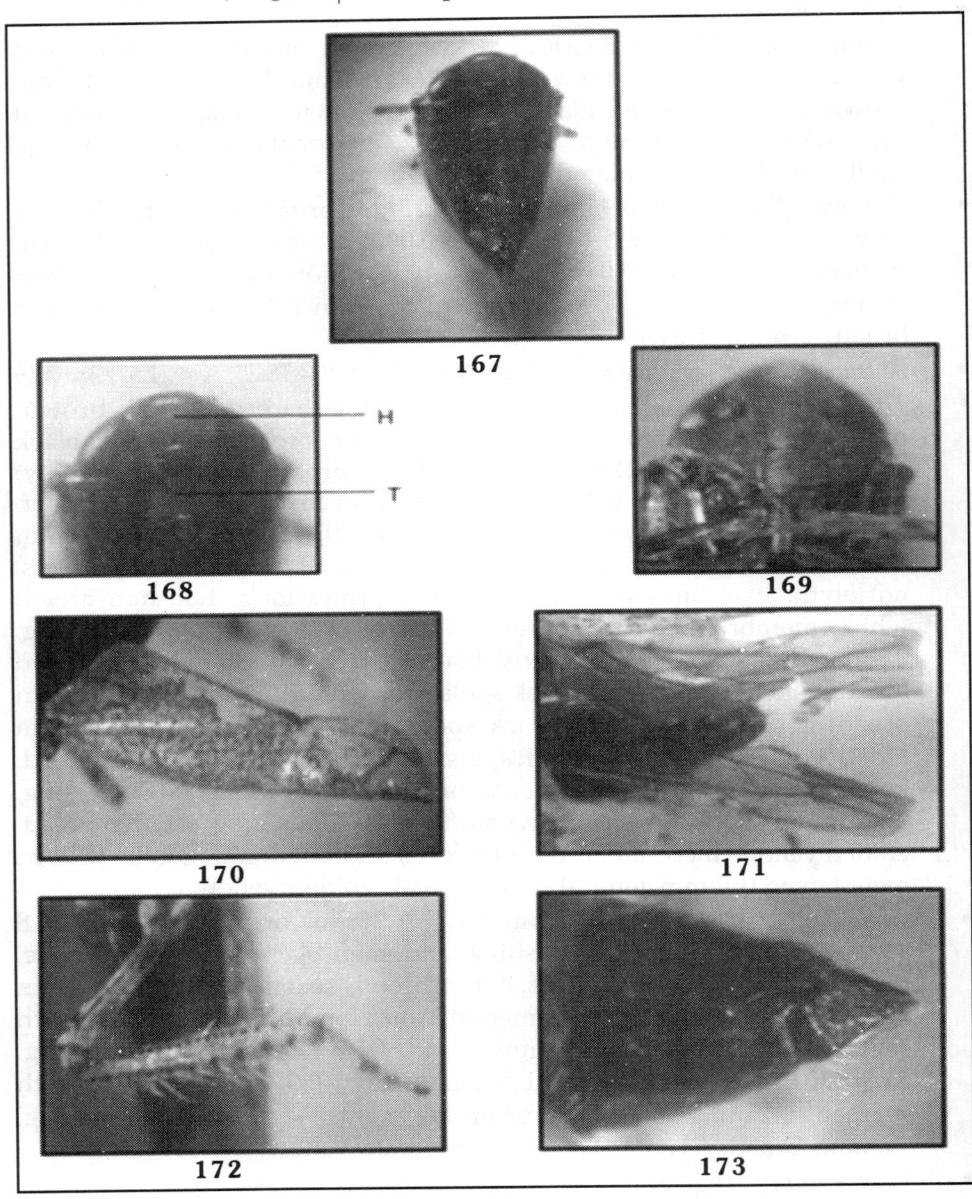

Plate – 23: ***M. lugubris:*** Fig. 4.167: **Adult male,** Fig. 4.168: **Dorsal view head and thorax,** Fig. 4.169: **Ventral view head and thorax,** Fig. 4.170: **Forewing,** Fig. 4.171: **Hindwing,** Fig. 4.172: **Hindleg,** Fig. 4.173: **Abdomen**

Subfamily-Deltocephalinae

Deltocephalus sp.

(Plate - 24: Figs. 4.174-4.180)

- *Male* (Fig. 4.174):
- *Head* (Fig. 4.175):

  0.63mm long, 0.78mm broad, broader than long, yellow in colour; crown (Fig. 4.175) 0.63mm long, 0.52mm broad, yellow, shiny, pentagonal in shape. Compound eye 0.52mm long, 0.26mm broad, greenish black, brown at lateral side, interocular distance 0.10 mm, ocelli two, brown, ocular distance 0.26mm.
- *Antenna* (Fig. 4.176) 0.94mm long, 0.10mm broad, pale yellow, long thread like; scape 0.10mm long, 0.10mm broad, yellow, shiny; pedicel 0.10mm long, 0.05mm broad; flagellum 0.75mm long, 0.05mm broad, whitish yellow; rostrum 0.26mm long, 0.10mm broad, brown.
- *Antennal formula* – S L/W = 1, P L/W = 2, F L/W = 15, A = 18/3 = 6
- *Thorax* (Fig. 4.175): 1.10mm long, 1.05mm broad, coffee brown; pronotum (Fig. 4.175) 0.42mm long, 1.05mm broad, golden brown, shiny, yellowish patch, not overlapping on scutellum (Fig. 4.175); mesonotum 0.31mm long, 0.52mm broad, coffee brown; scutellum 0.36mm long, 0.42mm broad, brown. *Wings*, fore wing (Fig. 4.177) 0.78mm long, 0.36mm broad, semitransparent, brown colour, not elytra like: *hind wing* (Fig. 4.178) 0.68mm long, 0.26mm broad, white, membranous, transparent. *Hind leg* (Fig. 4.179) 4.01mm long, 0.31mm broad pale yellow; coxa 0.36mm long, 0.31mm broad, pale; trochanter 0.31mm long, 0.26mm broad, pale yellow; femur 1.05mm long, 0.26mm broad, pale yellow, shiny; tibia 1.57mm long, 0.21mm broad, pale yellow with spines; tarsus 0.72mm long, 0.15mm broad, pale yellow; pre-tarsus 0.36mm long, 0.15mm broad, brown; meso-tarsus 0.26mm long, 0.15mm broad, brownish yellow; meta-tarsus 0.10mm long, 0.10mm broad, brown.
- *Abdomen* (Fig. 4.180): 2.26mm long, 1.68mm broad, yellow, 1 to 8 segments yellow dorsally, 1 to 4 tergites with black spots, at the centre of each segments contains two black spot. Abdomen whitish yellow from ventral side. First segment 0.21mm long, 1.68mm broad; second segment 0.21mm long, 1.68mm broad; third segment 0.26mm long, 1.57mm broad; fourth segment 0.26mm long, 1.52mm broad; fifth segment 0.26mm long, 1.15mm broad; sixth segment 0.26mm long, 0.89mm broad; seventh segment 0.26mm long, 0.63mm broad; eighth segment 0.26mm long, 0.52mm broad. Ovipositor 0.2mm long, pale yellow, shiny.
- *Host Plants* : Brinjal.
- *Holotype* : ♂, India, Maharashtra, Kolhapur. Coll. Chandani Kamble. 14-VIII-2014, Antenna, wings, legs, on slide labeled as above, rest part preserved in 70 per cent alcohol, labeled as above.

- *Paratype* : 3 ♂, 2 ♀, Coll. Chandani Kamble, Sept. to Dec. preserved in 70 per cent alcohol.
- *Distribution* : 2 ♂, 1 ♀, Amba Ghats (Kolhapur), 25-VIII-2015; 1 ♂, 0 ♀, Katyayani (Kolhapur), 30-XI-2014; 0 ♂, 1 ♀ Karad, 1-VII-2014.

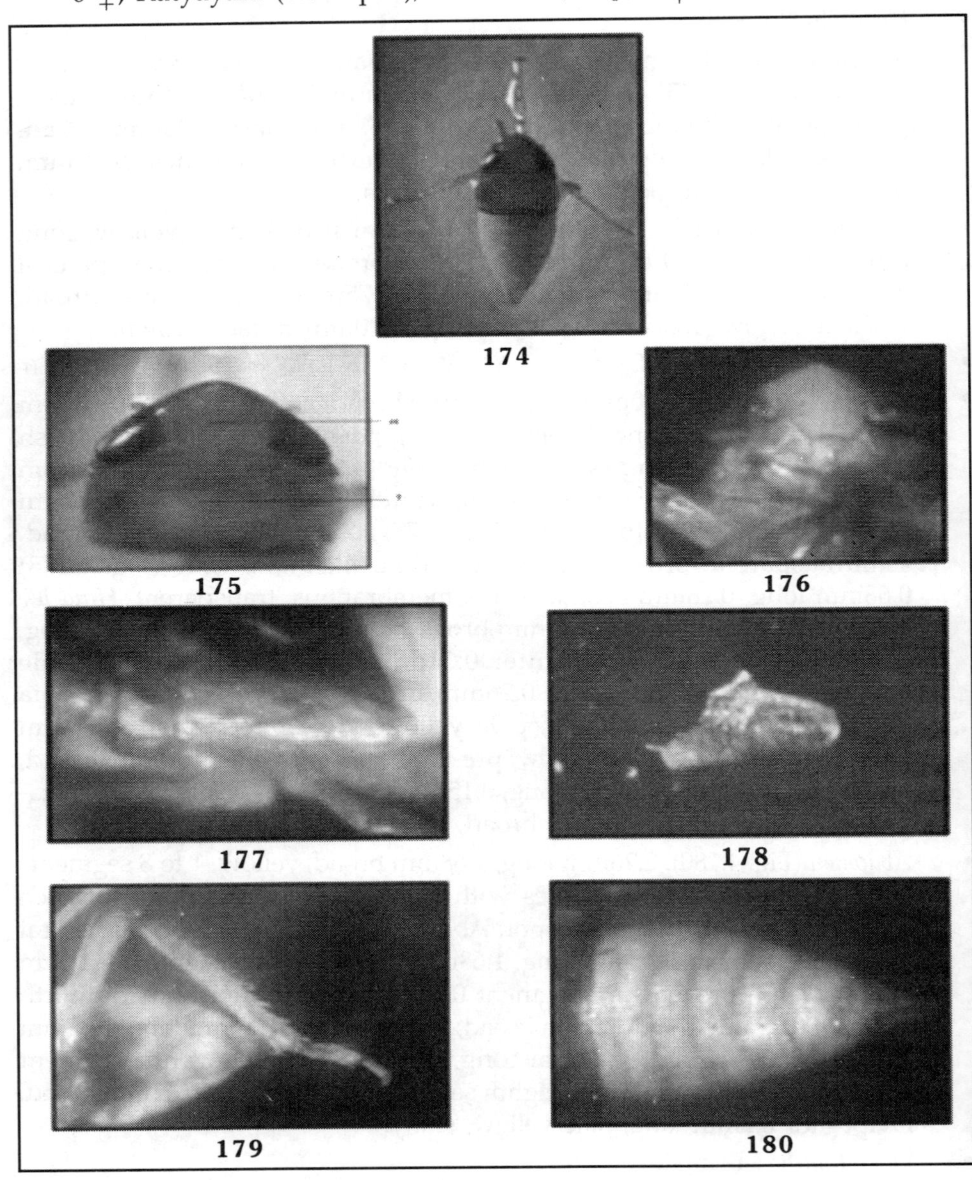

Plate - 24: ***Deltocephalus sp.*** Fig. 4.174: **Adult male,** Fig. 4.175: **Dorsal view head and thorax,** Fig. 4.176: **Ventral view head and thorax,** Fig. 4.177: **Forewing,** Fig. 4.178: **Hindwing,** Fig. 4.179: **Hindleg, Fig.** 4.180: **Abdomen**

Seasonal Abundance, Distribution and Damage of Jassids

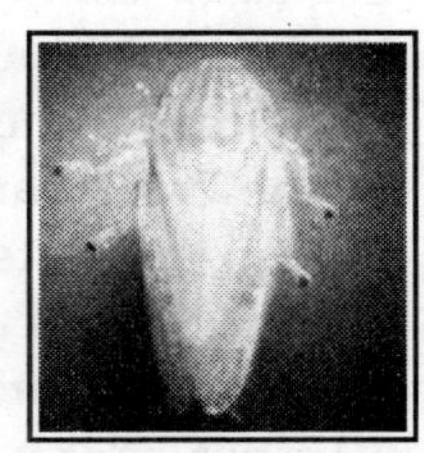

INTRODUCTION

Jassids (Hemiptera: Cicadellidae) are wedge shaped insects which walk diagonally and suck the cell sap with the help of piercing and sucking type of mouth parts and affect the growth and yield of crops. In past several workers (Baker, 1924; Datta, 1922; Distant, 1908, 1918; Pruthi, 1930, 1936; Hussain and Pruthi, 1923; Rao, 1980; Singh, 1989; Das and Vraktamath, 1998; Sathe and Margaj, 2001; etc.) Sathe and Kamble (2014); Kamble and Sathe (2015 a,b) worked on seasonal abundance, distribution and nature of damage of jassids from India. In the present topic attempts have been made on seasonal abundance, distribution and nature of damage of jassids. The present work will provide base line data for designing control strategies of jassids.

MATERIALS AND METHODS

Seasonal abundance of jassids was studied by collecting jassids from various ecosystems of Kolhapur, Sangli and Satara districts of Maharashtra. The collected samples were examined and identified by consulting appropriate literature (Distant, 1908, 1918; Datta, 1912; Pruthi, 1930 and 1936). Abundance, distribution and nature of damage of jassids were studied in various crop fields of Western Maharashtra by spot observation. The details of methodology are given in the chapter III materials and methods.

RESULTS

Results are recorded in Table 5.1 and Fig. 5.1 to 5.2. A total of 40 species of Jassids have been reported from Western Maharashtra especially from Kolhapur, Sangli and Satara districts. Most of the species were prevalent in the region in monsoon season. However, some of the species of genera *Nilaparvata, Sogatella* and *Deltocephalus* were found throughout the year. *Deltocephalus* genus was mostly associated with grassland ecosystems. The species of *Empoasca* were found most destructive to the cotton and castor crops in Maharashtra. Castor plants persist most of time of the year therefore; *Empoasca* complex was also more persistent on castor ecosystems. Mango Jassids were found throughout the year on the crop but during hot months, May-June and cold months, October-January only adults were found sitting in the cracks and crevices of tree trunk. The Jassids population peaks on mango ecosystem were from July-August which damaged new sprouting leaves. Second peak was observed in February synchronizing blossoming of the crop during which severe damage was caused this peak to the crop. Almost mango trees were made sterile by feeding on cell sap of inflorescence. Most of the flowering bodies dropped down and sticky substances were associated with the crop. Therefore, Jassids are supposed to be rank first pest of mango tree. However, jassid diversity was relatively more associated with paddy crops. Probably due to mono and continues culture of the crop from Kolhapur region. Many species of Jassids attract towards the light hence, they may be controlled with light sources (Traps) for avoiding pesticidal use on various crop ecosystems. In future, more attention should be given on this important group of destructive pests since pesticides are less effective against Jassids because they take their food by deeping their beak into plant tissues. The occurrence, distribution, host plants and nature of damage of jassids have been given in Table 5.1 and Figs. 5.1 to 5.2. The family Deltocephalinae was dominant over others.

DISCUSSION

Nakamuro *et al.* (1967) estimated the population density of the green rice leafhopper *Nephotettix cincticeps* Uhler in spring field by the capture-recapture method. *N. cineticeps* is an important pest of rice in Japan which injures the crop not only in direct way but also in carrying the rice dwarf virus. In the Kanto district, this species hibernates in the nymphal stage on gramineous weeds grown in resting paddy field and ridge and the adult emerges from late in March to mid-April. It completes three generations throughout a year. The capture-recapture method has been used for sampling many insect pests including: Orthoptera, Diptera, Lepidoptera, Coleoptera and others. This method used for sampling Hemipterans insect *N. cincticeps* was quite suitable. This method is based on two assumptions that is, the marked and remarked animals mingle completely with the unmarked ones and the sampling efficiency is performed equally on the marked and unmarked animals. The number of *N. cincticeps* in hibernated generation was rather small and the rate of recapture was also low.

Table: 5.1: Abundance, distribution, host plants and damage by jassids in Western Maharashtra (Kolhapur, Sangli, Satara)

Sl. No.	Scientific Name	Family	Host Plants	Nature of Damage	Occurrence	Locality
1	2	3	4	5	6	7
1.	Brown plant hopper *Nilaparavata lugsena* (Stal.)	Delphacidae	Paddy *Oryza sativa* L.	Suck the cell sap, cause yellowing and drying of leaves, flowering and fruiting of bodies. Cause sooty mould, affect photosynthesis, growth and yield of the crop.	Throughout year, abundant Oct-Feb.	K, S, St.
2.	White black plant hopper *Sogatella furcifera* (Horv.)	Delphacidae	Paddy *O. sativa*	-,,-	Throughout year	K, S, St.
3.	Green leaf hopper *Nephotettix nigropictus* (Stal.)	Cicadellinae	Paddy *O. sativa*	-,,-	July- Aug.	K, S, St.
4.	*Nephotettix virescens* (Distant)	Cicadellinae	Paddy *O. sativa*	-,,-	July- Aug.	K, S, St.
5.	*Nephotettix pavus* I and K	Cicadellinae	Paddy *O. sativa*	-,,-	July- Aug.	K, S, St.
6.	White leaf hopper *Cofana spectra* (Distant)	Cicadellinae	Paddy *O. sativa*	-,,-	July-March	K, S, St.
7.	*Cofana albida* Walker	Cicadellinae	*O. sativa*	Suck cell sap from leaves and flowering bodies	June-March	K, S, St.
8.	*Cofana maai* Young	Cicadellinae	*O. sativa*	Suck cell sap from leaves and flowering bodies	June- March	K, S, St.
9.	*Cofana jedarfa* Young	Cicadellinae	*O. sativa*	Suck cell sap from leaves and flowering bodies	June- March	K, S, St.
10.	*Cofana oryzae* sp. nov.	Cicadellinae	*O. sativa*	Suck cell sap from leaves and flowering bodies	June- March	K, S, St.

Contd…

1	2	3	4	5	6	7
11.	*Scaphoidus indica* sp. nov.	Deltocephalinae	*O. sativa*	Suck cell sap from leaves and flowering bodies	July-March	K, S, St.
12.	*Ishidaella albomarginata* Signoret	Deltocephalinae	*O. sativa*	Suck cell sap from leaves and flowering bodies	Oct.-Feb.	K, S, St.
13.	*Anoscopus albifrons* Linn.	Aphrodinae	*O. sativa*	Suck cell sap from leaves and flowering bodies	Oct.-Feb.	K.
14.	*Anoscopus sp.* 1	Aphrodinae	Grasses	Suck cell sap from leaves and flowering bodies	July-March	K, S.
15.	*Xestocephalus brunnens*	Aphrodinae	Grasses	Suck cell sap from leaves and flowering bodies	Nov.-Feb.	K.
16.	Zigzag leaf hopper *Recilia dorsalis* (Mots.)	Cicadellinae	Paddy *O. sativa*	Suck cell sap from leaves and flowering bodies	July-Oct.	K, S, St.
17.	Blue leaf hopper *Typhlocyba maculifrons* (Mots.)	Cicadellinae	Paddy *O. sativa,* Maize *Zea mays* L., Jowar *Sorghum vulgare* L. Sugarcane *Saccharum* sp.	Suck cell sap from leaves and flowering bodies	July-Oct.	K, S, St.
18.	*Amrasca* spp.	Cicadellinae	Wheat *Triticum* sp.	Suck cell sap from leaves and flowering bodies	Aug-Dec.	K, S, St.
19.	*Laodephax striatella* (Fall.)	Delphacidae	Wheat *Triticum* sp.	Suck cell sap from leaves and flowering bodies	Aug-Dec.	K, S, St.
20.	Grapevine leaf hopper *Erythroneura* sp.	Cicadellinae	Grape vine *Vitis vinifera* L.	Cause brownish spots to leaves and fruits	Spring	K, S, St.
21.	*Idioscopus clypealis* (Lethi.)	Cicadellinae	Mango *Mangifera indica* L.	Sucking cell sap of tender leaves and blooming, flowering and fruiting bodies drop down, cause sooty mold, affect photosynthesis, growth yield.	Feb-April	K, S, St.

Contd…

1	2	3	4	5	6	7
22.	*Idioscopus atkinsoni* (Lethi.)	Cicadellinae	Mango *M. indica*	Sucking cell sap of tender leaves and blooming, flowering and fruiting bodies drop down, cause sooty mold, affect photosynthesis, growth yield.	July-Aug.	K, S, St.
23.	Potato Jassid *Hishimonus phycitus* (Distant)	Cicadellinae	Potato *Solanum tuberosum* L.	Suck cell sap cause sooty mould, affect growth yield.	July-Nov.	K, S, St.
24.	Cotton Jassid *Empoasca devastan* (Distant)	Cicadellinae	Cotton *Gossypium arboretum* L. Ladies finger *Abelmoschus esculentus* L.	Suck cell sap, cause yellowing and curly leaves. Sooty moulds, affect growth yield.	July-Nov.	K, S, St.
25.	*Empoasca notata* (Mel.)	Cicadellinae	Cotton *Gossypium hirsutum* L.	Suck cell sap, cause yellowing and curly leaves. Sooty moulds, affect growth yield.	July-Jan.	K, S, St.
26.	*Empoasca flavescens* (Distant)	Cicadellinae	Castor *Ricinus communis* L.	Suck cell sap, cause yellowing and curly leaves. Sooty moulds, affect growth yield.	July-Jan.	K, S, St.
			Tea *Camellia sinensis* L. Mulberry *Morus alba* L.	—,,— Cause hopper burnt		
27.	*Empoasca kerri* (Pruthi)	Cicadellinae	Castor Ricinus communis L.	Suck cell sap, cause yellowing and curly leaves.Sooty moulds, affect growth yield.	July-Jan.	K, S, St.
28.	*Empoasca parathea* (Pruthi)	Cicadellinae	Castor *Ricinus communis* L.	Suck cell sap, cause yellowing and curly leaves. Sooty moulds, affect growth yield.	July-Jan.	K, S, St.
29.	*Deltocephalus vulgaris*	Deltocephalinae	Jowar *Sorghum vulgare* L.	Suck cell sap, cause yellowing and drying of leaves, cause sooty moulds, affect photosynthesis, growth and yield.	Aug-Sept.	K, S, St.
30.	*Deltocephalus trisuli*	Deltocephalinae	Grasses	Suck cell sap, affect growth	Aug-Sept.	K, S, St.

Contd…

1	2	3	4	5	6	7
31.	*Deltocephalus truncatus*	Deltocephalinae	Grasses	Suck cell sap, affect growth	Aug-Sept.	K, S, St.
34.	*Varta longula* Virakatmath	Deltocephalinae	Sugarcane,	Suck cell sap, affect growth	July- Sept	K, S, St.
35.	*Obornellus limosus* Delong	Cicadellinae	Grasses	Suck cell sap, affect growth	July- Sept	K, S, St.
36.	*Gyponana cacuminal*	Typhlocybinae	Cashew nut	Suck cell sap, affect growth	July- Sept	K, St.
37.	*Exitianus plebeius* Kirkaldy	Cicadellinae	Grasses	Suck cell sap, affect growth	July- Sept	K, S.
38.	Unknown-1	Tribe-Opsiini		Suck cell sap, affect growth	July- Sept	K.
39.	Unknown-2	Typhlocybinae		Suck cell sap, affect growth	July-Sept	K.
40.	Unknown-3	Deltocephalinae		Suck cell sap, affect growth	July- Sept	K, S.

Footnote: K = Kolhapur
S = Sangli
St = Satara

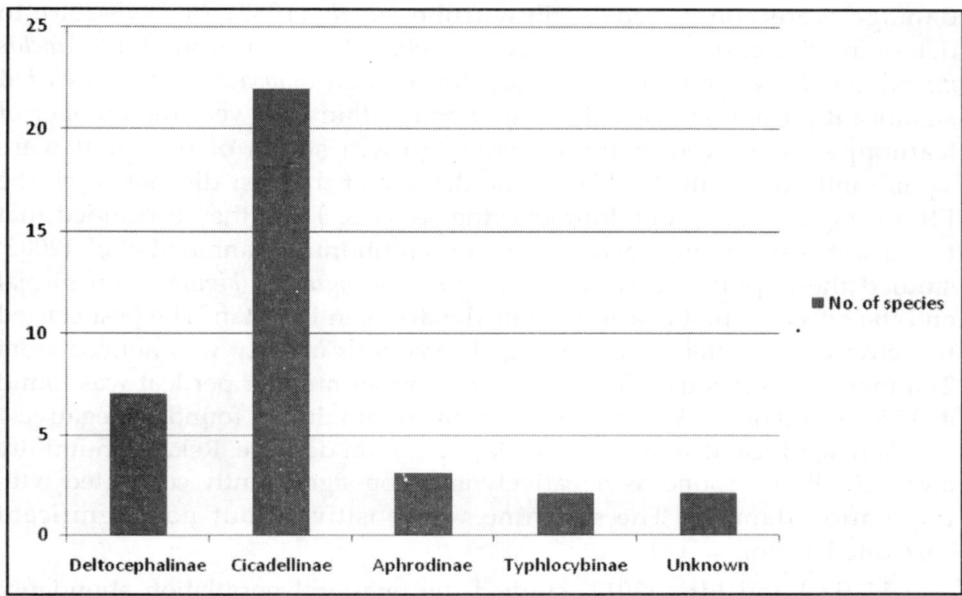

Fig. 5.1: **Abundance of Jassids from Western Maharashtra**

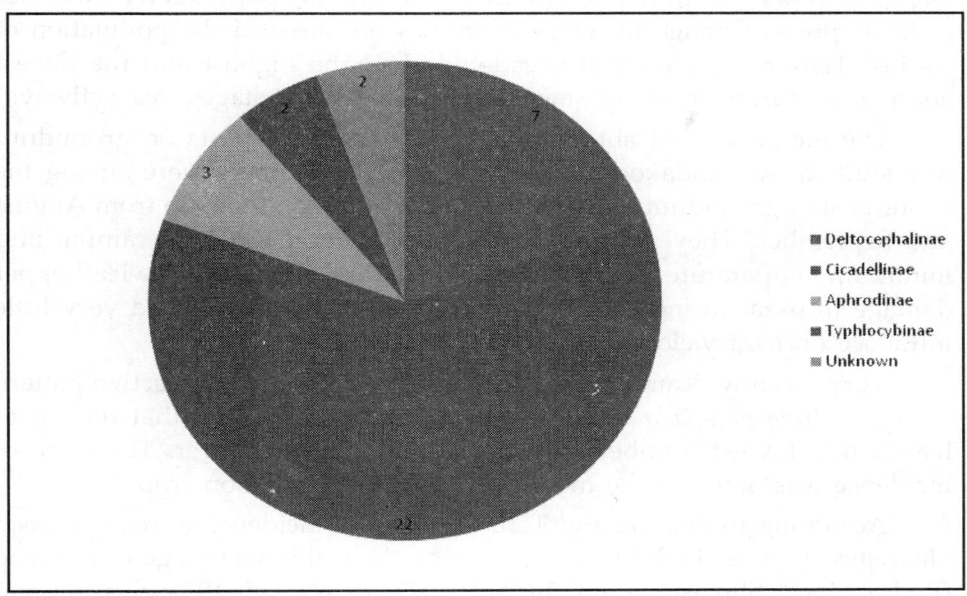

Fig. 5.2: **Species abundance of Jassids from Western Maharashtra**

Population studies and tests on the relationship between density and damage were conducted by Egwurube, *et al.* (1982) in 1999-2001 to determine the pests status of *Empoasca dolichi* Paoli on groundnut *Arachis hupogaea* L. in Nigeria. Their analysis showed that *Empoasca* numbers varied significantly from one year to another and within each year the number of leafhoppers observed at the different growth stages of the plant were significantly different (P = 0.01). The density of the pest did not reach the EIL throughout the groundnut growing seasons. Thus, they concluded that this insect was not an economic pest on groundnut. Mahmood *et al.* (2002) studied the population dynamics of *Amrasca biguttula biguttula* on brinjal and the effects of biotic factors on its dynamics in Pakistan. The pest started its activity soon after transplanting. The serious activity was noticed from 21st may to 6th August. The highest leafhopper number per leaf was found as 12.96 ± 0.93 on 9.7-96. Mean maximum and minimum found as negatively and non-significantly correlated with population damage. Relative humidity and rainfall was found as negatively and non-significantly correlated with population damage. The sunshine was positively but non-significant correlated factor.

Hafizal and Idris (2014) studied the temporal population abundance of leafhoppers on rice crop from Malaysia. Their results showed that the mean temperature and relative humidity were varied slightly during the rice growth period but not significantly affecting the population abundance of leafhoppers. Change in temperature has not affected the population of jassids. They concluded that Cicadellids had the highest and the lowest abundance during maturity stages and reproductive stages, respectively.

The incidence and abundance of sucking insect pests on groundnut was studied by Kandakoor *et al.* (2012). The leafhoppers were among the major pest of groundnut and were more abundant on the crop from August and September. They showed negative correlationship with rainfall and minimum temperature. According to Faleuro and Rai (1985) the leafhopper damage to okra during early and late stages of its growth had very little influence on fruit yield.

Very recently, Kamble *et al.* (2014) studied vertical destructive pattern of *A. biguttula biguttula* to sunflower wherein they noted that the lower leaves had lowest number of nymphs and upper highest. The peak of incidence was noted in the month of August on monsoon crop.

According to Sharma and Tara (2014) peak incidence of mango jassid *Idioscopus clypealis* (Leth.) was seen during the full bloom stage of the crop (Reddy, 1968; Shivastava and Butani, 1972; Patel *et al.* 1973; Sharma and Sharma, 2009; Sharma *et al.* 2010).

Biology of *Idioscopus nitidus* Walk, a mango jassid was studied by Nordin and Ibrahim (1995) from Malaysia. This is serious treat to mango industry in Malaysia due to its damage to crop by sucking cell sap down flowering and fruiting bodies.

Indian green jassid *A. biguttula biguttula* is serious pest of many agricultural crops in India and Australia. It attacks crops such as: soyabean, sunflower, cotton, tomato, maize, pigeon pea, mungbean and several others which is also prominent pest of several agricultural and other crop plants from Kolhapur.

Since, jassids suck the cell sap and cause sooty moulds over crop plants, affect photosynthesis, growth and yield of the crops and transmit various viral diseases to crops, the present work will add great relevance by providing base line for adopting their control strategies.

6 Control of Jassids

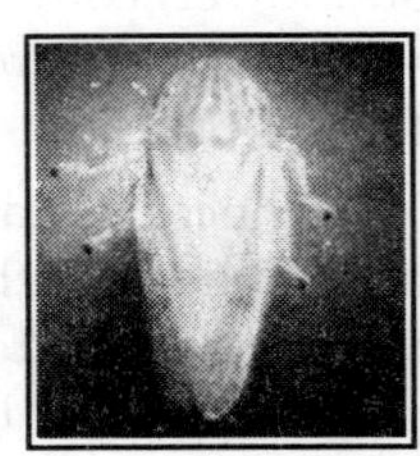

Following methods are adopted for control of jassids.

1. Preventive control.
2. Ecological control.
3. Biological control.
4. Cultural control.
5. Mechanical.
6. Chemical control.

1. Preventive control

(i) Jassid nymphs and adults are collected with the help of insect net and dipped into keratinized water or pesticides, emulsifiable concentrates for killing them.

(ii) Jassids lay eggs in plant tissues. Therefore, infected crop plants are collected and destroyed.

(iii) Clean cultivation and removal of grasses can control jassids.

(iv) Use Appropriate dose of nitrogenous fertilizers.

2. Ecological control

Ecological control has two important components *viz;*

(a) abiotic factors.

(b) biotic factors.

(a) abiotic factors

Abiotic factors such as: topography, water bodies, soil quality, climate, temperature, humidity, light, rainfall, wind, etc., have direct impact on jassid population.

Temperature, humidity, rainfall and topography are largely responsible for abundance of jassids. Temperature is the most important factor which determines the population size of jassids in various seasons. Warm days, spring and summer determines populations. Climatic conditions in the fall are the limiting factor of successful egg laying and thus influence the number of eggs laid. Temperature, humidity and light affect embryonic and post embryonic developments, thereby affecting the time of occurrence. In winter, development is slowed down in jassids.

It has been noted that relationship between temperature and rainfall controls the amount of crop damaged by jassids. Under hot dry conditions, a small jassids population can cause much damage. During the monsoon season jassid diversity was more due to increased diversity of food plants. There after, the population declines. Many species migrate to first ecosystem in search of food plants. Similarly, their insect predators like: ladybird beetles and lacewings also migrated (Sathe, 2014) in want of preys. (Sathe, 2014)

Environmental moisture can affect the size of jassid population. During an extended drought, scarcity of water may slow the development of jassids, especially during certain embryonic stages including eclosion. However, extremely dry conditions seriously affect the survival of jassids and the populations.

Rainfall has also severe effect on jassid populations. Heavy rainfall wiped out the jassid populations within no time. The cool and wet weather reduce the crop losses by hindering pest development and increasing adverse conditions to jassids.

3. Biological control

Natural enemies in the form of parasitoids and predators always play an important role in controlling insect populations. In some localized areas these enemies may even be more important factor than the weather. However for jassids unfortunately parasitoids are not reported. It needs continuous survey for parasitoids for jassids.

(a) *Insect predators*: The nymphs and adults are predated by predators like: insects and other arthropods. For example Lace wings, Ladybird beetles, Tiger beetles, Mantids, Dragon flies, crickets and Spiders.

- *(i)* Lace wings *Chrysiperla* spp.: Both nymphs and adults feed on jassid populations at day and night in field and at light sources respectively.
- *(ii)* *Grasshoppers:* Predatory grasshoppers feed on many species of jassids at light source. Jassids attracted to light source at field conditions and human dwelling. They predated by small grasshoppers. The adults of some species of grasshoppers feed directly on the nymphs and adults of jassids destroying up to 80 per cent population.

(*iii*) *Dragon flies and Damsel flies:* These belongs to order Odonata and visualized as exclusively predacious on many insects including jassids. Both dragon flies and damsel flies are found predating on various species of jassids in paddy ecosystems of Kolhapur.

(*iv*) *Crickets:* Jassid nymphs and adults are also predated by crickets in field condition and at light source in store houses/godowns/ human dwellings.

(*v*) *Tiger beetles:* Tiger beetles like: *Eudema polyphagi, Eudema angulatum, Anthia sexgutatta, Diacranoncus indicus* and *Diacranoncus pocillator* predates upon jassids in field conditions.

(*vi*) *Cicindellids:* Their are 20,000 species of Cicindellid beetles reported as exclusively predators of many insects including jassids. These beetles are also potential biocontrol agents of jassids.

(*vii*) *Mantids:* Mantids in various crop ecosystems largely feed on jassids and suppress pest populations. In mulberry, vegetables and cotton ecosystems, they play a very important role for jassid control.

(*viii*) *Spider:* Spiders are effective biocontrol agents of jassids both at field condition and at light sources in store houses, godowns or human dwellings.

Vertebrate Predators

Following vertebrate predators feed on jassids.

1. Toads *Bufo marinus*: In paddy ecosystems and at light source, jassids are attracted, the toads feed on jassids.
2. *Wall Lizard*: Wall lizards are good biocontrol agents of jassids. Very large number of jassids are taken by wall lizard as their diet in human dwelling at light source.
3. *Shrews:* Shrews at light feed on jassids when they attracted to light and drop down on ground.

4. Cultural control

The cultural control of jassid is least expensive. Under this method following strategies are visualized.

(*i*) Early sowing.

(*ii*) Crop rotation.

(*iii*) Tillage.

(*iv*) Trap strips/crops.

(*v*) Manipulation of Environment.

(*vi*) Manipulation of Nitrogenous fertilizers.

(*vii*) Use of resistance verities.

(*viii*) Removal of weeds.

Manipulation of Environment

The proper timing of sowing and harvesting of crop can play important role in jassid control. By modifying the environment at certain critical periods of life cycle, one can reduce pest population.

The effectiveness of cultural control methods are difficult to assess. Nevertheless, these methods have great relevance in keeping environment eco-friendly, although it takes time to work.

- *Early sowing*: Crops should be sown as early as possible. Older plants can withstand with more jassids feeding than younger plants. Early seeding will not prevent crop damage entirely but reduce the amount of damage to crops and will provide also more time for farmers to keep crop insecticide free. Early seeded crops mature early and pests are less attracted to them than young crops.
- *Crop rotation*: Whenever possible, avoid non suitable crop rotations in the fields. Cereals should be sown on stubble fields only where soil moisture is adequate and where one or more applications of an insecticide are given. Rotation of sugarcane-maize-cotton is not accepted but, paddy-sunflower is accepted for control of many pests including jassids. Similarly, maize-Sanji also accepted system for jassid control.
- *Tillage*: Cultivation of the soil is very good cultural practice performed by farmers for the reduction of pest populations and to keep crops healthy. Healthy crops can resists pest attack and or pests have less attack on them. Tillage control jassids primarily by eliminating the green plants on which jassids feed. Hence, this method has little value. Excessive tillage is harmful; it will reduce soil moisture level and increase the risk of soil erosion.

Weeds encourage jassids by providing alternate host for multiplication on them and early fall will discourage females from depositing their eggs on crops.

It is advisable to give the chemical treatment to eliminate all the developments of pests on crops, deprive the availability of food for young jassids or make unpalatable by treating the crops with repellents like Bordeaux mixture. This also checks fungal diseases of the crops and will starved jassids to death. Early tillage provides additional benefits that it gives good weed control and conserves moisture at no extra cost.

Pruning and thinning

In jowar thinning control jassids and Delphacids while in grapes thinning control jassids and also other pests like mealy bugs and thrips.

Trap Crops/Strips

Adequate control is by simply climinating all green plant materials in a field. Certain crops invite same pest problem found on other crops. Such crops are used as trap crops or as strip crop for attracting pest complex on the basis cost benefit ratio of the crops. Less economic crops are sacrificed for more economical crops. The pests on less economically important can also be controlled by using various appropriate control measures. But protected crop will grow in pesticides free environment/ecosystem and will be safely for humans. Hence, such methods have more importance in IPM strategies. For cotton pests, okra is used as trap crop. Trap crop models are to be detected in near future, since little is known on this concept.

After complete migration trap strips should be treated with insecticide for killing jassids. The highest recommended doses of insecticides be used for adequate control on such strip crops.

- *Use of appropriate dose of Nitrogenous fertilizers:* Excess use of Nitrogenous fertilizers lead increase in jassid populations. Ex. cotton ecosystem and several others.
- *Use of resistant varieties of crops:* Deshi varieties of cotton are less hairy, hence less affected by jassids than American varieties. Smooth and less hairy surface of crop plants is favorable for egg laying of jassids on plants. Cotton varieties like B-1007 and Badnawar are resistant to jassids while, PS- 1 and PS- 10 are nonresistant.

Sugarcane resistant varieties for jassids refer to CO- 312, CO-453, CO-213, CO-313, CO-615, CO-621, CO-628 etc.

Economic threshold

The economic threshold depends on several factors such as:

(*ix*) Stage of the insect.

(*x*) Type of crop.

(*xi*) Crop stage.

(*xii*) Growing conditions.

(*xiii*) Cost of control.

(*xiv*) Current market value of the crop.

The economic threshold of jassid can be detected in certain crops. The most serious economic damage may be related to specific instars on specific crop. The economic threshold in crops range from 5 to 15 jassids per 1 fit length of crop twig.

Fig. 6.1: ***Empoasca devastance*** **onokra**

Fig. 6.2: **Brinjal jassid**

Fig. 6.3: **Empoasca sp. on green pea**

Fig. 6.4: **Jassids on pigion pea**

Fig. 6.5: **Jassid nymph**

Fig. 6.6: **Sunflower field**

Fig. 6.7: **Paddy field**

Fig. 6.8: **Forest ecosystem**

Mango crop is preferred by the jassids. The jassid on mango have two peaks first is Sept-Oct and another is from Jan-March. For rest of the period jassids found sitting in cracks and crevices of tree trunk and can be treated with contact pesticides for their control. Similarly, grapes, vegetables and paddy crops are badly affected by jassids. Their survey and abundance should be taken into account for their treatments. Advance spray of pesticides before sprouting of blossoms or early stage blossoming can control jassids on mango.

In Maharashtra jassids cause severe damage to vegetables, grapes, mango, paddy, til, cotton etc. Therefore, they should be controlled by above said methods including chemical.

5. Mechanical control

(i) use of light traps.

(ii) use of sticky panels.

(iii) use of yellow coloured traps/sticky traps.

(iv) use of greessy or oil papers at light source.

6. Chemical control

1. *Repellents* - Use Bordeaux mixture as repellent.
2. *Antifeedants* - Azadirachtin 0.03 per cent acts as antifeedent against jassids and some soft bodied insects.
3. *Insecticides*: Spraying the crop with any of the following insecticides can control the jassids.
   - 0.1 per cent Carbaryl.
   - 0.05 per cent Malathion.
   - 0.02 per cent - 0.05 per cent endrin.
   - 0.02 per cent Formathion.
   - 0.02 per cent - 0.05 Phosphamidon.
   - 0.05 per cent endosulfan.
   - 0.05 per cent Fenitrothion.
   - 0.2 per cent BHC.
   - 0.5 per cent Lindane.
   - 0.02 per cent Rogor.
   - 0.05 per cent Diazinon.

1. On grapes, against *Erythroneura* sp. Fenitrothion 50 EC in 250 ml or Carbonyl 50 WP in 500 liters of water should be treated after rainy season, as their population increases during this period.

2. On mango, against *Idioscopus clypealis* (Leth.) Carbaryl 0.1 per cent/ Malathion 0.03 per cent/1 Kg., DDT 50 WP in 500 liters of water be used.
3. On potato, against *Amrasca* sp. spray 300 ml of Rogor 30 EC. or Methyl-Oxydemeton 25 EC in 300 ml in 150 liters of water per acre, Phosphamidon 0.02 per cent.
4. On cotton, against *Amrasca devastans* (Distant) spray Dimecron or metasystox or rogor in rainy season as systemic insecticides.
5. On til, against *Crocius albicinctus* Distant spray malathion 0.05 per cent.
6. On mango, 3 species of jassids are occurred. They should be controlled by 5 sprays as integrated part of pest management.

1st spray - (in September-October) when buds start sprouting on the crop, 25 per cent Cypermethrin/fenvalrate or deltamethrin in 450 ml in 750 lit./ha. is advised.

2nd spray of Carbaryl 0.1 per cent or endosulfan 0.05 per cent be given before occurrence of blossoming.

3rd spray of quinolphos or phesolon be given after 15 days of second spray.

4th spray of phosphamidon/Rogor/Monocotophos/Methyldemeton be given after 15 days of 3rd spray.

5th spray of Synthetic Purethroids be given as per the need. This will control all jassids and even other insect pests on mango.

(*b*) *Dusting:* BHC 10 per cent weekly 20-25 Kg/ha is useful for jassid control.

(*c*) *Granule application:*

(*i*) Phorate granules - On cotton crop, soon after emergence of jassids, Phorate granules 1.5 Kg/ha be applied.

(*ii*) Endrine granules be applied against jassids.

(*d*) On edible crops following insecticides are used.

Spray- 0.03 per cent Azadirachtin/Malathion/0.02 per cent Phosphamidon.

7 Summary and Conclusion

There are many endemic, rare, indeterminate and endangered species of animals and plants are found in Maharashtra. Western Maharashtra is gene rich area of Maharashtra by floral and faunal diversity. However, very little information is paid of jassid biodiversity from western Maharashtra. Kolhapur, Sangli and Satara districts are famous for advanced agricultural practices. However, jassids became one of the limiting factors of crop yields of the region. Jassids belongs to order Hemiptera of Class-Insecta containing 15, 000 described species from the world. From India 5300 species have been reported. Therefore, the present work was carried out from Western Maharashtra.

The book has been divided into seven chapters. First chapter is devoted for a general introduction which provides national and international status of topic and importance of the region.

Second chapter is devoted to review of literature on diversity, abundance, distribution and nature of damage of Jassids.

Third chapter deals with collection and preservation methods adopted for completion of present work. The Jassids have been collected with the help of insect collecting net and with the help of plastic containers and light sticky traps. The collected specimens have been preserved in alcohol and slides of body parts such as: wings, legs have been prepared for morphological studies in addition the body parts such as: head, thorax, abdomen and their appendages. The collection was done by visiting study spots at 15 days interval by one man one hour search method. Seasonal abundance, distributional and nature of damage and host plants have been studied by spot observations at different spots of Western Maharashtra.

Fourth chapter deals with the morphological diversity of Jassids and their distribution. A total of 20 species of Jassids belonging to 4 subfamilies, Deltocephalinae, Cicadeliinae, Aphrodinae and Typhlocybinae and 13 genera have been described from Western Maharashtra. Out of which 2 species *Scaphoidues indica* sp. nov. and *Cofana oryzae* sp. nov were newly reported and described, in addition two unidentified species. The species described refer to, *Nephotettix virescens* Distant, *Nephotettix parvus* Ishihara and Kawase, *Nephotettix nigropictus* Stal, *Recilia dorsalis* Motschulsky, *Varta longula* Viraktamath, *Osbornellus limosus* Delong, *Gyponana cacuminal* Ball, *Exitianus plebeius* Kirkaldy, *Doratura* sp., Sahlberg, *Scaphytopius* sp. Ball, *Cofana albida* Walker, *Cofana maai* Young, *Cofana jejarfa* Young, *Cofana ozyzae* sp. nov., *Scaphoidius indica* sp. nov., *Ishidaella albomarginata* Signoret, *Amrasca biguttula biguttula* Ishida, *Anoscopus albifrons* Linnaeus, *Anoscopus* sp., Linnaeus, *Xestocephalus brunnens, Amrasca* sp. Ghauri etc.

Chapter fifth embodies abundance, distribution, host plants and damage by a Jassids. A total of 40 species of Jassids belonging to four subfamilies found to be damaging various economical important plants from Western Maharashtra. Jassid host plant index of Western Maharashtra is given and nature of damage caused by jassids is also reported in the chapter. The jassids cause damage to various crop [plants by sucking the cell sap and injecting toxins into the plant body which resulted yellowing curling and drying of leaves flowering and fruiting bodies of several crops were found dropped down resulting in declining the yield of the crops.

Sixth chapter is devoted for control of jassids and Seventh contain summary and conclusion of the work presented in the book.

Lastly, the book is incorporated with bibliography referred.

Conclusion

Jassids are herbivorous insects; they cause serious damage either directly by sucking the cell sap or indirectly by transmitting plant pathogens including viruses and phytoplasmase. They secret honeydew likes: sticky substance over the plant body and cause sooty moulds. The sooty mould on the leaf affects photosynthesis and further growth and yield of the crop. Therefore, any advanced knowledge on the biodiversity, abundance and damage will add great relevance in jassid management and protecting various crops of the region from jassids. However, very little attention is paid on their diversity from western Maharashtra.

In present study 20 species have been described out of which two species were newly described. There is a need to give more attention towards this destructive group of insects in near future since Western Maharashtra is agriculturally very sound region of India and crop protection is the need of the day.

I feel that this work will be stimulatory to those workers working in the field of pest management, biodiversity and life sciences.

Bibliography

Afzal, M. and M.A. Ghani, (1953). Cotton Jassid in the Punjab. The Pakistan Association for the Advancement of Science, University Institute of Chemistry, The Mall Lahore. pp. 7-11.

Alam, S. and Alam, M.S., (1979). Hopperburn by the Orange-Headed Leafhopper in Bangladesh. *IRRN*, 4: 17.

Amjad, A. and G.M. Aheer, (2007). Varietal Resistance against Sucking Insect Pests of Cotton under Bahawalpur Ecological Conditions. *J. Agric. Res.*, 45: 205-208.

Arshad, M., A. Suhail, M.J. Arif and M.A. Khan, (2009). Transgenic Bt and Non-transgenic Cotton Effects on Survival and Growth of *Helicoverpa armigera*. *Int. J. Agric. Biol.*, 11: 473-476.

Atkinson, E.T., (1885). Notes on Indian Rhynchota No. 3, *J. Asiasti Soc. Bengal*, 54 (3): 91-113.

Atwal A.S., (1963). Insect Pest of Mango and their Control. *Punjab Hort*, J. 3 (2-4): 235.

Balakrishashnan, P. and K.M. Alexander, (1984). The Endangered Wildlife of India and their Conservation. *Bull. Ethol. Soc. India*. (Suppl.), 3, 181-190.

Balakrishnan, P. and K.M. Alexander, (1984). The Endangered Wild life of India and their Conservation. *Bull. Ethol. Soc. India*. (Suppl.), 3, 181-190.

Barnet, D.E., (1977). A Revision of the Nearctic Species of the genus *Scaphoideus* (Homoptera : Cicadellidae). *Transactions of the American Entomological* Society, 102, 485-593.

Berne, B.P. (1952). A New Species of Scaphytopins (Cloanthanus), with a key to the Canadian Species (Homoptera: Cicadellidae). Contributing No. 2948, Division of Entomology, Service, Department of Agriculture, Ottawa, Canada.

Bhoje, P.M. and T.V. Sathe, (2003). Faunistic Studies on Butterflies from Radhanagari Wildlife Sanctuary, India. *Indian J., Enviorn. and Ecpplan.*, 7 (3), 655-658.

Bindra, O.S. and Singh Joginder, (1970). Biology and Bionomics on *Orosius albicintus* Dist. The Jassid Vector of Sesamumphyllody virus. *Indian J. Agric. Sci.* 40 (4): 340-55.

Biswas, B. and L.K .Ghosh, (1998). Insecta: Hemiptera: Membracidae. *Zool. Surv. India: Fauna of Meghalaya,* Part 4: 51-67.

Blocker, H.D. and B.W. Triplehorn, (1985). External morphology of leafhoppers, pp. 41-60 *In* L. R. Nault and J. G. Rodriguez [eds.] The Leafhoppers and Planthoppers. John Wiley and Sons, New York.

Bohart, Richard Mitchell, (1943). New Species of *Halictophagus* with a key to General in North Americans (Strepsiptera, Halic to phagidae). *Ent. Soc. Amer. Ann.* 36: 341-359.

Bressan, A., Clair, D., Semetey, O., Boudon-Padieu, E., (2005). Effect of two Stains of florescence doreephytoplasmase on the Survival and fecundity of the Experimental leafhopper vector *Euscelidius variegates* Klrschbaum. *J. Invertebr. Pathol.* 89: 144-149.

Britton, David (2009). "Metamorphosis: a remarkable change (http://australianmuseum.net.au/metamorphosisaremarkablechange). Australian Museum. Retrieved 13 July 2015.

Buckton, G.B. (1903). A Monograph of the Membracidae. Monographiae entomologies, London, 1-296.

Buckton, G.B., (1903). A Monograph of the Membracidae. Monographiae Entomologiae, London, 1-296.

Carpriles, J.M., (1964). Studies on Idiocerinae Leafhoppers: II. The Indian Philippine Species of *Idiocerus*and the genus *Idioscopus. Proc. ent. Soc. Wash.,* 66(2) : 89-100, 1964.

Chauri, M.S.K., (1971). Revision of the genus *Nephotettix* Matsumura (Homoptera: Clcadelloidea: Euscelidae) based on the type of the material, *Bull. ent. Res.* 60: 481-512.

China, W.E., (1938a). Melichar's 'Monographie der Cicadellinen'. *Annals and magazine of Natural History* (2), 11, 182-185.

Chowdhury S., Rao V.R. and K. Sreedevi, (2011). Taxonomic Studies on Leafhopper Fauna Associated with Rice Ecosystems in Tripura. *Current Biotica*: 4(4); 397-404.

Dai W., Viraktamath C.A., Zhang Y.L., Webb M.D., (2009). A Review of the Leafhopper genus *Scaphotettix* Matsumura (Hemiptera, Cicadellidae, Deltocephalinae), with Description of a new genus. *Zoological Science* 26: 656-663.

Das, P.C. and C.A. Viraktamath, (1998). A Review of the Indian and Nepalese grass feeding leafhopper genus *Deltocephalus* (Homoptera: Cicadellidae) with description of new species. *Hexapoda,* 10(1&2), 1-59.

Datta, B. (1972). On Indian Cicadellidae (Homoptera) - II. *Zool. Anz.,* 188, (5/6), 412-419.

Datta, B. (1973). On Indian Cicadellidae (Insecta: Homoptera) - XXII. *Zool. Anz.,* 191, (5/6), 443-447.

Datta, B. (1988). On Indian Cicadellidae (Insecta : Homoptera). *Rec. Zool. Sur. India,* Occ. Paper 90, 1-256.

Datta, B. (1988). Records of the Zoological Survey of India. Miscellaneous Publication Occasional Paper No. 90., *Zoological Survey of India, Calcutta.* pp. 1.

Datta, B. and Dhar, M. (1984). On some Collections of Cicadellids (Homoptera: Cicadellidae) *Bull. Zool. Surv. India,* 6 (1-3) : 181-220.

Datta, B. and Ghosh, L.K. (1973). Three New Species of Typhlocybinae (Homoptera: Cicadellidae) from the Himalayan Region. *Zool. Anz.,* 191 (5/6): 415-419.

Datta, B. and Ghosh, L.K. (1974). On New and two known Cicadellidae (Homoptera: Cicadellidae) *Indian J. Ent.,* 36 (2): 118-124.

Datta, B., (1969). On Indian Cicadellidae (Homoptera) - I. *Zool. Anz.,* 182, (5/6), 391-392.

Datta, B., (1972). On Indian Cicadellidae (Insecta: Homoptera)-VII. *Zooloscher Anzeiger,* 189, 109-114.

Datta, B., Ghosh, L. K. and Dhar, M. (1978). Study on Population Density of Light Attracted Insects from Calcutta Air Port. *Proc. Ecol. Symp. Anim. Popul.* ZSI, pt. 3: 78-81.

Deitz, L.L., (1975). Classification of the Higher Categories of the New World Treehoppers (Homoptera: Membracidae). *North Carolina Agric. Exp. Sta. Tech. Bull.* 225: [i-iv] 1-177.

Dietrich, C.H., (2005). Keys to the families of Cicadomorpha and Subfamilies and Tribes of Cicadellidae (Hemiptera: Auchenorrhyncha). *Florida Entomologist,* 88(4); 502-517.

Dietrich, C.H., (2013). Overview of the Phylogeny, Taxonomy and Diversity of the Leafhopper (Hemiptera: Auchenorrhyncha: Cicadomorpha: Membracoidae: Cicadellidae) vectors of plant pathogens. International Symposium on Insect vectors and Insect-Borne Diseases. 47-70.

Distant W.L., (1916). *Fauna Brit. India, Rhynchota,* (Homoptera), VI. 217-40.

Distant, W.L., (1908). The Funna of British India Including Ceylon and Burma. Rhynchota-Vol. IV, Homoptera and Appandix (pt) Taylor and Framcie, London, 501 p.

Distant, W.L., (1918). The Funna of British India Including Ceylon and Burma. Rhynchota - Vol. VII. Homoptera and Appandix, Heteroptera: Addenda. Taylor and Framcie, London, 209 p.

Diver, C. and Appanna, M. (1934). Entomological Investigation on the Spike Disease of Sandal, Studies on Insect Transmission. *Insect Forest Rec.* 20(1): 1-25.

Dominguez, E. and Godoy, C. (2010). Taxonomic Review of the genus *Osbornellus* Ball (Hemiptera: Cicadellidae) in Central America. *Zootaxa.* 2702. 1-106.

Dreeze, J. and A. Sen, (1995). Economic Development and Social Opportunity, New Delhi. Oxford University Press, pp. 291-292.

Duan, Y. and Zhang, Y. (2013). Review of the Grassland Leafhopper genus *Exitianus* Ball (Hemiptera, Cicadellidae, Deltocephalinae, Chiasmini) from China (2014). Genus *Existances* (Anchenorrhyneha, Cicadaellide, Dettoce and Chiasmini) in Tando Jan *J. insect sci.*

Dworakowska, I. (1969). Two new Typhlocybine genera from the Oriental region with a remark on Synonymy (Homoptera : Cicadellidae : Typhlocybinae). *Bull. Acad. Pol. Sci. Cl. II. Ser. Sci. Biol.* 17 (8): 487-490.

Dworakowska, I. (1970). On some East Palaearctic and Oriental Typhlocybinae (Homoptera : Cicadellidae : Typhlocybinae). *Bull. Acad. Pol. Sci. Cl. II. Ser. Biol.* 18(4) : 211-217.

Dworakowska, I. (1976). On some Oriental and Ethiopian Typhlocybinae (Homoptera, Auchenorrhyncha, Cicadellidae). *Reichenbachia Mus. Tierk, Dresdan,* 16 (1): 1-51.

Dworakowska, I. (1977). On some North Indian Typhlocybinae (Homoptera, Auchenorrhyncha, Cicadellidae). *Reichenbachia Mus. Tierk, Dresdan,* 16 (29) : 283-346.

Dworakowska, I. (1979). On some Typhlocybinae from India and Adjoining areas (Homoptera, Auchenorrhyncha, Cicadellidae). *Reichenbachia Mus. Tierk, Dresdan,* 17 (18) : 143-162.

Dworakowska, I. (1980). On some Typhlocybinae from India (Homoptera, Auchenorrhyncha, Cicadellidae). *Ent. Abh. Mus. Tierk. Dresden,* 43 (8) : 151-201.

Dworakowska, I. (1981a). On Some Typhlocybinae from India and Nepal (Auchenorrhyncha, Cicadellidae, Typhlocybinae). *Bull. Acad. Pol. Sci. Cl. II. Seri. Sci. Biol.* 28 (10-11).

Dworakowska, I. (1981b). On some Typhlocybinae from India, Sri Lanka and Nepal. (Homoptera, Auchenorrhyncha, Cicadellidae). *Ent. Abh. Tierk. Dresden,* 44 (8) : 153-203.

Dworakowska, I. and Sohi, A.S. (1978). On some Typhlocybinae with Remarks on Synonymy of Indian Species (Auchenorrhyncha, Cicadellidae). *Bull. Acad. Pol. Sci. Cl. II Ser. Sci. Biol.,* 26 (1) : 35-44.

Dworakowska, I. and Viraktamath, C.A. (1975). On some Typhlocybinae from India (Auchenorrhyncha, Cicadellidae). *Bull. Acad. Pol. Sci. Cl. II Ser. Sci. Biol.,* 26 (8) : 539-548.

Dworakowska, I. and Viraktamath, C.A. (1978). On some Indian Typhlocybinae (Auchenorrhyncha, Cicadellidae). *Bull. Acad. Pol. Sci. Cl. II Ser. Sci. Biol.,* 26 (8) : 539-548.

Dworakowska, I. and Viraktamath, C.A. (1979). On some Indian Erythroneurini (Auchenorrhyncha, Cicadellidae, Typhlocybinae). *Bull. Acad. Pol. Sci. Cl. II. Seri. Sci. Biol.* 27 (1) : 49-59.

Dworakowska, I. Singh, S. and Nagaich, B.B. (1979). Two new Species of *Dikraneura* Hardy (Auchenorrhyncha, Cicadellidae, Typhlocybinae) from India with remark on the genus. *Entomon.* 4(3): 289-293.

Dworakowska, I., Sohi A.S. and Viraktamath, C. A. (1980). One New genus and two new Species of *Zyginellini* (Cicadellidae, Typhlocybinae) from India *Oriental Ins,* 14(3) : 271-277.

Edwards, J. (1881). A Synopsis of British Homoptera - Cicadina. Part - II. *Transactions of the Entomological Society of London* 1886: 41-129.

Edwards, J. (1886). An Additional Species of British Homoptera. *Entomologists Monthly Magazine* 17: 224.

Edwards, J. (1889). Fauna and Flora of Norfolk. XX. Hemiptera. *Transactions of the Norfolk and Norwich Naturalists' Society* 4: 702-711.

Edwards, J. (1922). A generic Arrangement of British Jassina. *Entomologist's Monthly Magazine* 58, 204-207.

Edwards, J., (1881). An Additional Species of British Homoptera. *Entomologists monthly magazine,* 17: 224.

Edwards, J., (1886). A Synopsis of British Homoptera-Cicadina. Part - II. *Transactions of the Entomological Society of London.* 1886: 41-129.

Edwards, J., (1889). Fauna and flora of Norfolk. XX. Hemiptera. *Transactions of the Norfolk and Norwich Naturalists' Society.* 4: 702-711.

Edwards, J., (1922). A generic Arrangement of British Jassina. *Entomologist's monthly magazine.* 58, 204-207.

Emeljanov A.F. (1964). Novyerody i Vidytsikadok (Homoptera, Cicadellidae) izSrednejAziii [New genera and Species of Cicadellidae from Middle Asia (Homoptera)]. Doklady *Akademii Nauk Tadzhikskoi SSR, DokladyAkademii Nauk Tadzhikskoi SSR* 7: 52"56.

Emeljanov, A.F. (1966). On the tuilestire Tribe nov and its Taxonomic Position (Homoptera : Cicadellidae) Zool. Zh. 45 : 609-610.

Evans, J.W. (1947). A Natural Classification of Leafhoppers (Jassoidea : Homoptera) Part 3. Jassidae. *Trans. R. ent. Soc. Lond.*

Fiber, F.X., (1885). Description des Cicadines d'Europe des genres *Cicadula et. Thamnotettix.* (Traduit de I'allemend sur le manuscript original, par F. Reiber). Avec des additions, per L. Lethierry. *Revista de Entomologia.* 4 : 40-110.

Gaonkar, H. (1996). The Butterflies of Western Ghats, India and Srilanka. A Biodiversity Assessment on the Ecological History of Western Ghats. Abst., pp. 99.

Ghauri, M.S.K. (1936). A New genus based on *Orosiusmaculata* and Generic Reassignment of some Pruthi's Species of Cicadelloidea (Auchenorrhyncha : Homoptera). *Ann. Mag. Nat. Hist.* 6 : 559-563.

Ghauri, M.S.K. (1963). New Fig Leaf-Hoppers (Homoptera : Cicadellidae) from India with Redescription of allied Species under new genera. *Ann. Mag. Nat. Hist.* 6 : 465-475.

Ghauri, M.S.K. (1967). New Mango Leaf-Hoppers from the Oriental and Ausro Oriental regions (Homoptera : Cicadellidae). *Proc. R. Ent. Soc. London* (B) 36 : (11-12) : 159-166.

Ghauri, M.S.K. (1971). Notes on the Hemiptera from Pakistan and adjoining areas. *Ann. Mag. Nat. Hist.,* 7 : 673-688.

Ghauri, M.S.K. (1975). A New genus and Species of Idiocerine leafhopper (Cicadellidae, Auchenorrhyncha, Homoptera) on pear tree from Simla. *Nevu. Rev. Ent.,* 5 : 287-290.

Ghosh M. and A. Bal (2007). Insecta: Hempera: Cicadelloidea. *Zool. Surv. India. Fauna of Mizoram, State Fauna Series,* 14.227-288.

Ghosh, L.K. and Ghosh M. (1993). Insecta : Hemiptera : Cicadellidae. *State Fauna Series* 3 : *Fauna of West Bengal,* pt. 5 : 29-68.

Ghosh, M., Biswas B. and L.K. Ghosh. (2000). Insecta: Hempera: Cercopoidea, Cicadelloidea, Cicadoidea and Fulgoroidea. *Zool. Surv. India. Fauna of Triura,* Part 2, 317-344.

Gupta, R.K. (2004). Advancements in Insect Biodiversity Agrobios (India), Jodhpur, pp. 1-324.

Hamilton K.G.A. (1975). Revision of the genera *Paraphlepsius* Baker and *Pendarus* Ball (Rhynchota: Homoptera: Cicadellidae). *Memoirs of the Entomological Society of Canada* 96: 1-129.

Hamilton, K.G.A. (1994). Evolution of *Limotettix* Sahlberg (Homopeta: Cicadellidae) in peat lands with Description of New Taxa. Mem.Can. Entomol. Soc. 169: 111-133.

Hamilton, K.G.A., (1975). Review of the Tribal Classification of the Leafhopper Subfamily Aphrodinae (Deltocephalinae of Authors) of the Holarctic region (Rhynchota: Homoptera: Cicadellidae). *The Canadian Entomologist* 107: 477-498.

Hamilton, K.G.A., (1980). Contribution to the Study of the World Macropsini (Rhynchota: Homoptera: Cicadellidae). *Canadian Entomologist*. 112: 875-932.

Hepner L.W. (1947). A Revision of the tribe Scaphytopiini (Homoptera, Cicadellidae) in North America. *University of Kansas Science Bulletin* 31: 413-541.

Hepner L. W. 1946. A New Subgenus and Several new Species of *Scaphytopius* (Homoptera : Cicadellidae). *Journal of the Kansas Entomological Society* 19: 87-109.

Hilder, V.A. and D. Boulter, (1999). Genetic Engineering of Crop Plants for insect Resistance - A Critical Review. *Crop Prot.*, 18: 177-191.

Hofs, J.L., A. Schoeman and M. Vaissayre, (2004). Effect of Bt Cotton on Arthropod Biodiversity in South African Cotton Fields. *Commun. Agric. Appl. Biol. Sci.*, 69: 191-194.

Hofs, J.L., M. Fok and M. Vaissayre, (2006). Impact of Bt Cotton Adoption on Pesticide use by Small Holders: A 2 - Year survey in Makhatini Flats (South Africa). *Crop Prot.*, 25: 984-988.

Hussain, M.A. and Pruthi, H.S. (1923). A Short Note on Life History of Mango Hoppers (*Idiocerous*) in the Punjab. *Rep.proc. 5th Ent. Meeting pusa*, pp. 252-60.

Ishishara, T. (1969). Families and genera of leaf-hopper vectors. In : Viruses Vectors and Vegetation edited by *K. Maramorosch John wiley and Sons.* : 245-254.

Jadhav, B.V. and Sathe T.V. (2006a). Biodiversity of aphids (Order: Hemiptea) from Satara district of Western Ghats. *Indian J. Enviorn. and Ecoplan.*, 12 (1), 237-240.

Jadhav, B.V. and Sathe T.V. (2006b). Biodiversity of aphids (Order: Hemiptea) from Poona district of Western Ghats. *J. Adv. Zool.*, 27 (1), 43-45.

Joseph, K.J. (1984). Insect Life and Eco-development of the Western Ghats. Proc. Semi. *On Ecodevelopment of Western Ghats*, 1986, pp. 84-89.

Kamble C.S. and T.V. Sathe, (2015a). Colour Preference of Sugarcane jassid *Cofana spectra* Distant (Homoptera: Cicadellidae). *Indian Journal of Applied Research;* 5 (7), 292-294.

Kamble C.S. and Sathe T.V. (2015b). Impact of Environmental Factors on Population of *Idioscopus clypialis* (Hemipetera: Cicadellidae) on Mango Mangifera Indica L. *Indian Journal of Applied Research,* 5(10), 84-85.

Kamble C.S. and Sathe T.V. (2015c). On a New Species of the genus *Scaphoideus* (Hemiptera: Cicadellidae) Reported on Grape wine *Vitis vinifera* L. *Indian Journal of Applied Research,* 5(11), 456-458.

Kamble C.S. and Sathe T.V. (2015d). Incidence and Host Plants for *Amrasca biguttula* (Ishida) from Kolhapur Region, India. *International Journal of Development Research,* 5(3), 3658-3661.

Kamble C.S. Sathe T.V. and Desai, A.S. (2014). Vertical Destructive Pattern of Amrasca biguttula Ishida to Sunflower and its Control in Kolhapur district of Maharashtra. *International Journal of Development and Research,* 4(11): 2230-2232.

Kimura. M. and J.F. Crow. (1964). The Number of Alleles that can be Maintained in a Finite Population. *Genetics,* 49: 725-738.

Kirkaldy, G.W. (1906). Leafhoppers and their Natural Enemies. Part IX, leafhoppers, Hemiptera. *Bulletin of the Hawaiian Sugar Planters Association division of Entomology,* 1 (9): 271-479.

Knight W.J., Fletcher M.J. (2007). New deltocephaline Leafhopper genus, *Melanetettix,* from Melanesia (Hemiptera: Cicadellidae: Deltocephalinae). *Systematics and Biodiversity* 5: 199-222.

Knight, W.J. (1987a). Leafhoppers of the Grass-feeding genus Balchutha (Homoptera : Cicadellidae) in the Pacific Region. *J. Mat. Hist.,* 21 : 1173-1224.

Knight, W.J. and Nielson, M.W., (1986). The Higher Classification of the Cicadellidae (Homoptera), the genus *Moonia. Orient Insects,* 12 (3) : 238-292.

Knight, W.J. (1970). A revision of the genus of *Hishimonus* Ishihara (Homoptera :Cicadellidae) *Soom. Hyont. Aikak,* 36 : 125-139.

Knight, W.J. (1983). The Cicadellidae of S.E. Asia - Present Knowledge and Obstacles to Identification. Proc. 1st International Symp. Leafhoppers and Planthoppers of Economic Importance London, C.I.E. 197-224.

Knight, W.J. (1987b). Metcalf Leafhoppers Catalogue up-date. *Tymbal* 9:7.

Kramer, S. (1950). The Morphology and phylogeny of Auchenorhynchous [sic] Homoptera (Insecta). *Illinois Biological Monographs* 20: 1-111.

Krebs, C.J. (1989). Ecological Methodology. Harper and Raw Publishers, New York.

Krishnankutty and Viraktamath (2008). Australian Ocean Biogeographic Inf. Syst. (OBIS Australia). (2015) : Interium Register of marine and nonmarine genera. Accessed via http:/www.gblf,ors/sp./107098063.

Li Z. Z., Dai R.H. (2004). Descriptions of Six new Species of *Scaphoideus* from China (Homotera, Cicadellidae, Euscelinae). *Acta Zootaxonomica Sinica* 29: 281-287. [In Chinese].

Li Z. Z., Kuoh C.L. (1993). Two New Species of the genus *Scaphoideus* from Fujian China (Homoptera: Euscelidae). *Journal of Guizhou Agricultural College* 12: 37-40.

Li Z. Z., Xing J.C. (2009). A New Species of the Genus *Scaphoidella* Vilbaste (Hemiptera: Cicadellidae: Euscelinae) from China. *Entomotaxonomia* 31: 99-101.

Linnavuori, R.E., (1978a). Studies on the family Cicadellidae (Homoptera: Auchenorrhyncha). 1. A Revision of the Macropsinae of the Ethiopian Region. *Acta Entomological fennica*, 33: 1-17.

Linnavuori, R.E., (1978b). Revision of the Ethiopian Cicadellidae (Homoptera). Paraboloponinae and Deltocephalinae: Scaphytopiini and Goniagnathini. Revue Zoologique Africaine, 92: 457-500.

Malhotra, T.R. and Sharma, Baldev (1977). Key to Identification of Common leaf-hopper (Homoptera : Cicadellidae) of Jammu Division of J and K State. *Off Print from the University Review* :19.

Malhotra, T.R. and Sharma, Baldev, (1974). A New Species of *Litura* from Jammu, India (Homoptera : Cicadellidae). *Oriental Ins.*, 11 (1) : 27-29.

Mathur, (1953). A Systematic Catalogue of the main Identified Entomological Collection at the Forest Research Institute, Dehradun, Part 21, Order Hemiptera, *Indian Forest Leaft,* 121 (3) : 138-187.

Melichar, L. (1903). Description of genera and Species, Many new. *Homop-Faunavon Celon*. p. 248.

Melichar, L. (1924). Monograph der Cicadellinen I. *Annales Historico-Naturales Musei Nationalis Hungarici* 21: 195-243.

Melichar, L. (1925). Monograph der Cicadellinen II. *Annales Historico-Naturales Musei Nationalis Hungarici* 22:329-410.

Melichar, L. (1926). Monograph der Cicadellinen III. *Annales Historico-Naturales Musei Nationalis Hungarici* 23: 273-394.

Melichar, L. (1932). Monograph der Cicadellinen IV. *Annales Historico-Naturales Musei Nationalis Hungarici* 27: 285-328.

Metcalf, Z.P. (1962). General Catalogue of the Homoptera. Fasc. VI. Cicadelliodea. Pt. 4 Ledridae. (U.S. Dept. of Agriculture). 147pp.

Metcalf, Z.P. (1963). General Catalogue of the Homoptera. Fasc. VI. Cicadelliodea. Pt. 9. Hecalidae. (U.S. Dept. of Agriculture). 35 pp.

Metcalf, Z.P. (1963a). General Catalogue of the Homoptera. Fasc. VI. Cicadelliodea. Pt. 7. Nirvanidae. (U.S. Dept. of Agriculture). 123pp.

Metcalf, Z.P. (1964). General Catalogue of the Homoptera. Fasc. VI. Cicadelliodea. Pt. 11. Coelidiidae. (U.S. Dept. of Agriculture). 182pp.

Metcalf, Z.P. (1965). General Catalogue of the Homoptera. Fasc. VI. Cicadelliodea. Pt. 1. Tettigellidae. (U.S. Dept. of Agriculture). 730pp.

Metcalf, Z.P. (1966). General Catalogue of the Homoptera. Fasc. VI. Cicadelliodea. Pt. 14. Agallidae. (U.S. Dept .of Agriculture). 173pp.

Metcalf, Z.P. (1966a). General Catalogue of the Homoptera. Fasc. VI. Cicadelliodea. Pt. 15. Iassidae. (U. S. Dept of Agriculture). 229pp.

Metcalf, Z.P. (1966b). General Catalogue of the Homoptera. Fasc. VI. Cicadelliodea. Pt. 16. Idioceridae. (U. S. Dept of Agriculture). 237pp.

Metcalf, Z.P. (1968a). General Catalogue of the Homoptera. Fasc. VI. Cicadelliodea. Pt. 10. Euscelidae. (U.S. Dept. of Agriculture). 2695pp.

Metcalf, Z.P. (1968b). General Catalogue of the Homoptera. Fasc. VI. Cicadelliodea. Pt. 17. Cicadellidae. (U.S. Dept. of Agriculture). 1513pp.

Metcalf, Z.P. (1962-68). General Catalogue of the Homoptera - Fascicle VI. Cicadellidae (17 parts) Agricultural Research Service, North Carolina, Entomology Department, United States Department of Agricultural Department, Washington.

Moaschulsky, V.I. (1863). Essai d'un catalogue des insects de Ceylan. *Bul. Moscou Nat. Soc.* 36: 1-153.

Moran, N.A., Tran, P., and Gerardo, N.M. (2005). Symbiosis and insect Diversification: An Ancient Symbiont of sap Feeding Insects from the Bacterial phylum *Bacteroidetes. Appl. Environ. Microbiol.* 71: 8802-8810.

Morrison, W.P. (1973). A Revision of the Hacalinae (Homoptera : Cicadellidae) of the Oriental Region. *Pacif. Insects,* 15(3-4) : 379-438.

Myers, N. (1988). The Environmentalists, 8, 187-208.

Nagendran, N.A. and M.S. Smija, (2004). A Seminal Report on Diversity of Higher Taxa of Aquatic Insects in three Hills Streams of Western Ghats, South India. A.P.H. Pub, Crop. New Delhi, pp. 1-659.

Nair, K.S.S., Mathew, G. and Shivrajan, M. (1973). Occurrence of bagworm pteroweaplagiophleps Hampsen (Lepidoptera: Psychidae) as a pest of the free Albiziafalcataria in Kerala, India. Entomon., 6,179-180.

Nast J. (1972). *Palaearctic Auchenorrhyncha (Homoptera): An Annotated Check List.* Institute of Zoology, Polish Academy of Sciences, Polish Scientific Publisher, Warsaw, 550 p.

Nath, D.K. Banerjee, D.K., Das M.K. and Das B. (1986). Key to the Jassid Leaf hoppers (Cicadellidae : Homoptera). Occurring on rice in West Bengal. *Proceeding of the National Seminar on* Ricehoppers. Hopperburn Viruses and their Integrated Management, B.C.K.V., October 24-26: 71-85.

National Centre of Biotechnology Information. (2015).http://www.gbif.org/species/104930142.

Nei, M. (1973). Analysis of gene Diversity in Subdivided Populations. *Proceedings of the National Academy of Sciences,* USA, 70:3321-3323.

Nei, M. (1978). Estimation of average Heterozygosity and genetic Distances from a Small Number of Individuals. *Genetics,* 89:583-590.

Nielson, M.W. (1918). The Leafhopper vectors of phytopathogenic Viruses (Homoptera : Cicadellidae). Taxonomy, Biology and virus transmission. *Agricultural Research Service, USDA* (August issue).

Nielson, M.W. (1977). A revision of the Subfamily Coelidiinae (Homoptera : Cicadellidae) 11 Tribe Thagriini. 1. *Pacif. Insects Monogr.* 34 : 1-218.

Nielson, M.W. (1982). A Revision of the Subfamily Coelidiinae (Homoptera : Cicadellidae) IV. Tribe Coelidiini. *Pacif. Insects Monogr.* 39 : 1-318.

Oman P.W., Knight W.J., Nielson M.W. (1990). *Leafhoppers (Cicadellidae):* A Bibliography, Generic check-list and Index to the World Literature 1956-85. CAB International Institute of Entomology, Wallingford, Oxon, United Kingdom, 368 p.

Oman P.W., Knight W.J. and Nielson, M.W. (1990). Leafhoppers (Cicadellidae). Bibliography Genetic check-list and index to World Literature, 1956-85 : 1-384. CAB International, Wallingford, Oxon.

Oman, P.W. (1931). New Jassinae, with notes on other Species. (Homoptera, Cicadellidae). *Journal of the Wshington Academy of Sciences.* 21: 430-436.

Oman, P.W. (1936). A Generic Revision of American Bythoscopine and South American Jassinae. *University of Kansas Sciences Bulletin.* 25(16): 343-420.

Oman, P. W. (1938). A generic Revision of American Bythoscopine and South American Jassinae. *University of Kansas Sciences Bulletin.* 24: 343-420.

Oman, P.W. (1943). A new leafhopper from Oceania (Homoptera Cicadellidae). *The Pan-Pacific Entomologist.* 19(1): 33-34.

Oman, P.W. (1943b). A Generic Revision of the Cicadellidae (Homoptera) [Summary of Doctral thesis]. The Washington University, Washington, D. C. Bulletin 1941-43, pp. 14-17.

Oman, P.W. (1949). The Nearctic leafhoppers (Homoptera: Cicadellidae). A Generic Classification and Check-list. *Memoirs of the Entomological Society of Washington* 3: 1-253.

Oman, P.W. (1949). The Nearctic leafhoppers (Homoptera; Cicadellidae). A Generic Classification and Check-list. *Memoris of the Entomological Society of Washington.* 3: 1-253.

Pandharbale, A.R., (2004). Biodiversity of Moths (Lepidoptera) from Western Ghats of Satara district (Maharashtra). Ph. D. thesis, Shivaji University, Kolhapur, pp. 1-240.

Paroda, R.B., (1993). Crop Science Research for Sustenance Agriculture in India. *Proc. Nat. Acad. Sci. India (B),* 63, 97-114.

Patil, B.C., S.B. Patil, S.S. Vdikeri and B.M. Khadi, (2003). Effect of Imidacloprid Seed Treatment on Growth, yield, Seedling vigour and Biophysical Parameters in Cotton (*Gossypium*spp.) genotypes. *Proc. World Cotton Res. Conf. 3, Cape Town, South Africa,* 9-13 March.

Pedigo, L.P., (2004). *Entomology and Pest-management.* Prentice Hall of India, New Delhi. 4th Edition, pp. 175-210.

Prasad, S.G. and Logiswaran, G., (1997). Influence of Weather Factors on Population Fluctuation of Insect Pest of Brinjal at Madurai, Tamilnadu. *Indian J. Ent.,* 59: 385-388.

Pruthi, H.S. (1930). Studies on Indian Jassidae (Homoptera) Part - I. Introductory and Description of some New Genera and Species. *Mem. Indian Mus.,* 11 (1), 1-68.

Pruthi, H.S. (1934). Studies on Indian Jassidae (Homoptera) Part - II. Description of the genotypes of some of the genera found by W.L. Distant with a revision of the genus *Moonia Distant. Mem. Indian Mus.* 11 (2) : 69-99.

Pruthi, H.S. (1936). Studies on Indian Jassidae (Homoptera) Part - III. Description of some new genera and Species with first Records of some known Species from India. *Mem. Indian Mus.* 11 (2) : 101-131.

Pruthi, H.S. (1940). Studies of some New Species of *Empoasca* Walsh (Eupterygidae, Jassoidea) from North India. *Indian J. Ent.* 2 (2) : 1-9.

Qin, D. and Zhang, Y., (2008). Two new Empoascine Leafhopper Genera and Species (Hom: Cic: Typhlocubinau) from southern China, with a key to Chinese genera of empoascini. *Zootaxa.* 1966: 62-68.

Radhakrishnan, L. (2003). India's Environmental Problems and Issues. In Environment and its Challenges. (Ed. Arvind Kumar). 13, 34-38.

Rakitov, R.A., (1998). On Differentiation of cicadellid leg chaetotaxy (Homoptera: Auchenorrhyncha: Membracoidea). *Russian Entomol. J.* 6: 7-27.

Ramakrishanan U. and Menon, M.G.R. (1971). Studies on Indian Typhlocybinae (Homoptera : Cicadellidae). 1. Five new genera and a new record of Dikraneurini. *Oriental Ins.*, 5 : 455-468.

Ramakrishanan U. and Menon, M.G.R. (1972). Studies on Indian Typhlocybinae (Homoptera :Cicadellidae). Three new genera with four Typhlocybinae. *Oriental Ins.*, 6 : (1) : 111-129.

Ramakrishanan U. and Menon, M.G.R. (1973). Studies on Indian Typhlocybinae (Homoptera : Cicadellidae). Seven new genera with fourteen new species of Erythroneurini. *Oriental Ins.*, 7 (1) : 15-48.

Ramakrishanan U. and Menon, M.G.R. (1974). Studies on Indian Typhlocybinae (Homoptera : Cicadellidae). The tribe of Erythroneurini. *Oriental Ins.*, 8 : 433-455.

Ranga Rao, G.V., and Shanower, T.G. (1999). Identification and Management of Pigeonpea and Chickpea Insect Pests in Asia. Information Bulletin no. 57. (In En. Summaries in En, Fr.) Patancheru, 502 324, A.P., India: International Crops Research Institute for the Semi-Arid Tropics. ISBN 92-9066-412-6.

Rao, K.R., (2001). Insecta: leafhoppers (Homoptera: Cicadellidae) *Zool. Surv. India., fauna of Conservation area Series 11: Fauna of Nilgiri biosphere Reserve*: 85-109.

Rao, K. Ramchandra, (1967). On a New Species of *Zizyphoides* Distant (Homoptera : Jassidae) from India. *Oriental Ins.*, 1 (3-4) : 239-241.

Rao, K. Ramchandra, (1969). On the Female of *Paralimnusconfuscus* Pruthi (Homoptera : Cicadellidae). *Oriental Ins.*, 3 (2) : 187-188.

Rao, K.R. A Note on *Neodartusaccocephaloides* Melichar (Homoptera : Cicadellidae) from Tamil Nadu. *Rec. zool. Surv. India.* (In Press).

Rao, K.R. Some Descriptive notes on *Changwhaniaceylonensis* (Baker) (Homoptera : Cicadellidae) from India. *Rec. zool. Surv. India* (In Press).

Rao, K.R. (1986). On a Collection of Leafhopper (Cicadellidae : Homoptera) from the Silent Valley. *Rec. zool. Surv. India.* 84 (1-4) : 49-58.

Rao, K.R. (1990). Studies on a Small Collection of Leafhoppers (Homoptera : Cicadellidae) from Khasi Hills, Meghalaya.

Ross. H.H. (1968). The Evolution and Dispersal of the Grassland leafhopper genus *Exitianus* with keys to the old World Species (Cicadellidae: Hemiptera) *Bull. Br. Mus. nat. Hist.* (Ent.) : 22 : 1-30.

Roy S.A. Mukhopadhyay, and G. Gurusubramanian, (2010). Development of Resistance to Endosulphan in Populations of the tea mosquito bug Helopeltistheivora (Heteroptera: Miridae) from Organic and Conventional tea Plantations in India. *Interenational Journal of Tropical Insect Science,* 30(2): 61-66.

Saha, D., S. Roy and A. Mukhopadhyay, (2012). Seasonal Incidence and Enzyme-based Susceptibility to Synthetic Insecticides in two Upcoming Sucking Insect pests of tea. *Phytoparasitica,* 40:105-115.

Sathe T.V. and Margaj G.S., (2001). Cotton pests and Biocontrol agents. Daya Publishing House, Delhi. pp. 1-147.

Sathe, T.V. (1992). Founa of aphids on Plants of Economic Importance Found in Western Maharashtra, India. *J. Curr. Biosci.*, 9 (1), 27-31.

Sathe, T.V. (2003). Agrochemicals and Pest Management. Daya Publication House, Delhi, pp. 1-217.

Sathe T.V. (2004). Vermiculture and Organofarming. Daya Publication House, Delhi, pp. 1-121.

Sathe, T.V. (2005). Basic Entomology: A Practical manual. Daya Publication House, Delhi, ISBN - 81-7035-353, pp. 1-118.

Sathe T.V. (2008). Biotechnological Approaches in Entomology. Mangalum Publication, Delhi, pp. 1-167.

Sathe, T.V. (2012). Pests of Ornamental Plants. Daya Publication House, Delhi. ISBN - 978-81-7035-757-5, pp. 1-199.

Sathe, T.V. (2013). Dragonflies Production Technology. Astral International Pvt. Ltd. New Delhi, pp. 1-121.

Sathe T.V. (2014). Recent Trends in Biological Pests Control. Astral International Pvt. Ltd. New Delhi, pp. 1-204.

Sathe T.V. (2015). Biological Control through Ichneumonids. Astral International Pvt. Ltd. New Delhi, pp. 1-117.

Sathe, T.V. and M. B. Jagtap, (2014). Barcoding in Mosquitoes. Mangalum Publication, Delhi, pp. 1-90.

Sathe, T.V. (2004). Biology and Behaviour of Coccinellid beetles, in Indian Insect Predators in Biological Control. Ed. K. Sahayaraj. 8, 177-198.

Sathe, T.V. and A.R. Pandharbale, (1999). Hawk moth (Shingidae: Lipidoptera) Diversity in Western Maharashtra including Ghats. *Geobios*, 18, 77-82.

Sathe, T.V. and A.T. Pandharabale, (2005). Biodiversity of Moths (Order-Lepidoptera) from Western Ghats of Satara district, India. *Bull. Biol. Sci.* 1, 81-88.

Sathe, T.V. and Pandharbale, (2008). Forest pests Lepidoptera. Mangalam Publication, Delhi, ISBN - 978-81-906650-63, pp. 1-186.

Sathe, T.V. and K.P. Shinde, (2006). Diversity of Butterflies from Western Ghats (Kolhapur district). *J. Nat. Con.*, 81 (1), 181-184.

Sathe, T.V., Inamdar, S.A. and R. Davale, (2001). Indian Pest Parasitoids. Daya Publishing House, New Delhi, pp. 1-169.

Sathe, T.V., Inamdar, S.A. and M.V. Santhakumar, (1986-87). Founa of Butterflies from Western Maharashtra and Western Ghats (Parts of Maharashtra only), India. *J. Shivaji Uni.* (Science), 23. 391-398.

Sathe, T.V., Shendage N. N. and Chandani Kamble, (2014). Biodiversity of Jassids from Agroecosystems of Kolhapur district, India. *International Journal of Science, Environment and Technology,* 3 (3), 1053-1058.

Sathe, T.V., Shendage N.N. and Chandani Kamble, (2014). Role of Brumus Species (Coccinellidae: Coleoptera) in Population Control of Jassid Amrasca kerri Pruthi (Cicadellidae: Hemiptera). The Pest of Cowpea in Kolhapur region of Maharashtra, India. *Global Journal for Research Analysis*, 13-14.

Satish, P.M. (1996). Moths and Butterflies of Bhandra Projects .M. Sc. Thesis submitted to Kuvempu University, Shimoga, pp. 80.

Saur-Kruh, L., Weintraub, P.G., Mozes-Daube, N., Robinson, W.E. , Perlman, S.J., and Zchori-Fein, E., (2013). Characterization of a Novel Rickellsiella in the Leafhopper Orosiusalbicinctus (Hemiptera: Cicadellidae). *App. Environ. Microbiol.* (In Press).

Sharma, H.C. and G. Pampapathy, (2006). Influence of Transgenic Cotton on the Relative Abundance and Damage by Target and Non-target Insect pests under different Protection regimes in India. *Crop Prot.*, 25: 800-813.

Shinde, K.P. (2006). Biodiversity of Dragonflies (Order-Odonata) from Koyana dam and around area. Ph. D. Thesis, Shivaji University, Kolhapur, pp. 1-275.

Signoret, V.A. (1853). Revue Iconographique des Tettigonides. *Annales de la Societe entomologique de France.* (3)1: 13-40, 323-374, 661-688.

Signoret, V.A. (1854). Revue Iconographique des Tettigonides. *Annales de la Societe entomologique de France.* (3)2: 5-28.

Singh-Pruthi, H. (1930, 1934, 1936). Studies on Indian Jassidae (Homoptera) *Mem. Indian Mus.,* 11, Part - 1, 1-68. Part - II, 69-99; Part - III, 101-131.

Singh, S. (1969). Fifteen new Species of Jassids (Cicadellidae) from Himachal Pradesh and Chandigarh. *Res. Bull. (N.S.) Punjab University,* 20: 339-361.

Sivaramkrishnan, K.G, Shridhar, S. and Venkataraman, K. (1990). Habitat, Micro Distribution, Lifecycle Patterns and Tropic Relationship of May Flies of Cardamam hills, Western Ghats. *Hexapoda,* 11, 59-64.

Skimmer, D.Z., and R. F. Camacho, (1995). Genetic Diversity within a Potato Leafhopper (Homoptera: Cicadellidae) Population infesting alfalfa. *Journal of Kansas Entomological Society*, 68: 35-42.

Sohi, A.S. and Dworakowska, I. (1983). A revision of the Indian Typhlocybinae (Homoptera :Cicadellidae) from India. *Oriental Ins.*, 17: 159-213.

Sohi, A.S., (1972). *Cestius (Cestius) indicus*new Species (Homoptera : Cicadellidae) from Punjab, India. *Oriental Ins.*, 6 (1) : 131-132.

Sohi, A.S., (1983). The Oriental Typhlocybinae with Special Reference to Pests of Cotton and Rice: A Review.

Stal, C. (1969). Bidrag till Membracidernas kannedom. *Ofversigt af Kongliga Svenska Vetenskaps-Akademiens Forhandlingar* 26: 231-300.

Takiya, D.M., Taran, P.L., Dietrich, C.H. and Moran, N.A., (2006). Co-cladogenesis Spanning three phyla: Leafhoppers (Insecta: Hemiptera: Cicadellidae) and their dual bacterial *symbionts. Mol. Ecol.* 15: 4175-4191.

Van Duzee, E.P. (1892). A Synoptical Arrangement of the genera of North American Jassidae, with Description of some new species. *Transactions of the American entomological Society*. 19: 295-307.

Van Duzee, E.P. (1894). A Catalogue of the Described Jassoidea of North America. *Transactions of the American entomological Society*. 21: 245-317.

Van Duzee, E. P. (1916). Scborder Homoptera Latr. 1810. Section Auchenorhyncha A. and S. 1843. In "Checklist of Hemiptera (excepting the Aphididae, Aleurodidae and kCoccidae) of America North of Maxico." 11 pp.

Van Duzee, E.P. (1933). The Templeton Crocker Expendition of the California Academy of Sciences, 1932, No. 4. Characters of twenty-four new species of Hemiptera from the Galapagos Island and lkthe coast and islands of Cental America and Mexico. *Proceedings of the California Academy of Sciences*. (4) 21: 25-40.

Van Duzee, E.P. (1937). The Hemiptera of the Templeton Crocker Expedition to Polynesia in 1934-1935. *Proceedings of the California Academy of Sciences*. (4)22: 111-126.

Vilbaste J. (1968). Systematic treatise of cicadas found on the edge of the coastal regions. Uber die Zikadenfauna des Primorje Gebietes. Valgus, Tallin, 195 p.

Viraktamath C.A., Mohan G.S., (2004). A Revision of the Deltocephalinae leafhopper genus *Scaphoideus* (Hemiptera: Cicadellidae) from the Indian subcontinent. *Zootaxa* 578: 1-48.

Viraktamath, C.A. and Anantha Murthy, H.V. (1999). A Revision of the Leafhopper Tribe Scaphytopiini from India and Nepal. Senckenbergiana Biologica 79 (1): 39-55.

Viraktamath, C.A. and Gnaneswaran, R. (2009). Three new Species of Goniagnathus (Hemiptera: Cicadellidae) from the Indian Subcontinent with Description of a New Subgenus. Zootaxa 2224: 51-59.

Viraktamath, C.A. and Mohan, G.S. (1994). Description of Scaphodhara a new genus Related to Scaphoideus (Homoptera: Cicadellidae) and five new Species from South India. Entomon 19 (1&2): 13-22.

Viraktamath, C.A. and Mohan, G.S. (2004). A Revision of the deltocephaline leafhopper genus Scaphoideus (Hemiptera: Cicadellidae) from the Indian subcontinent. Zootaxa 578: 1-48.

Viraktamath, C.A. (1980a). Indian Macropsinae (Homoptera : Cicadellidae) 1. New Species of *Macropsis* from South India. *J. nat. Hist.*, 14 : 319-329.

Viraktamath, C.A. (1980b). Notes on *Idoscopus*species (Homoptera : Cicadellidae) described by Dr. H.S. Pruthi with Description of New Species from Meghalaya, India *Entomon,* 5 : 227-231.

Viraktamath, C.A. (1981). Indian Macropsinae (Homoptera : Cicadellidae) II. Species described by W.L. Distant and Description of New Species from Indian Subconinent. *Ent. Scand.,* 12 : 295.

Viraktamath, C.A. (1982). A Generic Revision of old World Agallini (Homoptera : Cicadellidae) Ph. D. Thesis Submitted to the *Univ. Agril. Science, Bangalore, India,* 1-367.

Viraktamath, C.A. (1983). Generic to be Revised on a Priority basis. The Need for keys and illustrations of Economic Species of Leafhopper and Preservation of Voucher specimen in Recognized Institution. *Proc. 1st International Symp.* Leaf hoppers and plant hoppers of economic importance, *London,* C.I.E. : 471-492.

Viraktamath, C.A. (1998). A Revision of the leafhopper tribe Paraboloponini (Hemiptera: Cicadellidae: Selenocephalinae) in the Indian Subcontinent. Bulletin of the Natural History Museum (Entomology) 67 (2): 153-207.

Viraktamath, C.A. (1976a). Four new Species of Indiocerinae leafhoppers from India with a note on male *Balochaaututa* Melichar (Homoptera : Cicadellidae : Indiocerinae) *Mys. Agric. J.,* 10 : 234-244.

Viraktamath, C.A. (1976b). New Species of *Doratulina and Bumizana* (Homoptera : Cicadellidae) from Karnataka. *Oriental Ins.,* 10 (1): 79-86.

Viraktamath, C.A. (1979a). *Jogocerus* gen. nov. and New Species of *Idiocrine* of *Idioscopus* leafhoppers from Southern India. (Homoptera : Cicadellidae). *Entomon,* 4 : 173-181.

Viraktamath, C.A. (1979b). Few New Species of *Indioscopus* (Homoptera : Cicadellidae). 1. New Species of *Macropsis* from South India. *J. nat. Hist.*, 4 : 173-181.

Viraktamath, S. Viraktamath, C.A. (1980). Redescription of *Allectus, Divitiacus and Lampridius* (Homoptera: Cicadellidae) described by W.L. Distant. *Entomon,* 5 (2): 135-140.

Walker, F. (1850). List of the Specimens of Homopterous Insects in the Collection of the British Museum. 3: 637-907.

Walker, F. (1858b). Homoptea. Insecta Saundersiana: or Characters of Undescribed Insects in the Collection of William Wilsonn Saunders Esq. *J. van Voorst,* London. 117 pp.

Walker, F. (1862). Characters of undescribed Species of Homoptera in the Collection of F.P. Pascoe, F. L. S. *Journal of Entomology* 1: 303-319.

Wang L. M., Li Z. Z. (2004). Three New Species of the genus *Scaphoideus* (Homoptera: Cicadellidae: Euscelinae) from Yunnan. *Entomotaxonomia* 26: 15-18.

Webb, M.D. and Heller, F.R. (1990). The leafhoppers genus *Pseupalus* in the World tropics with a Check-list of the Afrotropical and Oriental paraliminini (Homoptera : Cicadellidae : Deltocephalinae) *Stuttgarter. Beitr., Natur K. Serv.* A. No. 452. 1-10.

Wilson, M.R. (1983). A Revision of the genus *Paramesodes* Ishihara (Homoptera : Archenorrhyncha : Cicadellidae) with description of eight new species. *Ent. Scand.* 14 : 17-32.

Wyner, Blyth, M. A. (1957). Butterflies of Indian Region. *Bom. Nat. Hist. Soc. Bombay,* 1-523.

Xing J.C., Dai R.H. and Li Z.Z. (2008). A new Species of genus *Scaphoidella* from Hainan Province in China (Hemiptera: Cicadellidae: Euscelinae). *Sichuan Journal of Zoology* 127: 963-964.

Yang, M., Meng, Z.H., and Li, Z.Z. (2015). Taxonomic Study on the leafhopper genus Cofana Melichas (Hemeptera: Cicadellidae: Cicadellinae) from China with description of two new Species - *Zootaxa.,* 3994(2): 253-264.

Yeh, F., R.C. Yang, and T. Boyle, (2000). Popgene (v.1.32), Microsoft Windows - based Freeware for Population Genetic analysis. http://www.ualberta.ca/*fyeh/Pop32.exe.

Young, D.A. (1965). Cicadelline typers in the British Museum (Natural History) (Homoptera: Cicadellidae). *Bulletin of the British Museum (Natural History), Entomology.* 17 (4): 163-199.

Young, D.A. (1968). Taxonomic Study of the Cicadellinae (Homoptera: Cicadellidae). Part 1. Proconiini. *U.S. National Museum Bulletin* 261: 1-287.

Young, D.A. (1979). A Review of the leafhoppers genus *Cofana* (Homoptera: Cicadellidae) *Proc. Ent. Soc. Wsh.* 8 : 1-21.

Young, D.A. (1952). A Reclassification of Western Hemisphere Typhlocybinae (Homoptera : Cicadellidae). *Univ. Jans. Sci. Bull.*, 35 (1) : 1-217.

Young, D.A. 1986. Taxonomic study of the Cicadellinae (Homoptera: Cicadellidae) Part 3, Old World Cicadellini *Technical Bull. N. Carolina agric. Expt. Stn.* 281, 1 : 1-639.

Zachuvatkin, A.A. (1933). Sur quelques Homopteres interessants de la faune Italienne. Memoria della Scoieta Entomologica Italiana. 12: 262-272.

Zachuvatkin, A.A. (1935). Notes on the Homoptra-Cicadina of Jemen. *Wissenschaftliche Berichte Moskauer Statsuniversitat* 4: 106-115.

Zachuvatkin, A.A. (1946). Studies on the Homoptera of Turkey. I-VII. *Transactions of the Entomological Society of London.* 97: 149-176.

Zachuvatkin, A.A. (1947). Homoptera Cicadina from north-western Persia. I. Revue d'Entomologique de I;URSS 28: 106-115.

Zachvatkin, A.A. (1929). Description d'une nouvelle espece du genre Edwardsiana Jaz. 1929 (Homoptera, Eutomologidae) des environs de Moscou. *Revue Russe d'Entomologie* 23: 262-265.

Zahniser J.N., Dietrich, C.H. (2010). Phylogeny of the leafhopper Subfamily Deltocephalinae (Hemiptera: Cicadellidae) based on molecular and morphological data with a revised family-group classification. *Systematic Entomology* 35: 489-511.

Zahniser, J.N. (2008). *Systematics of the leafhopper subfamiCy Deltocephalinae (Hemiptera: Cicadellidae) and the tribe Chiasmini: phylogeny, classification, and biogeography*. Ph.D. dissertation, University of Illinois, Urbana-Champaign, 196 p.

Zahniser, J.N., Dietrich C.H. (2008). Morphology-based phylogeny of the leafhopper subfamily Deltocephalinae and related groups (Hemiptera: Cicadellidae). *Systematics and Biodiversity* 6: 1-24.

Zhang, Y. L., Dai W. (2006). A Taxonomic Study on the leafhopper genus *Scaphoidella*Vilbaste (Homoptera: Cicadellidae: Deltocephalinae). *Zoological Science* 23: 843-851.

Young, B.A. (196[illegible]). Taxonomic study of the [illegible] (Chloropidae). Part 1. [illegible]

Young, B.A. (195[illegible]). A Review of the [illegible] (Chloropidae). Proc. [illegible]

Young, [illegible] (195[illegible]). A Revised [illegible] [illegible]

Young, [illegible] (1956). Taxonomic study of the [illegible] (Chloropidae). Part 3. [illegible]

Zachvatkin, A.A. (19[illegible]). [illegible] Memorie della Società Entomologica Italiana, [illegible]

Zachvatkin, A.A. (19[illegible]). [illegible]

Zachvatkin, A.A. (19[illegible]). [illegible]

Zachvatkin, A.A. (19[illegible]). [illegible]

Zachvatkin, A.A. (19[illegible]). [illegible] Moscow. [illegible]

Zahradník, [illegible] Dietrich [illegible] [illegible]

Zahniser, [illegible] (Diptera: Chloropidae) [illegible] Ph.D. Dissertation, [illegible] Urbana-Champaign, [illegible]

Zahniser, [illegible] Dietrich, [illegible] (Chloropidae) [illegible]

Zhang, [illegible] [illegible] Zoological [illegible]

Index